Praise for *The War That Killed Achilles*

"Spirited and provocative . . . a nobly bold even rousing venture . . . it would be hard to find a faster, livelier, more compact introduction to such a great range of recent Iliadic explorations."

—Steve Coates, *The New York Times*

"*The War That Killed Achilles* will engage a reader who may not be ready to take on all twenty-four books of the original [the *Iliad*], and will be illuminating for those who already know them. . . . [Alexander's] exposition of Hector's death becomes a virtuoso rendering of one of the most riveting books in Homer, and we can see from what she has done that a fine translation may well be the most elegant and revealing form of commentary. . . . Alexander's selection of material is consistently judicious and arresting." —G. W. Bowersock, *The New York Review of Books*

"Excellent . . . *The War that Killed Achilles* is an original and stimulating reintroduction to an enduring work and valuably recasts the ancient story for our own age. Muscular and thoughtful, it is a fitting companion to the great epic it celebrates. [Alexander] gives us an *Iliad* that is in essence a powerful piece of antiwar literature, savage in its condemnation of the folly and cost of war, and brutal in its depiction of the human consequences." —*Financial Times*

"Penetrating . . . reflecting her own skills [Alexander] provides her own translation of an entire chapter. . . . A real bonus for the reader, comparing favorably with Lattimore and Fagles." —*The Boston Globe*

"Alexander pulls off the trick of doing several things at once and doing them all well." —*The Seattle Times*

"Caroline Alexander has written an invaluable study of the *Iliad*. Profound, learned, and strikingly original, *The War That Killed Achilles* takes us inside an ancient Middle Eastern war and makes it a chilling mirror of our Middle Eastern wars today—the same tragic loss of young lives, the same futility, the same heroism. It will change how we read the *Iliad*, but it will also change how we read the daily news."   —Russell Banks

"An insightful analysis of command responsibility in war. Caroline Alexander's superb use and account of the Trojan War raises issues as relevent in today's conflict as they were in Homer's time. This is a must-read for all who aspire to command."

—General Anthony C. Zinni USMC (Retired) and author of *Battle Ready*

"Although Caroline Alexander packs her books with information, she never forgets that the best aspects of the *Iliad* and the worst aspects of war lie in the realm of human emotion. She makes us fume with Achilles, grieve with Andromache, and, most moving of all, weep with Priam as he begs for the return of his son's body. As we turn these sad pages, the millennia fall away."   —Anne Fadiman, author of *The Spirit Catches You and You Fall Down*

"In her spectacular and constantly surprising new book, Caroline Alexander has taken the 'original' war book and turned it upside down, making it, as all wars are, an excruciating story of loss. . . . *The War That Killed Achilles* is a triumph."   —Ken Burns

"This riveting tale of ancient wars, legendary warriors, and mythical gods is at once a great adventure story and a cautionary tale of the enduring perils of hubris and ego. Achilles' life and death are instructive lessons for all of us today."   —Tom Brokaw

PENGUIN BOOKS

THE WAR THAT KILLED ACHILLES

Caroline Alexander is the author of the international bestsellers *The Endurance* and *The Bounty*. A Rhodes scholar, she was a lecturer at the University of Malawi, where she established a department of classics. She received her doctorate in classics at Columbia University, where she was a Mellon Fellow in the Humanities. Alexander is a contributing writer for *National Geographic* and has written for *The New Yorker*, *Smithsonian*, and *Outside*.

CAROLINE ALEXANDER

The
WAR That
KILLED
ACHILLES

The True Story of Homer's *Iliad*
and the Trojan War

PENGUIN BOOKS

PENGUIN BOOKS
Published by the Penguin Group
Penguin Group (USA) Inc., 375 Hudson Street, New York, New York 10014, U.S.A.
Penguin Group (Canada), 90 Eglinton Avenue East, Suite 700, Toronto,
Ontario, Canada M4P 2Y3 (a division of Pearson Penguin Canada Inc.)
Penguin Books Ltd, 80 Strand, London WC2R 0RL, England
Penguin Ireland, 25 St Stephen's Green, Dublin 2, Ireland (a division of Penguin Books Ltd)
Penguin Group (Australia), 250 Camberwell Road, Camberwell,
Victoria 3124, Australia (a division of Pearson Australia Group Pty Ltd)
Penguin Books India Pvt Ltd, 11 Community Centre, Panchsheel Park, New Delhi – 110 017, India
Penguin Group (NZ), 67 Apollo Drive, Rosedale, North Shore 0632,
New Zealand (a division of Pearson New Zealand Ltd)
Penguin Books (South Africa) (Pty) Ltd, 24 Sturdee Avenue,
Rosebank, Johannesburg 2196, South Africa

Penguin Books Ltd, Registered Offices:
80 Strand, London WC2R 0RL, England

First published in the United States of America by Viking Penguin,
a member of Penguin Group (USA) Inc. 2009
Published in Penguin Books 2010

10 9 8 7 6 5 4 3 2 1

Grateful acknowledgment is made for permission to reprint excerpts from *The Iliad of Homer*,
translated by Richmond Lattimore. Copyright 1951 by the University of Chicago.
Copyright renewed 1979 by Richmond Lattimore.
Used by permission of the University of Chicago Press.

THE LIBRARY OF CONGRESS HAS CATALOGED THE HARDCOVER EDITION AS FOLLOWS:
Alexander, Caroline, 1956–
   The war that killed Achilles: the true story of Homer's *Iliad*
and the Trojan War / Caroline Alexander.
      p.   cm.
   Includes bibliographical references and index.
   ISBN 978-0-670-02112-3 (hc.)
   ISBN 978-0-14-311826-8 (pbk.)
1. Homer. Iliad.   2. War in literature.   3. Trojan War—Literature and the war.
4. Achilles (Greek mythology)   I. Title.
   PA4037.A5955 2009
   883'.01—dc22   2009020160

Printed in the United States of America
Map by David Cain
Designed by Carla Bolte • Set in Warnock

TO SMOKEY

❖

οὐ μὲν γὰρ ζωοί γε φίλων ἀπάνευθεν ἑταίρων
βουλὰς ἑζόμενοι βουλεύσομεν

CONTENTS

PREFACE

The *Iliad* is generally believed to have been composed around 750 to 700 B.C. and has been in circulation ever since.[1] The reason for this is not difficult to fathom. In addition to being a poem of monumental beauty and the origin of some of literature's most haunting characters, the *Iliad* is first and foremost a martial epic, its subject warriors and war. If we took any period of a hundred years in the last five thousand, it has been calculated, we could expect, on average, ninety-four of these years to be occupied with large-scale conflicts in one or more parts of the world.[2] This enduring, seemingly ineradicable fact of war is, in the *Iliad*'s wise and sweeping panorama, as intrinsic and tragic a component of the human condition as our very mortality.

Today, headlines from across the world keep Homer close by. The dragging of the bodies of U.S. Rangers behind their killers' jeeps through the streets of Mogadishu evoked the terrible fate of the Trojan hero Hektor. A young American widow was reported as saying that she had tried to close the door against the soldier who appeared at her home in dress greens, believing that if she could keep him from speaking his news of her husband in Iraq, she could keep his news at bay—a small domestic scene that conjured the heartbreaking words of Hektor's widow, Andromache: "May what I say come never close to my ear; yet dreadfully I fear . . ." The *Iliad*'s evocation of war's devastation, then, is as resonant today—perhaps especially today—as it was in Homer's Dark Age. Now, as at any time, Homer's masterpiece is an epic for our time.

The classical age of ancient Greece knew the *Iliad* well, and the events surrounding the Trojan War furnished subjects for the great tragedians. Plato quoted and criticized Homer; Aristotle commented on him; Aristotle's most famous pupil, Alexander the Great, is alleged to have slept with a copy of the *Iliad* annotated by Aristotle under his pillow. More tellingly, it is said that when the conqueror of the known world himself arrived at what remained of Troy, he lamented the fact that unlike the hero Achilles, he, Alexander, had no Homer to glorify his deeds.

Knowledge of Homer was brought to Rome in the third century B.C. by one Livius Andronicus, who composed Latin versions or imitations (as opposed to faithful translations) of the *Odyssey*, Homer's sequel to the *Iliad*, as well as of the works of the Athenian playwrights. Perhaps more important, he established a curriculum of study of the Greek language and letters, of which Homer's epic poems took pride of place. The centrality of Homer's epics to the education of the Roman elite was never displaced, and indeed, the works of Homer formed the foundation of Greek studies in the schools of the empire. Young Octavian, the future emperor Augustus, is reported to have quoted the *Iliad* following the death of his uncle Caesar: "I must die soon, then; since I was not to stand by my companion / when he was killed."[3] Horace and Pliny knew Homer, Cicero criticized him, while Virgil's epic imitation borders at times on plagiarism.

When the Roman Empire split in the sixth century A.D., knowledge of Greek, which flourished in Byzantium, or the Eastern Empire, all but vanished in the West. The *Iliad* itself was forgotten, and in its stead stories about the war at Troy flourished, which, along with romantic sagas about Alexander the Great, formed the most popular "classical" material of the Middle Ages. The primary sources for these post-Homeric renderings of the matter of Troy, as the body of romance came to be called, were the Latin prose works of Dictys of Crete and Dares of Phrygia, dated to the third and fifth or sixth centuries A.D., respectively—both of whom were fancifully believed to have been eyewitnesses to the Great War at

Troy. In these Latin renderings, Achilles, the complex hero of Homer's *Iliad*, stripped of his defining speeches, devolved into a brutal, if heroically brave, action figure. In the hands of medieval writers, sentiment hardened further against him. The twelfth-century *Roman de Troie* takes pains, in thirty thousand lines of French verse, to ensure that Achilles is depicted as in all ways inferior, even in martial prowess, to the noble Trojan hero Hektor. Such interpretive touches would remain potent down the ages, arguably into the present time.[4]

England, as late as the Elizabethan age, was largely Greekless, and the first translation of a substantial portion of the *Iliad* (ten books) into the English language was made by way of a French text and published in 1581 by Arthur Hall, a member of Parliament until he suffered disgrace for, among other offenses, "sundry lewd speeches" and debt. His translation flirts with doggerel:

> And often shall the passers-by say, Look who yonder is,
> The wife of valiant Hector lo! Who in the field with his
> Such fame and great renown did get, when Grecians compassed
> round
> The great and mighty town of Troy and tore it to the ground.

Then, between 1598 and 1611, George Chapman's landmark translation of the *Iliad* appeared, made from Greek and other texts (and Latin translations), and was followed in five years by his translation of the *Odyssey*. It was the latter that, two hundred years later, Keats, who did not know Greek, read and commemorated unforgettably in his sonnet "On First Looking into Chapman's Homer":

> Much have I travelled in the realms of gold,
>   And many goodly states and kingdoms seen;
>   Round many western islands have I been
> Which bards in fealty to Apollo hold.

Oft of one wide expanse had I been told
   That deep-browed Homer ruled as his demesne;
   Yet did I never breathe its pure serene
Till I heard Chapman speak out loud and bold:
Then felt I like some watcher of the skies
   When a new planet swims into his ken;
Or like stout Cortez when with eagle eyes
   He stared at the Pacific—and all his men
Looked at each other with a wild surmise—
   Silent, upon a peak in Darien.

The ice had been broken, and "there is since the late sixteenth century hardly a generation in the English-speaking world which has not produced its 'Homers.'"[5]

But as knowledge of Homer was disseminated by English translations, as well as by knowledge of the original Greek, the perception of the *Iliad*'s central hero, Achilles, shifted, and so accordingly did the perceived meaning of the epic. Not only had Achilles been tarnished by the medieval lays, but from the time of Augustan England of the eighteenth century, he was further diminished by the ascendancy of another ancient epic: Virgil's *Aeneid,* which related the deeds and fate of the Roman hero *pius Aeneas*—Aeneas the pious, the virtuous, dutiful, in thrall to the imperial destiny of his country. In contrast to this paragon of fascism, Achilles, who asserts his character in the *Iliad*'s opening action by publicly challenging his commander in chief's competence and indeed the very purpose of the war, was deemed a highly undesirable heroic model.[6]

Thus, while the *Iliad*'s poetry and tragic vision were much extolled, the epic's blunter message tended to be overlooked. Centuries earlier, tragedians and historians of the classical era had matter-of-factly understood the war at Troy to have been a catastrophe: "For it came about that, on account of the length of the campaign, the Greeks of that time, and the barbarians as well, lost both what they had at home and what they had acquired by the campaign," wrote Strabo in the early first century B.C., in what can be seen as a summation of the ancient view of the Trojan War, "and so, after the destruction of Troy, not only did the victors turn to piracy because of their poverty, but still more the vanquished who survived the war."[7] But now, later ages marshaled the *Iliad*'s heroic battles and heroes' high words to instruct the nation's young manhood on the desirability of dying well for their country. The dangerous example of Achilles' contemptuous defiance of his inept commanding officer was defused by a tired witticism—that shining Achilles had been "sulking in his tent."

Homeric scholarship goes back to the dawn of literary scholarship, to the work of Theogenes of Rhegium, around 525 B.C., and in most Western—and some non-Western—universities continues to this day. Thousands of books, articles, and lectures, beyond tabulation, have been composed on this epic, and an incalculable mass of scholarship has examined and analyzed the *Iliad* from almost every conceivable angle of approach.

This book is not about many of the things that have occupied this scholarship, although inevitably it will touch on the same themes. This book is not an examination of the transmission of the Homeric text or of what Homer has meant to every passing age. It is not an analysis of the linguistic background of the epic, and it is not about the oral tradition behind the poem; it is not about formulaic expressions or whether "Homer" should refer to an individual or a tradition. It is not about Bronze Age Greece nor the historicity of the Trojan War. This book is about what the *Iliad* is about; this book is about what the *Iliad* says of war.

NOTE TO THE READER

The translation used throughout this book, with one exception, is that of Richmond Lattimore, whose landmark *Iliad* was first published in 1951 by the University of Chicago Press. It was Lattimore's translation that introduced me to the *Iliad* at the age of fourteen and inspired me to learn Greek, and my appreciation of its plain diction but epic gravitas and tone has only increased over the years. I am very grateful to the University of Chicago Press for permission to quote from this work.

The excerpts used in this book are faithful to Lattimore's translation with a few exceptions. The more familiar "Achilles" has been substituted for Lattimore's strictly correct transliteration of the Greek name "Achilleus," just as "Achaeans" has been substituted for his "Achaians" and "Mycenae" for "Mykenai." There is no single orthography for the rendering of Greek names, and readers will therefore encounter, in the quoted translation and in transliterations used by editors of the many other works cited, both "Athene" and "Athena," "Hektor" and "Hector," "Aias" and "Ajax," the Greek "Aineias" and the Roman "Aeneas," and so forth. In addition, the "Greeks" of Homer's *Iliad* are called variously Achaeans, Argives, and Danaans, just as some Trojans are also Dardanians.

The ninth chapter of this book, "The Death of Hektor," is the author's own translation of the *Iliad*'s Book Twenty-two. The translation was not made because it was felt that Lattimore's work could be improved upon, but because this Book is too perfect to be fragmented by commentary, and it seemed an impertinence to lift an entire chapter of another scholar's work.

THESSALY
Iolkos
PHTHIA
Troy
TROAD
Hellespont
Aegean Sea
ANATOLIA
LESBOS
BOIOTIA
Lefkandi
Argos
Mycenae
PELOPONNESE
Sparta
Pylos
CRETE

CAPE HELLE
Hellespont
SIGEU
PROMONTO

Aegean
Sea
SIGEUM RANGE
PLAIN
Tumulus of
Achilles
Ancient Cemetery
Besik
Bay
PRESENT-DAY
SHORELINE

CITY of TROY

Dardanelles)

PRESENT-DAY SHORELINE

Troy Bay

T R O Y

Troy

Simoeis River

Ancient Skamandros River

Modern Skamandros River

River

The War That Killed Achilles

The Things They Carried

It is the epic of epics, the most celebrated and enduring of all war stories ever told. In sparest outline, the ancient legend of the Trojan War tells of the ten-year-long siege of the Asiatic city of Troy, or Ilion, by a coalition of Greek forces to regain Helen, a famously beautiful Greek noblewoman, who had been taken to Troy by the Trojan prince Paris. The war was won by the Greeks—or Achaeans, as they were known—who finally gained entrance to the fortified city by hiding their best men inside the belly of a gigantic wooden horse alleged to be an offering to the god Poseidon. After the deceived Trojans dragged the horse inside their own fortifications, the hidden Achaeans emerged at night, sacked the city, set it aflame, and killed or enslaved all remaining Trojans.

The greatest war story ever told commemorates a war that established no boundaries, won no territory, and furthered no cause. The war is cautiously dated to around 1250 B.C. Its story was memorialized by the *Iliad*, an epic poem attributed to Homer and composed some five centuries later, around 750–700 B.C. Homer's *Iliad* is the only reason that this inconclusive campaign is now recalled.

Across the perilous gulf between the Bronze Age and Homer's time, generations of poetic storytellers had passed the legend of the war down the centuries. Many of the episodes evoked by these forgotten bards in their now-lost poems were ignored or rejected by the *Iliad*. Homer's epic does not tell of such seemingly essential events as the abduction of Helen, for example, nor of the mustering and sailing of the Greek fleet, the first hostilities of the war, the Trojan Horse, and the sacking and burning of Troy.

Instead the 15,693 lines of Homer's *Iliad* describe the occurrences of a roughly two-week period in the tenth and final year of what had become a stalemated siege of Troy. Thus the dramatic events that define the *Iliad* are the denouncement by the great Achaean warrior Achilles of his commander in chief as a mercenary, unprincipled coward; the withdrawal of Achilles from the war; and the declaration by Achilles that no war or prize of war is worth the value of his life. Homer's *Iliad* concludes not with a martial triumph but with Achilles' heartbroken acceptance that he will in fact lose his life in this wholly pointless campaign.

In Homer's day, the ruins of what had once been the well-built walls of Troy, on their commanding site overlooking the Hellespont, as the Dardanelle Straits were then known, were visible to any traveler; the *Iliad*'s close description of the Troad, the region around Troy, suggests that it was known to its poet at first hand. The war, then, was real, not mythic, to Homer and to his audience. Similarly, the major Greek principalities named by the *Iliad* as participating in the war also existed. Their ruins, too, were visible to any traveler.

Knowledge of Troy and Troy's time has been advanced by archaeology. The Trojan War itself, however, the terrible conflagration that unmoored whole nations, remains mysterious. Regardless of whatever facts may come to light, the *Iliad*'s unambiguous depiction of what this war *meant* remains unchanged. Reaching deep into his already ancient story, Homer had grasped a savage and enduring truth. Told by Homer, the ancient tale of this particular Bronze Age war was transported into a sublime and sweeping evocation of the devastation of all war of any time.

"Divine Homer," according to the ancient Greeks, was a professional poet from Ionia, a region of Greek settlements along the western coast of Anatolia (now Turkey) and its outlying islands. This plausible tradition apart, his identity is lost in the mythic past; according to one testament, for example, his father was the river Meles and his mother a nymph.[1]

The *Iliad*'s own origins are similarly murky. Certain poetic features (such as a complex system of metrically useful phrases and a marked use of repetition of passages and words) indicate that behind the *Iliad* there lay a long tradition of oral storytelling. The *Iliad*'s references to geographical place-names and to types of armament and other artifacts that can be correlated with finds of modern archaeology, combined with linguistic evidence, indicate that some of its elements date back to the Bronze Age. These historic relics were melded with themes, language, and characters borrowed from other traditions, folklore and Near and Middle Eastern poetry and mythology being particularly rich sources. Some elements are even of pre-Greek origin. Helen's name, for example, can be traced to the Indo-European *Swelénā, from the root *swel—"sun," "solar glare," "burn," "grill." Her prototype was a Daughter of the Sun, the abduction of the Sun Maiden being a recurrent motif in old Indo-European myth.[2]

Certain of the *Iliad*'s features can be teased out to suggest at least the character, if not the actual storyline, of the Bronze Age epic tradition. The hero Aias, for example, with his distinctive towerlike shield and huge size, belongs to the Greek Bronze Age, as do the easy communion between gods and men, similes comparing men to lions, and heroes of a stature with the gods. Above all, we can infer that the early tradition sang of battle and of death in combat.[3]

◈

The epic's journey can be traced in the history of two extinct peoples: the Bronze Age Greeks—known to Homer as "Achaeans" and to modern historians as Mycenaeans, after their principal settlement—and the Trojans, a Hittite-related people of western Anatolia.

The Mycenaeans came to power on the Greek mainland in the seventeenth century B.C., and while the large southern peninsula called the

Peloponnese was the main region of their strongholds, they were sailors, raiders, and warriors as well as traders and by the mid-fifteenth century B.C. had assumed political and cultural ascendancy throughout the Aegean. Golden and other precious objects unearthed from their graves reveal that they were a wealthy people. Some of this wealth came from legitimate trade, but fragmentary references to Mycenaean troublemakers in the records of the contemporary Hittites suggest that bands of individuals, if not organized armies, roamed the Anatolian coast looking for plunder: possibly the dramatic action of early epic had followed such seaborne raids.[4] Certainly the determinedly militaristic themes of Mycenaean art, with its depictions of sieges, marching warriors, and departing fleets, give every indication that the Mycenaeans were a martial people.[5]

The height of their wealth and power was reached in the late fourteenth and thirteenth centuries B.C., an era known as the "palatial" period in deference to the great palace complexes that were now built. Often set on strategic heights and encircled by massive fortification walls, the palaces functioned as both defensive strongholds and the headquarters of a sophisticated, feudal bureaucracy. Archives of documents found at some of the sites, written on baked clay tablets in an early form of Greek using a syllabic ideogram script dubbed "Linear B," contain seemingly inexhaustible lists—of tributes, taxes, commodities, stores, and military equipment—a glimpse at once of the wealth, organization, military character, and naked materialism of the ruling order.[6] No diplomatic documents, characteristic of other Bronze Age societies in the Near and Middle East, have been found amid the piles of Linear B tablets; no treaties or letters between embassies or rulers, no historical accounts of skirmishes or battles; no poems or prayers or fragmentary epics—nothing but the careful, acquisitive lists of possessions:

Kokalos repaid the following quantity of olive oil to Eumedes: 648 litres of oil.

One footstool inlaid with a man and a horse and an octopus and a
    griffin in ivory.
One footstool inlaid with the ivory lions' heads and grooves . . .
One pair of wheels, bound with bronze, unfit for service.
Twenty-one women from Cnidus with their twelve girls and ten boys,
    captives.
Women of Miletus.

And:

To-ro-ja—Woman of Troy.[7]

How women of Troy ended up as the inventory of a Mycenaean palace
cannot be known from one slender entry, but the most straightforward
explanation is that, like the women of Cnidus and Miletus—and Lemnos
and Chios and other named settlements in Anatolia or the Aegean
islands—they were, in the language of the tablets, "women taken as
booty," or captives, carried off to serve as "sewing women," textile work-
ers, "bath pourers," and probably in their masters' beds.[8] A letter written
around 1250 B.C., the conjectural time of the war, by the Hittite king
Hattusili III to an unnamed Mycenaean king, referring to the transportation and resettlement of some seven thousand Anatolians, by capture
and inducement, in Mycenaean land, indicates the scale of Mycenaean
interference.[9] A few Hittite documents and the Linear B entry, together
with a wealth of Mycenaean pottery discovered at Troy itself, are evidence that in the course of their travels—for trade, plunder, or colonization along the Anatolian coast—significant contact had been made
between the people of Mycenae and the inhabitants of Troy.[10]
    Situated at the entrance of the Hellespont (now the Dardanelles), Troy
itself had a history more ancient than that of any of the Mycenaean palaces. The earliest, very small Trojan settlement had been built around
2900 B.C., perched on a low hill above a marshy and perhaps malarial

plain that was cut by two rivers, the Simoeis and the Skamandros.[11] Seven major levels of settlements were built on the site between the date of its foundation and its abandonment nearly two thousand years later, in 1050 B.C.[12] Of these seven levels, that dubbed Troy VI (dated from 1700 to 1250 B.C.) spanned the period of Mycenaean dominance in Greece. Itself built in eight distinct phases, on the ashes of its predecessors, Troy VI was constructed with discernible novel skill and style, suggesting that a new people had claimed the ancient site; the Luwians, an Indo-European people related to the powerful Hittites, are known to have settled at this time in northwest Anatolia and are the most likely candidates for these new Trojans.[13]

On the hill, the palatial citadel was rebuilt and refurbished, with graceful, gently sloping defensive walls constructed of blocks of carefully finished limestone. Standing some seventeen feet in height, the stone walls were in turn surmounted by a mud-brick superstructure, so that from stone base to brick summit the walls rose to nearly thirty feet; strategic towers strengthened the defenses, and stone ramps led to gateways in and out of the city. These details would be retained by the epic tradition, for the *Iliad* knows of Troy's wide ways and gateways, its towers and "well-built walls." Below the citadel, a lower city housed a population of approximately six thousand souls.[14]

Thus at the time of Mycenae's height of power, in the fourteenth to thirteenth centuries B.C., Troy was a substantial settlement, surmounted by a palace citadel and happily situated at the entrance to the Dardanelles, which in turn controlled access to the Sea of Marmara and the Black Sea beyond.[15] Its influence extended not only throughout the Troad but as far as islands such as Lesbos, in the eastern Aegean, where the archaeological record, evidenced principally in pottery (and even by the lead element in copper objects), shows that from at least 3000 B.C. these islanders had shared the material culture of the Trojans.[16]

For all this, however, Troy was never more than a local power. The great Hittite kingdom that ruled Asia Minor from its capital in Hattusa (now Boğazköy, in central Turkey) held ultimate sway, and clay documents from the extensive Hittite archives show that Troy was merely one of its vassal states.[17] Mined by scholars for evidence of the "real" Troy and Trojan War since they were first deciphered, the Hittite archives have yielded tantalizing clues, made more substantial by discoveries of recent years. A reference to the "Ahhiyawa," ruled by a Great King across the sea, for example, is now generally taken to refer to the Achaeans—the name most commonly used in the *Iliad* for the Mycenaeans.[18] Similarly, Hittite "Wilusa" is now confirmed to be the Homeric Ilios; or more properly, with the restoration of its original ancient *w*-sounding letter, the "digamma"—"Wilios."[19] Particularly intriguing is a reference made in a letter from the Hittite king Hattusili III to an unnamed king of Ahhiyawa, around 1250 B.C.: "in that matter of Wilusa over which we were at enmity . . ."[20] This, then, is evidence that, on one occasion at least, a Mycenaean king had engaged in hostilities over Ilios.

No documents have yet been found at any of Troy's levels; a single seal stone unearthed at Troy VI, inscribed in Luwian, remains the only written evidence.[21] How Troy survived, how it amassed wealth enough to build its impressive walls, can only be guessed. The number of spindle whorls unearthed by excavators has been interpreted as evidence of a long-established textile industry, while horse bones found at Troy VI may be evidence of horse breeding: in the *Iliad*, Homer's Troy is "famed for its horses."[22] Particularly suggestive, however, is the small, late–Bronze Age cemetery discovered close to Troy's western harbor, in which roughly a quarter of the miscellaneous cremations and burials contained Mycenaean objects. Independent of Troy, it appears to have been a burial ground for foreign mariners, or traders.[23] At the same time, evidence of Mycenaean contact beyond the Hellespont and Bosporus is very sparse, indicating that most trade did not venture farther, but stopped at Troy. Whether this was because the Trojans actively controlled the strait, perhaps exacting tariff as was done in later eras, or simply because of the difficulty of sailing Bronze Age keelless ships against a stiff prevailing current and wind cannot be known.[24]

In Greek mythology and epic, the war between the Greeks and Trojans was directly caused when Paris, a son of King Priam of Troy, visited the Greek king Menelaos of Sparta and abducted, or seduced—even in antiquity there was a difference of opinion—the king's wife, Helen, taking with him many possessions. There is no reason this tradition could not reflect some historical truth. Given that the Linear B inventory lists clearly indicate that women were captured in Mycenaean raids along the Anatolian coast, it is at least possible that raids were also made in the other direction. The union in myth of Greek Helen with Asian Paris could also reflect a dim memory of a—perhaps resented—politically arranged marriage between a Hittite prince and his Greek bride.[25] On the other hand, the cause of the "Trojan War" may simply have been cold-blooded quest for plunder, with a series of raids romantically conflated into the Bronze Age's single Great War. Significantly, early mythological and epic stories refer to two sacks of Troy by Greeks over two successive generations, as well as, intriguingly, a failed campaign to the region led by Agamemnon, the king of Mycenae.[26]

The last of Troy VI's phases—Troy VIh—ended in 1250 B.C., falling to what appears to be a combination of natural disaster and enemy fire. The same population, much reduced in both size and circumstances, remained on the site, crowding the once-palatial citadel with what would appear to have been a clutter of small tenements: either the ruling elite were remarkably accommodating of these new inhabitants or they had fled, abandoning their palace to humbler folk.

If Troy VIh fell to Mycenaean invaders, the Mycenaeans did not have long to savor their victory. Despite the strength and watchfulness of their own great citadels, with their lookout posts and stockpiles of prudent stores, the Mycenaeans could not forestall the cataclysmic disaster that ended their own civilization, dramatically and suddenly, around 1200 B.C., a generation or so after the fall of Troy. Various reasons for the collapse have been speculated—natural disaster, internal unrest, disruption of trade, foreign marauders. That it was the Trojan War itself that left the Greek world vulnerable to such discord was the view of later ancient writers. This view is also reflected in the *Odyssey*, the second, later epic also attributed to Homer: on his return after the war to his native land, the hero Odysseus discovers that his estate has been plundered by usurpers in his absence. "It was long before the army returned from Troy, and this fact in itself led to many changes," Thucydides wrote in the fifth century B.C. "There was party strife in nearly all the cities and those who were driven into exile founded new cities."[27]

As at Troy, some local Mycenaean populations attempted to rebuild on the sites of devastation, returning to the rubble of what had been their homes to scavenge what they could from the citadels' damaged walls and sanctuaries and storerooms; but as with modern disasters, those with the means to move on did so. Although sharing the same culture, religion, and language throughout Greece, the Mycenaeans were distinguished among themselves by regional differences, and when their world collapsed, they chose different routes of escape. Those who had lived in Boiotia, in central Greece, and in wild Thessaly, on the northern extremity of the Mycenaean world, drifted eastward to the island of Lesbos, possibly joining small settlements of kin who had settled here earlier, before or during the time of the Trojan War. Significantly, passing references are scattered throughout the *Iliad* to Achaean raids made in the Troad and eastern Aegean islands: "'I have stormed from my ships twelve cities / of men, and by land eleven more through the generous Troad,'" says the Greek hero Achilles, in a passage that undoubtedly recalls his people's conquest of the region.[28] Excavations on Lesbos show that the indigenous culture was an extension of the Troad's—by chance or ironic destiny, then, the Mycenaeans had settled among a people who were culturally akin to Trojans.[29] Later Greeks, recounting fragmentary knowledge of their post-Mycenaean history, called these colonists Aeolians, from Aeolis, a son of Hellen, the eponymous clan hero of the Hellenes, or Greeks, and the term is used by historians today.

Behind the Mycenaean immigrants lay their land, their cities, the graves of their ancestors. As refugees they had undoubtedly carried with them whatever they were able of their former lives—gold and precious goods, if feasible, the clothes on their back, household wares—or so one presumes, for this is the way of all refugees, down to the present day. Many things they were unable to preserve, however, and valuable assets evaporated with the disintegration of their civilization: literacy, for example, vanished and was not to reappear for nearly five hundred years.

Of all the things the refugees carried from their shattered world, the most significant were also the least tangible—the gods they worshipped, the language they spoke, the stories they told. Here, in the region of Lesbos, memories of the lost Mycenaean world were handed down to subsequent generations in stories and poems: tales of great cities, rich in gold; remembrances, often muddled, of battles fought and types of armor. Their poems sang of the exploits of warriors who fought like lions and communed with the gods, of favorite heroes, such as the great Trickster whose wily devices always got the better of his foes, and a stubborn giant of a man who fought behind a shield that covered him like a wall—heroes who would later be known to the world as "Odysseus" and "Aias."[30]

Along with such common elements, the refugees also carried traditions that were specific to Thessaly. At some point, a new and electrifying character strode into the evolving narrative about warriors and war, a semidivine hero indelibly associated with rugged, faraway Thessaly, who was called "Achilles." The old martial tradition also adopted a specific conflict, shaping itself around the siege of an actual town whose ruins now lay just a day's sail away, on the Hellespont, in western Anatolia: "Taruisa," in the language of the Hittites, "Troia" in Greek—Troy.[31]

Presumably the Trojan allies among whom the Mycenaeans were now settled possessed stories of their own about the city—its people, its plight, and its destruction; scattered Anatolian words and phrases embedded in the *Iliad* are evidence of contact between the colonizers and local inhabitants.[32] With the ruins of their own cities behind, and the ruins of another a day's sail ahead, the Aeolic poets entrusted with the old epic narrative might have come to see, from their new vantage, that the old story of Troy's destruction was inextricably bound to the story of their own.

The evolving epic was still centuries from completion, with other critical stages yet to come. Possibly in the late tenth or early ninth century B.C., the Aeolic epic was absorbed by poets working in Ionic Greek.[33] Sophisticated and innovative, the Ionians enhanced the old Aeolic epic with parallel traditions and made it their own. Despite its discernible strand of well-embedded Aeolisms, the *Iliad* we have today is composed in Ionic Greek, and ancient tradition held Homer to be a poet of Ionia.[34]

Such, then, was the mix of elements that were passed down by epic poets over the five centuries that followed the collapse of the Mycenaean civilization, into the era historians have dubbed variably as Greece's "Dark" or "Iron Age"—the age in which Homer lived. During this still-little-known period, populations declined, as did material culture. Yet for all its relative poverty, life and society must not only have endured but eventually thrived, for when the "Dark Ages" ended, a vibrant, new human landscape was revealed. City-states had replaced the feudal palace settlements of Mycenaean times, expeditions abroad had led to the colonization by Greek settlers of new lands, writing had been reestablished, using an alphabet adapted from the Phoenician—and Homer's *Iliad* had been composed.

Little at all is known about how the *Iliad* received its final form. Was it dictated? Was it written? For whom was it performed? Recitation of the entire poem would last for days, suitable entertainment perhaps for occasional festivals, but it seems more likely that the epic was performed in episodes. The *Odyssey* gives portraits of two professional singers, both belonging to the courts of noble families, who perform short "lays";[35] one of these singers, Demodokos, is blind, a fact that inspired a tradition that Homer himself was a blind bard.[36] The small, aristocratic, and mostly—but by no means exclusively—male gatherings for whom the poets of the *Odyssey* perform are plausible models for the audiences of the *Iliad*.[37]

When the *Iliad* opens, the Achaean and Trojan armies are mired in a stalemate after a decade of hostilities. The huge fleet of ships drawn from all parts of the Greek world lie beached on the sands below Troy's fortified city, their ropes and wooden hulls rotting with disuse; and, as the epic makes very clear, the troops are desperate to go home.

Within the first of its total 15,693 lines, the *Iliad* tells of the confrontation between the hero Achilles and his inept commander in chief, Agamemnon, the ruler of wealthy Mycenae. Following their confrontation, Achilles angrily withdraws himself and his men from the common cause and threatens to return to his home in Thessaly. These events occur in Book One (by early convention—or possibly by Homer himself—the *Iliad* is divided into twenty-four chapters or "Books"),[38] and Achilles remains withdrawn until Book Eighteen; most of the epic's action, then, takes place with its main hero absent. When his closest companion, Patroklos, is killed by the Trojan hero Hektor, Achilles returns to battle with the single-minded intent of avenging his friend. This he does, in a momentous showdown that ends with the death of Hektor. After Achilles buries Patroklos with full honors, Hektor's father, Priam, the king of Troy, comes at night to the Greek camp to beg for the body of his dead son. Achilles relents and returns the body, and Hektor is buried by the Trojans. The epic ends with the funeral of Hektor. From ancient times, this epic has been called the *Iliad* (the first mention of its title is made by Herodotus[39])—"the poem about Ilios," Ilios and Ilion being the alternative names for Troy. Remarkably, there are no accounts, in Greek epic or mythology, of the fall of any of the Greek cities; all emotional pathos was invested in the loss of the Asiatic settlement of Troy.

While Homer's epic told of the events of a very narrow slice of the ten-year war, the full legend supported a sprawling web of subplots and a broad cast of both momentous and minor characters. The complete story of the war was once told by a series of six other epics, known collectively as the Trojan War poems of the Epic Cycle. Composed at various dates, all considerably later than the *Iliad*, they also, like the *Iliad*, drew on much older, common traditions. The *Iliad* itself shows a keen awareness of these other, possibly competitive narratives by making allusion to events and characters distinctive to them. Those places where it does so are always worth close study, for they can reveal traditional elements that the *Iliad* adapted or rejected—junctures, in other words, where our *Iliad* made deliberate, transforming choices. The epics of the cycle have long been lost to time, and only their rough outlines and a few stray lines survive, the primary source being a compendium of "useful literary knowledge" cautiously believed to have been written by a philosopher named Proclus, in the fifth century A.D. From these summaries we learn that the epic *Cypria* had told of the origins of the war, for example, while the *Aethiopis* told of the death and funeral of the war's greatest hero, Achilles. Other epics told of the capture of Troy by the Greeks, the destruction of Troy, and the return of the Greek veterans to their homes.[40]

Given the wide array of topics available, the *Iliad*'s selection of the narrowest sliver of the least consequential period of this all-encompassing war—a quarrel between a warrior and his commander during the protracted stalemate of the siege—is striking. Behind this choice there undoubtedly lay a much older epic song built on the familiar theme of wrath, revenge, and the return of a slighted warrior. As it is, the *Iliad*'s chosen structure necessarily rivets attention on Achilles. This epic rendering thus focuses less on the launching of fleets or the fall of cities than on the tragedy of the best warrior at Troy, who, as the *Iliad* makes relentlessly clear, will die in a war in which he finds no meaning.[41]

There is much evidence within the *Iliad* to suggest that Achilles was originally a folk hero possessed of magical traits and gifts that made him invulnerable, and that he was brought into epic at a relatively late date. In the *Iliad,* he bears the indelible traces of his earlier folk origins but has been stripped of all magically protective powers. Homer's Achilles, the son of the goddess Thetis and the hero Peleus, is wholly mortal, and indeed his mortality is one of the unmoving poles around which the epic turns.

Achilles is the vehicle for the *Iliad*'s greatness. It is his speeches that galvanize the defining events, his thrashing questioning that gives the poem its powerful meaning. "'I for my part did not come here for the sake of the Trojan / spearmen to fight against them, since to me they have done nothing,'" he rages at his commander in chief, Agamemnon, in the heat of the quarrel that sets off the epic; "'but for your sake, / o great shamelessness, we followed, to do you favour.'"

"'Nor, son of Peleus,'" says the Achaeans' aged adviser Nestor, seeking to rein Achilles in, "'think to match your strength with / the king, since never equal with the rest is the portion of honour / of the sceptred king to whom Zeus gives magnificence.'"

"'So must I be called of no account and a coward'" is Achilles' response, ignoring old Nestor and speaking directly to Agamemnon, "'if I must carry out every order you may happen to give me. / Tell other men to do these things, but give me no more / commands, since I for my part have no intention to obey you.'"[42]

Thus, drawing on its long tradition, the *Iliad* used conventional epic events and heroes to challenge the heroic view of war. Is a warrior ever justified in challenging his commander? Must he sacrifice his life for someone else's cause? How is a catastrophic war ever allowed to start—

and why, if all parties wish it over, can it not be ended? Giving his life for his country, does a man betray his family? Do the gods countenance war's slaughter? Is a warrior's death compensated by his glory? These are the questions that pervade the *Iliad*. These are also the questions that pervade actual war. And in life, as in epic, no one has answered them better than Homer.

Chain of Command

Sing, goddess, the anger of Peleus' son Achilles
and its devastation, which put pains thousandfold upon the Achaeans,
hurled in their multitudes to the house of Hades strong souls
of heroes, but gave their bodies to be the delicate feasting
of dogs, of all birds, and the will of Zeus was accomplished
since that time when first there stood in division of conflict
Atreus' son the lord of men and brilliant Achilles.

—*Iliad* 1.1–7

In the tenth year of the war against Troy, the two armies, Achaean and Trojan, are locked in what has become a long stalemate. In lieu of sacking Troy itself, the Achaeans have taken to raiding cities and settlements throughout the region, both on foot and from the sea, in the old Mycenaean manner.

Now the victim of a recent raid comes forward to supplicate the plunderers. Chryses is a priest of the god Apollo, and among the war booty the Achaeans carried away was his daughter, Chryseis. With great courage, the old priest has traveled to the Achaean camp, displaying the gold staff of his priesthood and "carrying gifts beyond count" to supplicate the Achaeans and in particular "Atreus' two sons, the marshals of the people," Menelaos and Agamemnon.

In his brief appearance, Chryses makes a sympathetic figure, as evidenced by the reaction of the Achaean army, which shouts its assent to his plea. Compliance with the priest's humble and respectful request, then, will earn countless gifts of ransom, the support of the Achaeans, and undoubtedly the goodwill of Apollo, the god whom Chryses serves. There is, as it turns out, only one individual within the broad Troad for whom this straightforward act of both compassion and self-interest is unacceptable, and that is the commander in chief of the Achaean army, who also happens to be the person to whom, when the spoils were divided, the priest's daughter was given:

> Yet this pleased not the heart of Atreus' son Agamemnon,
> but harshly he drove him away with a strong order upon him:
> "Never let me find you again, old sir, near our hollow
> ships, neither lingering now nor coming again hereafter,
> for fear your staff and the god's ribbons help you no longer.
> The girl I will not give back; sooner will old age come upon her
> in my own house, in Argos, far from her own land, going
> up and down by the loom and being in my bed as my companion.
> So go now, do not make me angry; so you will be safer."

Thus does Agamemnon, son of Atreus and king of Mycenae, the wealthiest of all the coalition states, make his appearance in the *Iliad*, in a manner that has been found offensive down the ages. The ancient commentator Aristarchus, writing in the second century B.C., wished to delete his words on the grounds that it was "unfitting that Agamemnon should say such things," while a modern commentator characterizes them as being "typical of Agamemnon at his nastiest."[1] The immediate consequence of Agamemnon's arrogant dismissal of the priest is that he angers Phoibos Apollo—the god of healing, the archer who shoots from afar, and also, as it turns out, the bringer of plagues: Smintheus, "mouse-slayer," is the epithet by which the priest Chryses addresses Apollo, from *sminthos*—"mouse"—the bringer of plagues, in Mysian, one of the languages of the Troad.[2]

High on Mount Olympos, Apollo hears the prayer of his aggrieved priest and, enraged, strides down from the mountain pinnacles, his arrows clattering in his quiver. Taking aim first at the army's animals, the mules and dogs, he then lets fly his arrows against the men:

> The corpse fires burned everywhere and did not stop burning.
>   Nine days up and down the host ranged the god's arrows,
> but on the tenth Achilles called the people to assembly.

From this, his first action, Achilles declares himself the hero of the Achaean army and the hero of the epic. The son of the Thessalian king Peleus and an immortal goddess, Achilles is not Agamemnon's equal in rank. Nonetheless, he takes charge of the crisis with authoritative confidence, displaying the leadership that his commander in chief lacks. Before the assembled men, he calls for "'some holy man, some prophet, / even an interpreter of dreams . . . who can tell why Phoibos Apollo is so angry.'" In response, Kalchas, "the best of the bird interpreters," such as every good army carries, steps forth with trepidation. Kalchas knows that his words will incite Agamemnon's anger, and only after Achilles personally offers assurances for his safety does the old man speak.

Apollo's anger, and the plague, Kalchas declares, will continue to rage until Chryseis is returned to her father, "'without price, without ransom.'" Agamemnon's reaction to this pronouncement, which is tantamount to a public rebuke, is immediate and unseemly. Insulting Kalchas, he nonetheless sourly agrees to surrender his prize—but only if he receives another prize as compensation. Once more it is Achilles who takes the initiative, stepping in to reason with his commander:

> "Son of Atreus, most lordly, greediest for gain of all men,
> how shall the great-hearted Achaeans give you a prize now?
> There is no great store of things lying about I know of.
> But what we took from the cities by storm has been distributed;
> it is unbecoming for the people to call back things once given.

No, for the present give the girl back to the god; we Achaeans
thrice and four times over will repay you, if ever Zeus gives
into our hands the strong-walled citadel of Troy to be plundered."

"'What do you want?'" is Agamemnon's outraged and panicked response. "'To keep your own prize and have me sit here / lacking one? Are you ordering me to give this girl back?'" Lashing out, he issues the threat to Achilles that will haunt him and the entire Achaean army for the rest of the epic: "'Either the great-hearted Achaeans shall give me a new prize . . . or else . . . I myself shall take her, / your own prize, or that of Aias, or that of Odysseus.'" And in this way Agamemnon unleashes the wrath of Achilles.

"Sing, goddess, the anger of Peleus' son Achilles." The anger of Achilles is the engine that drives the epic. How that wrath is aroused, however, the fact that Achilles' protagonist is Agamemnon as opposed to any of his other companions, is of singular importance.

The summaries of the lost Trojan Cycle poems indicate that quarrels between allied heroes was a favorite theme of ancient epic.[3] In the lost epic *Cypria*, for example, "Achilles quarrels with Agamemnon because he received a late invitation" to a feast. In the *Aethiopis*, "Achilles kills Thersites after being abused by him and insulted over his alleged love" of the Amazon queen. Also in the *Aethiopis*, "a quarrel arises between Odysseus and Ajax over the arms of Achilles," which were to be awarded after his death to the best of the Achaeans.[4] Finally, the *Odyssey* relates at some length a quarrel between Achilles and Odysseus. This last example is particularly noteworthy, as the story is sung by a Homer-like singer of tales:

But when they had put away their desire for eating and drinking,
the Muse stirred the singer to sing the famous actions
of men on that venture, whose fame goes up into the wide heaven,
the quarrel between Odysseus and Peleus' son, Achilles,

how these once contended, at the gods' generous festival,
with words of violence . . .

—*Odyssey* 8.72ff.

Given that he appears as a protagonist in most of the heroic quarrels cited, Achilles was evidently a character who attracted *éris,* or strife: "'Forever quarrelling is dear to your heart,'" Agamemnon says to Achilles in the heat of their confrontation, a knowing nod toward his wider reputation. Audiences of Homer's time, therefore, would not necessarily have found the *Iliad*'s opening lines to be fully explanatory, since the "anger" or "wrath" of Peleus' son could have referred to any of several possible epic stories.

Epic tradition, then, appears to have offered numerous possibilities for igniting Achilles' dramatically necessary anger. The fact that the *Iliad* rejected traditions about a quarrel between Achilles and a comrade-in-arms and chose instead to pit him against his commander in chief immediately establishes a more dangerous and interesting arena of contention. The *éris* is now more than a "quarrel," and not only because Achilles is guilty of insubordination. What interests Homer are issues of authority and leadership on the one hand and duty and individual destiny on the other, issues brought swiftly to the fore by Achilles himself:

"I for my part did not come here for the sake of the Trojan
spearmen to fight against them, since to me they have done nothing.
Never yet have they driven away my cattle or my horses,
never in Phthia where the soil is rich and men grow great did they
spoil my harvest, since indeed there is much that lies between us,
the shadowy mountains and the echoing sea; but for your sake,
o great shamelessness, we followed, to do you favour."

It is a great gauntlet-throwing speech, particularly remarkable for occurring at the very outset of the epic. What Achilles is challenging is the bedrock assumption of military service—that the individual warrior submit his freedom, his destiny, his very life to a cause in which he may have no personal stake. In modern times, the speech finds its counterpart in Muhammad Ali's famous refusal to fight in Vietnam:

> I ain't got no quarrel with the Viet Cong. . . . No Viet Cong ever called me nigger. . . . I am not going 10,000 miles to help murder, kill and burn other people to simply help continue the domination of white slavemasters over dark people.

Like Ali's, Achilles' words are particularly dangerous in that one can assume he is speaking aloud words that other, less charismatic men had long thought.

The critical exchange, with the full tide of Achilles' eloquence is as follows:

> " . . . but for your sake,
> o great shamelessness, we followed, to do you favour,
> you with the dog's eyes, to win your honour and Menelaos'
> from the Trojans. You forget all this or else you care nothing.
> And now my prize you threaten in person to strip from me,
> for whom I laboured much, the gift of the sons of the Achaeans.
> Never, when the Achaeans sack some well-founded citadel
> of the Trojans, do I have a prize that is equal to your prize.
> Always the greatest part of the painful fighting is the work of
> my hands; but when the time comes to distribute the booty
> yours is the greater reward, and I with some small thing
> yet dear to me go back to my ships when I am weary with fighting.
> Now I am returning to Phthia, since it is much better
> to go home again with my curved ships, and I am minded no longer
> to stay here dishonoured and pile up your wealth and your luxury."

"'Run away by all means'" is Agamemnon's retort, and recklessly he repeats, and now confirms, his earlier threat to strip Achilles of his prize, a captive woman named Briseis:

> ". . . that you may learn well
> how much greater I am than you, and another man may shrink back
> from likening himself to me and contending against me."

Achilles' instinct is to draw his sword and kill the king; he is checked, hand on hilt, by the sudden intervention of the goddess Athene, visible to Achilles alone, who offers sympathetic words but counsels him to stay his hand. Whether Athene's appearance is taken literally or metaphorically—the sober second thought sent by the goddess known for wisdom—Achilles is receptive and sheathes his sword.

The full import of Achilles' rebellion is difficult to gauge given the *Iliad*'s vagueness on the nature and basis of Agamemnon's power. In other legend, related in detail by Hesiod, an epic poet following Homer, the coalition of Achaean forces was the result of a vow made years earlier by each of Helen's many suitors to her father: each man pledged that, regardless of whom she married, he would unite with her other suitors to come to her aid, if the need should ever arise. All the major Greek heroes at Troy appear to have made this pledge—save Achilles, who was too young to have been a suitor (but, according to Hesiod, "neither warlike Menelaus, nor any other human on the earth would have defeated him in wooing Helen, if swift Achilles had found her still a virgin"). [5] The *Iliad* makes no mention of this legendary pact, but some kind of agreement like it nonetheless informs the epic. Consequently, Agamemnon appears to be commander in chief not only because he is king of the wealthiest kingdom of the coalition but because he is brother to Menelaos, husband of Helen, whose cause the coalition fights. Minor kings such as Achilles, Diomedes, and Odysseus, then, have come to Troy with their own troops voluntarily, not as vassals beholden to the Great King.

The weight of Agamemnon's authority is spelled out most unambiguously by Nestor, king of Pylos, the Achaean army's aged counselor-at-large, who was famously long-lived: "In his time two generations of mortal men had perished, ... and he was king in the third age." Characteristically, his pronouncements betray him as being stuck in his own past; Nestor's many war memories date from the First World War, so to speak, and we are in Vietnam. Now, seeking to mollify Achilles and the king of Mycenae, Nestor intervenes in the quarrel, reminding both men that in his time he has "'dealt with better men than / you are, and never once did they disregard me.'" After a long and rambling narration of his former exploits fighting and destroying "'the beast men,'" or centaurs, who lived in the mountains, Nestor offers his counsel: to Agamemnon— "'great man that you are'"—his advice is to give up the girl. To Achilles he offers a rebuke:

> "Nor, son of Peleus, think to match your strength with
> the king, since never equal with the rest is the portion of honour
> of the sceptred king to whom Zeus gives magnificence. Even
> though you are the stronger man, and the mother who bore you was
> immortal,
> yet is this man greater who is lord over more than you rule."

Nestor is the spokesman for the status quo, for the tradition-hallowed belief that institutional power equates with unquestioned authority. Both Nestor and Agamemnon can smell the danger that Achilles himself does not yet know he threatens. Already Achilles has taken charge, instinctively, of the assembly; he has confidently extended unqualified protection to Kalchas; by making the commonsensical assertion that Chryseis should be returned, he is in essence distributing war prizes, the prerogative of kings; and in his manifestation of concern for the men under Agamemnon's charge he has assumed, again instinctively, the responsibility of a genuine leader. Were Agamemnon to submit to Achilles' injunction and return his prize, he would surrender the last vestige of ceremonial authority he possesses.

As the *éris* between the two men goes from bad to unmanageable, Achilles takes hold of the scepter of the assembly, a symbol of royal authority, and unleashes another blistering assessment of his commanding officer:

"You wine sack, with a dog's eyes, with a deer's heart. Never
once have you taken courage in your heart to arm with your people
for battle, or go into ambuscade with the best of the Achaeans.
No, for in such things you see death. Far better to your mind
is it, all along the widespread host of the Achaeans
to take away the gifts of any man who speaks up against you.
King who feed on your people, since you rule nonentities;
otherwise, son of Atreus, this were your last outrage.
But I will tell you this and swear a great oath upon it:
in the name of this sceptre, which never again will bear leaf nor
branch, now that it has left behind the cut stump in the mountains,
nor shall it ever blossom again, since the bronze blade stripped
bark and leafage, and now at last the sons of the Achaeans
carry it in their hands in state when they administer
the justice of Zeus. And this shall be a great oath before you:
some day longing for Achilles will come to the sons of the
    Achaeans."

After speaking, Achilles "dashed to the ground the sceptre" of the assembly; to Achilles this revered and potent object is only a piece of wood stripped of foliage.[6] His action neatly encapsulates the crisis of command: if the traditional trappings of authority are simply not recognized, then leadership of the gathered host is up for grabs. "'So must I be called of no account and a coward / if I must carry out every order you may happen to give me,'" says Achilles, toward the end of this confrontation. "'Tell other men to do these things, but give me no more / commands, since I for my part have no intention to obey you.'"

The altercation breaks off when Achilles stalks away to his quarters with his companions; in withdrawing from the war, he also withdraws the twenty-five hundred Myrmidon comrades who sailed with him.[7] A delegation under Odysseus, proverbially known for his smooth talking and diplomacy, is sent to return Chryseis to her father and to make propitiatory offerings and "perfect hecatombs" to Apollo; a hecatomb is believed to be a sacrifice of "a hundred cows"—in Greek *hekatòn boûs*—an appalling slaughter, but the term seems to have become generalized over time to mean something along the lines of "a worthy number."[8] While this delegation is busy, Agamemnon, making good on his threat, sends his heralds to Achilles' shelter to confiscate Briseis, Achilles' prize.

The heralds set out "against their will beside the beach of the barren / salt sea." On their arrival at Achilles' camp, set confidently at the extreme end, and thus the most exposed position, of the long line of ships stretched along the beach, "These two terrified and in awe of the king stood waiting / quietly, and did not speak a word at all." Achilles, however, receives them graciously, and the heralds duly return to Agamemnon with Briseis, who "all unwilling went with them." While Briseis is still a silent cipher at this point, her reluctance is quietly suggestive of a tender relationship with her captor.

Once the little delegation has departed, Achilles drops his hauteur, and, going down to the sea, weeping, he calls upon his mother, the sea nymph Thetis:

"Since, my mother, you bore me to be a man with a short life, therefore Zeus of the loud thunder on Olympos should grant me honour at least."

Hearing her son, Thetis rises like mist from the sea and sits beside him, while Achilles tearfully relates all that has happened: the plague, the quarrel, the loss of Briseis and with her loss the assault to his honor. He then asks of Thetis the single favor that will define the rest of the epic: that she supplicate almighty Zeus, the son of Kronos, for a favor, reminding the king of the gods that she once saved him from destruction:

"... that time when all the other Olympians sought to bind him,
Hera and Poseidon and Pallas Athene. Then you,
    goddess, went and set him free from his shackles, summoning
in speed the creature of the hundred hands to tall Olympos,
that creature the gods name Briareus, but all men
Aigaios' son, but he is far greater in strength than his father.
He rejoicing in the glory of it sat down by Kronion,
and the rest of the blessed gods were frightened and gave up
    binding him.
Sit beside him and take his knees and remind him of these things
now, if perhaps he might be willing to help the Trojans,
and pin the Achaeans back against the ships and the water,
dying, so that thus they may all have profit of their own king,
that Atreus' son wide-ruling Agamemnon may recognize
his madness, that he did no honour to the best of the Achaeans."

It is a weird and ultimately savage speech: "'pin the Achaeans back against the ships and the water, / dying'" is the summation of Achilles' murderous request. His references to obscure events of the Olympian past briefly part the elegant drapery that encloses the Homeric world, allowing a glimpse into the murky realm of mythology and folklore from which the *Iliad* was fomented. Characteristically, Homer eschews such outlandish, implausible creatures as hundred-handed monsters, but here it seems this creature—Briareus—was too closely associated with Thetis and her role as Zeus' savior to edit him out.[9] And in fact, Thetis' powerful claim on Zeus, the King of Heaven, can be shown to rest not so much on her rescue of him from rebellious gods as on a single detail submerged in the bizarre story of Briareus: "'he is far greater in strength than his father.'"

In the *Iliad*'s heroic world, the attribute of being superior to one's father is very dangerous, associated above all with usurpation. Zeus, the king of gods, came to power by overthrowing his father, Kronos—as Kronos had overthrown his father before him. Among gods, a son greater in strength than his father, then, can, and usually does, overturn the cosmic order. [10]

Among men, a central tenet of the heroic code is that the younger generation is inferior to the elder, or to the generation of its fathers. Old Nestor's authority among the Achaeans rests exclusively upon the fact, which he never tires of proclaiming, that he belongs to the age of heroes of old: "'I fought single-handed, yet against such men no one / of the mortals now alive upon earth could do battle.'" In heroic society, a hero is cajoled, bullied, or persuaded into line by being reminded of the illustrious deeds his father committed. Deference to the tenet that the fathers of old are greater than the heroes of today is part of the moral cement that holds heroic society together. [11]

The full significance of monstrous Briareus, however, is not only that he is, anomalously and dangerously, greater than his father; it is that he is evoked at just this juncture in the epic, in Achilles' own speech. The *Iliad*, as has been seen, is the product of a long and variegated tradition, arising and defining itself over centuries amid other, sometimes competitive, sometimes complementary, traditions. Knowledgeable of these other stories, audiences of Homer's own time would have recognized the *Iliad*'s allusions; indeed, sometimes the allusions are explicit enough to suggest that the *Iliad* is deliberately playing upon its audience's familiarity with the wider epic material. Often, however, as here, the allusion is obscure, compressed to a telltale phrase buried in the larger narrative. Modern readers, ignorant of the lost traditions, might be led to such subtle references by an outside source—a scene on a vase painting, for example, or a passage in other poetry—that makes more explicit the submerged myth. Those places in the *Iliad*, therefore, where an unknown myth is touched upon bear close study—and such is the case with Achilles' passionate evocation of Thetis' rescue of Zeus with the aid of a being superior in strength to his father.

From later poetry it is known that Achilles' mother, divine Thetis, bore a unique destiny: to bear a son who would be stronger than his father, whoever that father might be. The most explicit evidence comes from the poet Pindar, who although writing some two and a half centuries after the *Iliad* can be shown to draw upon very old, even pre-Iliadic traditions. The subject of the poem in question is the marriage of Peleus and Thetis, a favorite subject of both poetry and art:

This the assembly of the Blessed Ones remembered,
When Zeus and glorious Poseidon
Strove to marry Thetis,
Each wishing that she
Should be his beautiful bride.
Love held them in his grip.
But the Gods' undying wisdom
Would not let the marriage be,

When they gave ear to the oracles. In their midst
Wise-counselling Themis said
That it was fated for the sea-goddess
To bear for son a prince
Stronger than his father,
Who shall wield in his hand a different weapon
More powerful than the thunderbolt
Or the monstrous trident,

If she wed Zeus or among the brothers of Zeus.
"Put an end to this. Let her have a mortal wedlock
And see dead in war her son. . . ."

—*Isthmian* 8.29–40[12]

It seems, then, that the minor sea goddess Thetis was pursued by the two most powerful gods of the cosmic order—Zeus and Poseidon—and that when her destiny was disclosed to her suitors, their ardor turned to fear and a marriage with a mortal—Peleus—was quickly arranged. Her offspring would not be the most powerful god in the universe, the lord of heaven, but instead the "best of the Achaeans," a mortal who will die. A cosmic crisis was thus averted, but the price, to Thetis' eternal sorrow, would be the certain, untimely death of her short-lived son, Achilles.[13]

Honor for death—this seems to have been the bargain. If Achilles is dishonored at Agamemnon's hands, the bargain has been transgressed and he loses all. This small scene between the sorrowing mother and her weeping son is, as it now turns out, one of the most potent in the epic, representing the moment from which all subsequent action will be unfolded. Revealed, too, is the high import of the *Iliad*'s choice of what had at first appeared to be the least significant period in the long Trojan War. In the few days covered by the *Iliad*'s narrative, no cities will be stormed and the war will not be brought to conclusion. But the rebellion that would have played in heaven will take place on earth. Achilles will assert his birthright—not as the lord of heaven but as the best of the Achaeans. Stronger than all his father's generation, the legendary men of old, he will also operate beyond the reach of the conventional moral code of their society.

It is against this charged history that Thetis comes to Olympos to make her plea. Finding Zeus, her former suitor, sitting apart from the other gods, she goes directly to him, taking her place beside him, "with her left hand embracing / his knees, but took him underneath the chin with her right hand"—the supplicant's posture. Her plea to him is strikingly brief, eight lines only:

"Father Zeus, if ever before in word or action
I did you favour among the immortals, now grant what I ask for.
Now give honour to my son short-lived beyond all other
mortals. Since even now the lord of men Agamemnon
dishonours him, who has taken away his prize and keeps it.
Zeus of the counsels, lord of Olympos, now do him honour.
So long put strength into the Trojans, until the Achaeans
give my son his rights, and his honour is increased among them."

Zeus' initial response is an ominous silence, and Thetis, clinging to his knees, has to plead again:

"Bend your head and promise me to accomplish this thing,
or else refuse it, you have nothing to fear, that I may know
by how much I am the most dishonoured of all gods."

Zeus' reluctance, as it turns out, is not on account of the enormity of the request or the toll of human life entailed but because it will put him on a collision course with his wife (and sister), the goddess Hera, who is an unflagging champion of the Achaeans and an inveterate, pathological hater of Trojans. Nonetheless, reluctantly, he complies, bending his head in promise. Her petition granted, Thetis descends from Olympos to the ocean in a single leap, leaving Zeus to handle Hera, who immediately, as he had feared, speaks "revilingly" to him, charging him with treachery.

Then in return Zeus who gathers the clouds made answer:
"Dear lady, I never escape you, you are always full of suspicion.
Yet thus you can accomplish nothing surely, but be more

distant from my heart than ever, and it will be the worse for you.
If what you say is true, then that is the way I wish it.
But go then, sit down in silence, and do as I tell you,
for fear all the gods, as many as are on Olympos, can do nothing
if I come close and lay my unconquerable hands upon you."

He spoke, and the goddess the ox-eyed lady Hera was frightened.

Elsewhere, Zeus similarly threatens other gods; the point of the scene with Hera is not that he is an abusive husband but that there exists no agency that can stand up to his might. This point is underscored by the exchange immediately following between Hera and her son, the lame smith of the gods, Hephaistos. Cautioning his mother against causing unpleasantness on Olympos "'for the sake of mortals,'" he also reminds her of an earlier occasion on which he had once tried to intervene on her behalf and was himself hurled by Zeus from Olympos: "'all day long I dropped helpless, and about sunset / I landed in Lemnos, and there was not much life left in me.'" Zeus, as Hephaistos declares, "'is far too strong for any.'"

Zeus' threat to Hera at the end of this first Book echoes that of Agamemnon's threat to Chryses at the beginning, just as Hera's fright is reminiscent of that of Kalchas. The little scene on Olympos ironically shadows Agamemnon's strutting of power on earth below and is a reminder of the unassailable magnitude of the real thing: the authority of Zeus is that against which the combined forces of all the other gods cannot contend—this is what it means to be the lord of heaven. Book One ends peacefully on Olympos. The gods resume their feasting, and when the sun goes down, Zeus goes to bed with Hera beside him.

❖

During the night, Zeus ponders the promise he has made to Thetis. How best to make the Achaeans feel Achilles' absence? How best to turn the tide of battle against the Achaeans in favor of the Trojans? The strategy he eventually devises is one of breathtaking cynicism: the most straight-forward way to undo a great army, he decides, is to send a delusional dream of victory to its leader. Accordingly, Zeus dispatches "evil Dream" to Agamemnon's bedside, who whispers in the king's ear that Troy is his for the taking. "He thought that on that very day he would take Priam's city," Homer says of Agamemnon, in a rare editorializing aside; "fool, who knew nothing of all the things Zeus planned to accomplish."[14]

Released by Dream, Agamemnon wakes and dons his tunic, "beauti-ful, fresh woven," takes up his "sword with the nails of silver"—in Greek *xíphos arguróēlon*, a true relic of both Mycenaean language and equipment[15]—along with the "sceptre of his fathers, immortal forever," on which his status depends, and goes forth to summon the heralds to call an assembly.

While the rank and file are mustered, Agamemnon holds a prelimi-nary council with the princes and shares with them the splendid vision of his dream: Significantly, evil Dream had appeared to Agamemnon in the likeness of his most trusted adviser, the perhaps too-aged Nestor. Nestor's own reaction to Agamemnon's description of this landmark apparition—Troy to be taken on this very day!—is curious: "'had it been any other Achaean who told of this dream / we should have called it a lie and we might rather have turned from it,'" he says, with diplomatic caution. Having faithfully recounted the dream, Agamemnon adds a complicating twist. At some point as events were swiftly unfolding, he devised his own astonishing plan—he will test his men, a spur-of-the-moment ploy that he has apparently dreamed up alone:

"Yet first, since it is the right way, I will make trial of them
by words, and tell them even to flee in their benched vessels.
Do you take stations here and there, to check them with orders."

To the place of assembly, the thousands of troops swarm, so many that the earth groans beneath them. Here, leaning upon his father's scepter, Agamemnon delivers a speech to this grand host in one of the more bizarre episodes in the *Iliad*. He has had a dream, Agamemnon tells his men, and proceeds to relate the exact opposite of the dream he actually received. There is nothing to be done, he concludes, except to go home:

> "And now nine years of mighty Zeus have gone by, and the timbers
> of our ships have rotted away and the cables are broken
> and far away our own wives and our young children
> are sitting within our halls and wait for us, while still our work here
> stays forever unfinished as it is, for whose sake we came hither.
> Come then, do as I say, let us all be won over; let us
> run away with our ships to the beloved land of our fathers
> since no longer now shall we capture Troy of the wide ways."

What Agamemnon hoped to achieve by his "test" is never stated; presumably he expected the army to rise as a man and declare they would never cut and run, that Troy could be won, that success was just around the corner.[16] The actual results of the speech, in any event, are disastrous:

> All of that assembly was shaken, and the men in tumult
> swept to the ships, and underneath their feet the dust lifted
> and rose high, and the men were all shouting to one another
> to lay hold on the ships and drag them down to the bright sea.
> They cleaned out the keel channels and their cries hit skyward
> as they made for home.

At the height of the crisis, there arises another outspoken critic: Thersites, said to be "the ugliest man who came beneath Ilion," bandy-legged and hunch-shouldered. "Beyond all others Achilles hated him, and Odysseus. / These two he was forever abusing, but now at brilliant /

Agamemnon he clashed the shrill noise of his abuse."[17] Alone of the epic's major, speaking characters, Thersites has no patronymic, or name that identifies him by his father ("son of Atreus," "son of Peleus"), an absence indicating his unseemliness, if not low birth. His character may have been invented to serve the single purpose of being an attack dog; his name, Thersites, is derived from *thérsos*, an Aeolic word meaning "overbold" or "audacious," well suited to his confrontation here with Agamemnon:[18]

> "It is not right for
> you, their leader, to lead in sorrow the sons of the Achaeans.
> My good fools, poor abuses, you women, not men, of Achaea,
> let us go back home in our ships, and leave this man here
> by himself in Troy to mull his prizes of honour
> that he may find out whether or not we others are helping him.
> And now he has dishonoured Achilles, a man much better
> than he is. He has taken his prize by force and keeps her.

The mass desertion advocated by Thersites is averted only by Odysseus, who turns upon the little man, threatening to strip away his clothing and send him "'howling back to the fast ships,'" and then beats him with the royal scepter, which he has snatched from the impotent hands of Agamemnon. "Frightened, / in pain, and looking helplessly about," Thersites wipes away his tears, while the diverted host "laughed over him happily." After this scapegoating, order is restored. Odysseus bolsters morale with a long, eloquent speech, reminding the army of an earlier omen, made ten years previously, that promised eventual success. Nestor steps in with saber-rattling words, urging, among other things, that the Achaeans not go home until each man "'has lain in bed with the wife of a Trojan'" to avenge Helen. Finally Agamemnon reappears, rueful and shaken, and credited with not a single word or action to dispel the disaster he has caused:

"Zeus of the aegis, son of Kronos, has given me bitterness,
who drives me into unprofitable abuse and quarrels.
For I and Achilles fought together for a girl's sake
in words' violent encounter, and I was the first to be angry.
If ever we can take one single counsel, then no longer
shall the Trojans' evil be put aside, not even for a small time.
Now go back, take your dinner, and let us gather our warcraft."

Thus ends Agamemnon's test of his army. That this was only a test is never explained to the bewildered men, and the episode remains strangely open-ended. Over the years, many subtle theories have been floated to explain the intent and effect of the astounding act of idiocy represented by Agamemnon's trial of the army: by "wisely . . . diminishing his soldiers' own reserves of honor," Agamemnon "increases their need for battle" is one such example.[19] The most straightforward explanation, however, is that as illogical and disastrous as the trial may be, it is entirely consistent with the *Iliad*'s carefully drawn depictions of Agamemnon in action. His rough handling of Chryses caused the catastrophic plague in the first place, and his tactless pride caused the withdrawal of his most valuable warrior. In Zeus' judgment, Agamemnon and his delusions were the most effective instrument to turn the course of war against his own army. In fact, Agamemnon's every word and action in these first, important, stage-setting episodes of the epic has been disastrous. The trial scene is simply one more example—starker and uncomplicated by any other agency—of Agamemnon's unfitness to command. Is this not the point?[20]

The political world the poem purports to evoke is, of course, Bronze Age Mycenaean Greece, when strong rulers controlled centralized bases of wealth and power from palace-citadels such as Mycenae; but the end of the poetic tradition, in Homer's time, occurred in the late eighth century B.C., on the threshold of an age of extraordinary social innovation that included the establishment of citizen-ruled city-states and of colonies abroad by enterprising individuals and clans. Already, in the last

phase of the *Iliad*'s evolution, questions concerning the nature of authority and power, of individual rights and duties had to have been in the
air.[21] Those men who, like Achilles, found themselves constrained by the
unreasonable authority of lesser men over them or disaffected rabble-
rousers like Thersites would have been prime candidates to pick up their
tent pegs and start their own colony elsewhere.

There is no way of knowing how an audience of Homer's time viewed
this pointed portrayal of a traditional king who is unworthy of command,
but it is unlikely that they had no memory of a real-life analogy to color
the portrait, for the realization that a god-sent leader may not be up to
the job cycles through many ages of many people, up to the present time;
undoubtedly the last wave of Tommies to head dutifully over the top at
the Somme had realized that the authority of king and country did not
equate with military acumen. The articulated awareness that the authority above may be inferior to the individual soldier below is the beginning
of a dangerous wisdom. Achilles' contempt for Agamemnon is expressed
in the words of the highborn hero; Thersites' in the words of the people,
the men in the trenches. Dangerously, both views coincide.

Behind the straightforward narration of events, from Agamemnon's
first appearance through to the conclusion of his failed trial—the third
crisis of his manufacture—is a warning rumble of a not-so-distant political storm. The undisguised ineptness of the king, a shrill but eloquent
rabble-rouser in the person of Thersites, a demoralized army, and a charismatic warrior whose outstanding strength and prowess are matched
by a dangerous, unconventional independent-mindedness—in the cluster of these disjointed elements lurks the specter of a coup.

That Agamemnon is threatened by Achilles is manifest from his first
reactions in their confrontation. What the king does not know, however,
is that the usurpation he fears has in effect already taken place: Achilles
controls the army's fate and will continue to do so, present or absent, as
Achilles controls the epic. In the rebellion of Achilles, two powerful the-
matic lines have converged, one historical, one mythic: the historic reas-

sessment of an individual's unquestioned duty to his ruler and the playing out of Achilles' inherently subversive destiny.

Using the traditional set piece of *éris* between heroes, the *Iliad* deliberately probes the consequences of unexamined leadership; the kind of prosaic narrative line hinted at in the summaries of the quarrels of the other, lost epics that fell by the wayside has thus been elevated to cosmic heights. When the *Iliad* opens, the son of Thetis, who was almost lord of heaven, is taking orders from an ineffectual king. Agamemnon, for whom rank and power, authority and honor are equated with a careful calibration of wealth and prizes, can have no idea of the monstrous scale of real, absolute power, authority, and honor. By taking back a prize of war, he has broken the rules that, had he been wise enough to perceive them, both afforded him his status and were all that kept Achilles' terrible strength in check. "'Zeus, exalted and mightiest, sky-dwelling in the dark mist,'" Agamemnon prays at the conclusion of his disastrous trial, offering accompanying sacrifice:

> "let not the sun go down and disappear into darkness
> until I have hurled headlong the castle of Priam
> blazing, and lit the castle gates with the flames' destruction; . . ."
>
> He spoke, but none of this would the son of Kronos accomplish,
> who accepted the victims, but piled up the unwished-for hardship.

The king cannot know how wholly he is outranked, that it is Achilles' prayers, not his, that are heard in heaven. The honor Achilles seeks now will be absolute, such as is demanded by the gods. "Sing, goddess, the anger of Peleus' son Achilles" are the words of the proem. Achilles will bring his king and the mortal comrades who did not follow him to their knees.

To the epic's deliberate, painstaking portrayal of Agamemnon's ineptness are juxtaposed Achilles' most pointedly damaging words:

"I for my part did not come here for the sake of the Trojan
spearmen to fight against them, since to me they have done nothing.
               . . . but for your sake,
o great shamelessness, we followed, to do you favour,
you with the dog's eyes, to win your honour and Menelaos'
from the Trojans."

As any audience familiar with the story of the Trojan War would have
known, this charge—that Achilles and the Achaeans are at Troy solely
on behalf of Agamemnon and his brother—is wholly true. Thus, from
the *Iliad*'s first scenes, Homer has unambiguously established that the
demoralized Achaean army fights under failed leadership for a question-
able cause and wants to go home. It is, to say the least, a remarkable way
to introduce a great war epic.

Terms of Engagement

When Agamemnon has finished his sacrifice and prayers to Zeus, Nestor reminds him of his duty, urging him to muster the Achaeans for battle. As the heralds are duly summoned and the men marshaled with their proclamations and cries, Athene, the warrior goddess, sweeps through the great throng, holding her aegis, "ageless, immortal," and urges them on:

> She kindled the strength in each man's
> heart to take the battle without respite and keep on fighting.
> And now battle became sweeter to them than to go back
> in their hollow ships to the beloved land of their fathers.
> As obliterating fire lights up a vast forest
> along the crests of a mountain, and the flare shows far off,
> so as they marched, from the magnificent bronze the gleam went
> dazzling all about through the upper air to the heaven.
> These, as the multitudinous nations of birds winged,
> of geese, and of cranes, and of swans long-throated
> in the Asian meadow beside the Kaÿstrian waters
> this way and that way make their flights in the pride of their
>   wings, then
> settle in clashing swarms and the whole meadow echoes with them,
> so of these the multitudinous tribes from the ships and
> shelters poured to the plain of Skamandros, and the earth beneath
>   their
> feet and under the feet of their horses thundered horribly.

They took position in the blossoming meadow of Skamandros,
thousands of them, as leaves and flowers appear in their season.[1]

The same great host which, provoked by Agamemnon's trial, had risen
as a man to flee to the ships intent on home is now intent on action. The
change of heart was brought about in part by the rallying words of Odysseus and Nestor, but mostly by the sinister shadow of Athene's great
aegis. Like the goddess herself, the aegis is invisible to the men, its
terror-inducing powers being transmitted to them in some mystical way.
In statues and painted art, the aegis is depicted as a short mantle of goat-
skin (*aígeios*) worn over the shoulders or carried on the arm, its scalloped
edges bordered with serpents. Elsewhere in the *Iliad*, it is described as
"the betasselled, terrible / aegis, all about which Terror hangs like a gar-
land, / and Hatred is there, and Battle Strength, and heart-freezing
Onslaught / and thereon is set the head of the grim gigantic Gorgon, /
a thing of fear and horror." Associated with Zeus, his warrior daughter
Athene, and Apollo, all of whom appear to have their own, an aegis
is used to incite outright terror or, in Zeus' case, fearful storm clouds.[2]
This, then, is the object that ensures that battle for the Achaeans becomes "sweeter to them than to go back . . . to the beloved land of
their fathers." The descent of Athene to the field and the shadow of her
terrifying aegis—like the rousing speeches of Nestor and Odysseus—are
part of Zeus' plan to honor his vow to Thetis. The Achaean host must be
reassembled and the men's spirits aroused for war so that they can die
at the hands of their enemy and by their great losses bring Achilles
honor.

With bronze armor seemingly ablaze, the tumultuous host marches
in all their confident, shouting magnificence into Zeus' trap. The cascade
of extraordinary similes drawn from the natural world, as often in the
Iliad, is double-edged, underscoring both the sheer spectacle of a great
army on the move and the inherent poignancy of its deadly march. Linguistic evidence shows that the *Iliad*'s similes are generally "late," mean-

ing that they were introduced toward the end of the poetic tradition.[3] Often they undercut the very martial scenes they so vividly evoke with the sudden flare of a vision from the world of peace; here the apocalyptic image of blazing fire on the mountain heights swiftly gives way to that of a meadow full of migrating birds, a scene of teeming, clamorous life.

> Tell me now, you Muses who have your homes on Olympos.
> For you, who are goddesses, are there, and you know all things,
> and we have heard only the rumour of it and know nothing.
> Who then of those were the chief men and the lords of the
>   Danaans?
> As for the multitude, I won't put them in speech, nor give them
>   names,[4]
> not if I had ten tongues and ten mouths, not if I had
> a voice never to be broken and a heart of bronze within me,
> not unless the Muses of Olympia, daughters
> of Zeus of the aegis, remembered all those who came beneath Ilion.

This second invocation, far more expansive than the invocation that announces the *Iliad* itself, intrudes abruptly into this majestic flow of images. Its purpose is to introduce a long list of 226 verses naming each of the twenty-nine contingents that make up the Achaean army. "The Catalogue of Ships," as it is dubbed, has been variously interpreted as an authentic survival from the Mycenaean age to a pseudo document postdating Homer; several medieval manuscripts omit the list entirely or place it at epic's end, as a kind of appendix.[5]

> Leïtos and Peneleos were leaders of the Boiotians,
> with Arkesilaos and Prothoenor and Klonios;
> they who lived in Hyria and in rocky Aulis,
> in the hill-bends of Eteonos.

Of the 175 named places, a significant number can be identified with mostly late Mycenaean (circa 1250–1200 B.C.) sites, bolstering the claim that the Catalogue is a surviving relic from the Bronze Age.[6] On the other hand, late linguistic forms—the critical, much-repeated word for "ship" is a striking example[7]—along with certain geographical oddities, such as the omission of important Bronze Age place-names, also indicate that while the main contents of the Catalogue may possibly date to Mycenaean times, the list as a composition does not; this is not, in other words, an authentic muster roll lifted from the late Bronze Age.[8] The Catalogue's strangely qualified prelude—"For you, who are goddesses, are there, and you know all things, / and we have heard only the rumour of it and know nothing"—may point to the fact that the origin of the list was unclear even to the epic poet.[9]

According to all surviving traditions about the Trojan War, the Achaean armada was first launched for Troy from Aulis, in Boiotia, which, significantly, is where the Catalogue begins its circuit. Its original *poetic* purpose, then, was surely to describe the mustering of forces for the Trojan campaign. Like many other favorite events of the Trojan War that fall outside the parameters of the *Iliad's* chosen time frame, the muster has been opportunistically relocated here, in different guise.[10]

Tedious as it can be to modern audiences, the Catalogue with its grave roll call of long-deserted places was undoubtedly warmly received by audiences who knew these names from folk and family lore, an anticipated feature, perhaps, of performances relating the saga of bygone times—and one that a professional singer of tales would omit only at his peril.[11] Striking, too, is the epic's apologetic disclaimer of not being able to cite the names of "the multitude," or the troops—possibly a hint that this set piece received its final shape at a late stage, when the audience's sympathetic interest in a huge military venture extended beyond the top tier of kings to the common soldier.[12] Relocated here, as a prelude to the *Iliad's* first specifically martial action, the Catalogue magnificently evokes the massed and varied army and the high cost in manpower of commitment to this cause:

> They who held Arkadia under the sheer peak, Kyllene,
> beside the tomb of Aipytos, where men fight at close quarters,
> they who dwelt in Orchomenos of the flocks, and Pheneos,
> about Rhipe and Stratia and windy Enispe;
> they who held Tegea and Mantineia the lovely,
> they who held Stymphalos, and dwelt about Parrhasia . . .

One thousand one hundred and eighty-six ships, under the guidance of forty-four named leaders, are cited. With the average complement of a ship estimated at fifty, the Achaean force was at a minimum approximately sixty thousand men strong. Together with a more abbreviated list of Trojan allies, emphasizing the many languages spoken among them, the Catalogue conjures the epic nature of this almighty war; all the gods in heaven will be involved, and many, many nations of men. This, the *Iliad* asserts, was not some backwater campaign between undistinguished peoples; this was the war of wars.

> Tell me then, Muse, who of them all was the best and bravest,
> of the men, and the men's horses, who went with the sons of Atreus.
> Best by far among the horses were the mares of Eumelos . . .

The list of horses that the invocation seems to promise concludes abruptly, begging the question whether there was at one time a Catalogue of Horses; traditional songs in praise of domestic animals are attested in other cultures.[13] As it is, the brief citation of the two perfectly matched mares is followed awkwardly by the notice that "among the men far the best was Telamonian Aias / while Achilles stayed angry," which in turn leads by association to the observation that Achilles' own horses are now as unoccupied as he is: "standing each beside his chariot, / champed their clover and the parsley that grows in wet places, / resting, while the chariots of their lords stood covered / in the shelters"; it is a pleasant image. One ancient commentator notes that this marshland parsley (*sélinon*) differs from parsley that grows in rocks, an insight into how zealously Homer's works have been scoured and fathomed since ancient times.[14] Curtailed and clumsily placed as the "list" of horses is, it and its aftermath draw attention away from the ships that have been so thoroughly cataloged, back down to the plain of the "horse taming" (*hippódamos*) Trojans, where so much of the *Iliad*'s action will take place.

The Trojan plain and its surroundings are a landscape that commentators, past and present, agree that the poets of the epic tradition, if not Homer himself, knew at first hand. Writing in the early first century B.C., Strabo declared Homer to be "the first geographer" based upon his descriptions of the Troad, which Strabo himself had traveled (erratically; he was led by a local authority to misplace the actual site of Troy).[15] "As much as Lesbos . . . out to sea holds within its bounds / and Phrygia inland, and the boundless Hellespont" is the characterization Achilles gives of the territory of the Trojans. Possibly "the boundless Hellespont" referred not only to what is in fact the narrow modern Dardanelle Straits but to the entire surrounding sea—off Thrace to the north, off the Trojan plain to the south.[16] As the Hellespont, or Dardanelles, accounts for the northwest border, Mount Ida inland anchors the Troad's southeast corner. These and other landmarks, such as the hulking outlines of the islands of Tenedos and Lesbos and, on a very good day, Samothrace in the blue distance, are all as the *Iliad* describes. Below and around the actual city of Troy extends the level floodplain of the Skamandros and the Simoeis rivers, edged with rushes. While the *Iliad*'s grasp of the geography of Greece is hazy, notwithstanding the confident Catalogue of Ships, in both grand overview and telling detail, its acquaintance with "Troy land," and the northern Troad in particular, is secure.

So as to hasten the reengagement of the armies, Iris, the messenger of the gods, is sent from Olympos "with the dark message from Zeus of the aegis" to the Trojans. She finds them in assembly "gathered together in one place, the elders and the young men" in the city, and in the likeness of one of the many sons of Troy's King Priam she announces that the Achaeans are on the march and urges the Trojan hero Hektor to rouse his company:

> "In my time I have gone into many battles among men,
> yet never have I seen a host like this, not one so numerous.
> These look terribly like leaves, or the sands of the sea-shore,
> as they advance across the plain to fight by the city.
> Hektor, on you beyond all I urge this, to do as I tell you:
> all about the great city of Priam are many companions,
> but multitudinous is the speech of the scattered nations:
> let each man who is their leader give orders to these men,
> and let each set his citizens in order, and lead them."
> She spoke, nor did Hektor fail to mark the word of the goddess.
> Instantly he broke up the assembly; they ran to their weapons.
> All the gates were opened and the people swept through them
> on foot, and with horses, and a clamour of shouting rose up.

And so we meet the enemy. Surging onto the plain, the Trojans and their many foreign allies are mustered not far from the city, by "the Hill of the Thicket."[17]

"'Hektor, on you beyond all I urge this, to do as I tell you'": the words of Zeus' messenger serve as the best possible introduction to the Trojan hero who will be Achilles' greatest antagonist.[18] His name is Greek, at least as old as the Linear B tablets, where it appears as *e-ko-to*, derived from *échein*—"to hold," "to hold together," "to hold back," "to hold ground."[19] While it is his brother, Paris, who is responsible for causing the war, and his father, Priam, who rules the Trojans, it is on Hektor that the burden of the war falls most squarely—"on you beyond all," as Iris salutes him.

Hektor's Greek name and the fact that he features in no stories except the *Iliad* have led to the speculation that his character was Homer's own brilliant invention. But the role of the heroic defender is a traditional one and wholly necessary to a story of a besieged city. Moreover, in keeping with his status as an Asiatic king, Priam has, by many concubines, many sons: "'Fifty were my sons, when the sons of the Achaeans came here,'" Priam says later in the epic. "'Nineteen were born to me from the womb of a single mother, / and other women bore the rest in my palace.'" The establishment of so many warrior princes opens dramatic possibilities, as there is now scope, if not necessity, for them to play opposing roles. "'I have had the noblest / of sons in Troy,'" Priam declares, but also "'the disgraces, / the liars and the dancers, champions of the chorus, the plunderers / of their own people in their land of lambs and kids.'" The motif of paired brothers, one shining and one dark (like Abel and Cain), is also a common one in folklore and mythology.[20] It is possible that Priam's traditionally established, sprawling household provided both the inspiration and the latitude to expand the roles of different ones of his many sons. "'You said once / that without companions and without people you could hold this city / alone, with only your brothers and the lords of your sisters,'" a Trojan ally reminds Hektor, and the exchange suggests that there may have been an older tradition in which the sons of Priam formed a fighting band of brothers. Hektor is probably not a Homeric invention, then, but a brilliant Homeric development.[21]

Standing by the Hill of the Thicket, surrounded by the best and bravest fighting men, Hektor is formally presented as leader of the Trojans by the epithet that will most frequently describe him—*koruthaíolos*— from *kórus*, "helmet," and *aiólos*, "the notion of glancing light passing into that of rapid movement";[22] in the Linear B tablets, "Aiólos" is the name of what one must imagine was an affectionately regarded ox. "Of the shimmering helm" gives good sense of Hektor's epithet, evoking the changeable play of light off his glistening bronze, plumed helmet. Presumably many warriors at Troy have bronze helmets, but this term, used repeatedly (thirty-eight times) of Hektor, is associated with no other man.[23]

With the Achaeans roused by Athene and the Trojans stirred by a direct message from Zeus, the two armies advance across the plain to meet each other, the Trojans "with clamour and shouting, like wildfowl," the Achaeans in silence, with renewed, deadly intent. Suddenly Paris springs from the ranks, dressed in elaborate battle finery—a leopard skin is flung across his shoulders, and he is equipped with a bow, a sword, and two javelins, which he brandishes at the Achaeans, challenging the best to combat. Spying the man who stole his wife, Menelaos strides forth, ready to oblige, and at the sight of him Paris' courage falters and, like "a man who has come on a snake in the mountain valley," he shrinks back into the ranks:

But Hektor saw him and in words of shame rebuked him:
"Evil Paris, beautiful, woman-crazy, cajoling,
better had you never been born, or killed unwedded.
Truly I could have wished it so; it would be far better
than to have you with us to our shame, for others to sneer at.
Surely now the flowing-haired Achaeans laugh at us,
thinking you are our bravest champion, only because your
looks are handsome, but there is no strength in your heart, no
    courage.
Were you like this that time when in sea-wandering vessels
assembling oarsmen to help you you sailed over the water,
and mixed with the outlanders, and carried away a fair woman
from a remote land, whose lord's kin were spearmen and fighters,
to your father a big sorrow, and your city, and all your people,
to yourself a thing shameful but bringing joy to the enemy?

And now you would not stand up against warlike Menelaos?
Thus you would learn of the man whose blossoming wife you have
    taken.
The lyre would not help you then, nor the favours of Aphrodite,
nor your locks, when you rolled in the dust, nor all your beauty.
No, but the Trojans are cowards in truth, else long before this
you had worn a mantle of flying stones for the wrong you did us."

Alone of the *Iliad*'s heroes, Paris bears two names: the Greek "Alexandros," which is the epic's name of preference (an ancient name appearing in Linear B tablets), and "Paris," which like "Priam" is likely to have originated in pre-Greek Asia Minor: tantalizingly an "Alaksandu" of Wilusa is named in Hittite texts.[24]

The encounter between Paris and Menelaos through the dust of impending battle is, like a number of events of Book Three, more reasonably suited to the first weeks than to the tenth year of the war. But certain iconographic scenes, such as the encounter between the two most personally inimical protagonists—the cuckolded husband and the interloping lover—are necessary to the emotional, if not the logical, completeness of this story. Moreover, the introduction of Paris in this manner, his cowardice directly contrasting with Menelaos' old-fashioned, lionhearted courage as he steps from the ranks to meet the young pretender, is particularly effective and naturally leads to one of the most determinedly presented realities of this war—the hatred and contempt with which Paris is held by his own people.

"'Evil Paris,'" says his own brother Hektor, "'. . . better had you never been born.'" Disparagement of the Trojan responsible for the war is to be expected, of course, in a Greek epic performed before mostly Greek audiences. The vehemence of the disparagement, however, is striking, as is the fact that it comes from his brother. In the entire epic, no Trojan ever attempts to mitigate or diminish either Paris' crime or the unfair, intolerable burden it has placed on the Trojan people: "'the Trojans are cowards in truth, else long before this / you had worn a mantle of flying stones for the wrong you did us,'" as Hektor says—in other words, Paris should have been stoned. Bound by tribal and familial bonds of unyielding if resentful loyalty, the whole of Troy is engulfed in a war fought for what is universally acknowledged as a wrongful, hateful cause.

Paris' response to his brother's contemptuous rebuke is entirely characteristic of his response to the several stinging rebukes he receives throughout the epic. Swiftly, almost agreeably, he acknowledges the correctness of Hektor's words—"'you have scolded me rightly, not beyond measure'"—demurring only with the scorn his brother shows for his beauty and infatuation with the fair sex: "'do not / bring up against me the sweet favours of golden Aphrodite. / Never to be cast away are the gifts of the gods.'" Paris never exerts the energy of a defense and instead evinces languid self-acceptance that he is only as the gods have made him and does only what the gods direct. That the gods initiate and direct all human events is, in fact, a view supported by the epic. Paris is unheroic, however, not because of his religious belief in divine agency but because of his passive acquiescence to it; as will be seen, heroism is achieved by striving in the face of unconquerable destiny.

Now, languidly, Paris offers up to his brother one of his intermittent acts of courage; as he is without shame, so Paris is sometimes without fear, again on the principle that the gods alone will in any case determine the outcome. His suggestion is that he and Menelaos fight a duel, man to man, for "'Helen and all her possessions'":

"That one of us who wins and is proved stronger, let him
take the possessions fairly and the woman, and lead her homeward.
But the rest of you, having cut your oaths of faith and friendship,
dwell, you in Troy where the soil is rich, while those others return
    home
to horse-pasturing Argos, and Achaea the land of fair women."

On hearing his brother's suggestion—the fantasy of all fighting men that the individuals personally responsible for a war be the ones who actually fight it—Hektor "was happy." Striding into the dangerous open space between the advancing armies, he "forced back the Trojan battalions / holding his spear by the middle until they were all seated." Gradually the Achaeans see that he is trying to speak, and Agamemnon shouts for quiet.

In the silence, Hektor proclaims Paris' offer. The Achaean reaction to the prospect of a duel between young Paris and the older Menelaos is ambiguous: "all of them stayed stricken to silence." This could be simply because they are stunned at this unexpected development—or it could reflect the epic's several gentle hints that brave Menelaos may not rank among the very top tier of warriors; the stricken silence is perhaps a symptom of the Achaeans' instinctive alarm for him. Menelaos himself, however, does not hesitate to accept the challenge and rises to speak to the assembly, urging that whether it is he or Paris who is killed, "'the rest of you be made friends with each other.'"

So he spoke, and the Trojans and Achaeans were joyful,
hoping now to be rid of all the sorrow of warfare.

Not trusting the word of frivolous young men, Menelaos demands that Priam himself be summoned to cut the oath sanctifying the terms of the duel. While they wait for the aged king to come, the men of both armies pull their chariots into line and dismount, stripping off their armor and settling on the field "so there was little ground left between them." Leaving them to wait, the epic shifts the action dramatically away from the plain to a chamber in the palace complex inside the walls of Troy, an inner sanctuary removed from the world of dust and men. Here, sitting at her loom, is Helen of Troy, the prize sought by both armies and the prize shortly to be fought over by the two men who both claim her. Iris, the tireless messenger of Zeus, once again in the guise of a mortal, in this case Laodike, "loveliest looking of all the daughters of Priam," comes to Helen with a message:

> She came on Helen in the chamber; she was weaving a great web,
> a double folded cloak of crimson,[25] and working into it the
>   numerous struggles
> of Trojans, breakers of horses, and bronze-armoured Achaeans,
> struggles that they endured for her sake at the hands of the war god.
> Iris of the swift feet stood beside her and spoke to her:
> "Come with me, dear girl, to behold the marvellous things done
> by Trojans, breakers of horses, and bronze-armoured Achaeans,
> who just now carried sorrowful war against each other,
> in the plain, and all their desire was for deadly fighting;
> now they are all seated in silence, the fighting has ended;
> they lean on their shields, the tall spears stuck in the ground beside
>   them.
> But Menelaos the warlike and Alexandros will fight
> with long spears against each other for your possession.
> You shall be called beloved wife of the man who wins you."

Elsewhere in the *Iliad*, warriors are said to "weave" speeches and counsels, plots and schemes; by setting certain events in motion, such masculine weaving, then, shapes reality.[26] The women of Troy weave only the representations of events. The gentleness of all imagery in this scene—the quiet chamber where Helen sits spinning the story of her own life and the calm delivery of Iris' shattering news—places the domestic world of Troy and its women at an almost surreal remove from everything that exists on the plain outside. For this moment, from within these walls, even the actual war appears peaceful, as the soldiers sit unarmed together in unnatural passivity. The remoteness of this inner world of spinning and weaving from the rending and tearing that is the work of war is also a symptom of its powerlessness.[27] At the very moment Helen sits calmly weaving her own story, she is entirely ignorant of the fact that her story is being changed yet again—her fate rewoven, as it were, by Paris' off-the-cuff offer and Menelaos' acceptance. The hosts of two entire armies, thousands of men, know the terms of her fate before she does. "'You shall be called beloved wife of the man who wins you,'" says gentle Iris, and her categorical matter-of-factness has a sinister ring.

The goddess's words, the speaking of Menelaos' name, stir Helen:

> Speaking so the goddess left in her heart sweet longing
> after her husband of time before, and her city and parents.
> And at once, wrapping herself about in shimmering garments,
> she went forth from the chamber, letting fall a light tear.

Going out onto the roof above the Skaian Gates, one of two named entrances to the city and of all features of Troy the most fated, Helen passes Priam and the Trojan elders, men too old to fight, who remain now inside the gates with the women and children:

> . . . these, as they saw Helen along the tower approaching,
> murmuring softly to each other uttered their winged words:
> "Surely there is no blame on Trojans and strong-greaved Achaeans
> if for long time they suffer hardship for a woman like this one.
> Terrible is the likeness of her face to immortal goddesses.
> Still, though she be such, let her go away in the ships, lest
> she be left behind, a grief to us and our children."

Helen's timeless beauty is evoked with not a single physical attribute—her hair, her features, her eyes—but by the reaction of those who should hate her most. "Terrible"—*ainōs*—"is the likeness of her face to immortal goddesses"; the word *ainōs* carries the same double edge as its literal English counterpart—"in an extreme degree," "strongly," but also "to such a degree as to cause apprehension," "dreadfully."[28] This charged word and the men's conclusion—"'Still . . . let her go away in the ships'"—eloquently establishes Helen's precarious existence in the city of her people's enemy.

The only man to turn to her with wholehearted warmth is Priam himself, who calls her to join him in watching her "'husband of time past'" and inquiring as to the identity of one of the Achaean warriors, who given his splendid, lordly appearance "'might well be royal.'" Helen's response, the first words she utters in the epic, is roundabout, and tellingly begins with a devastating self-characterization:

> Helen, the shining among women, answered and spoke to him:
> "Always to me, beloved father, you are feared and respected;
> and I wish bitter death had been what I wanted, when I came hither
> following your son, forsaking my chamber, my kinsmen,
> my grown child, and the loveliness of girls my own age.
> It did not happen that way: and now I am worn with weeping.
> This now I will tell you in answer to the question you asked me.
> That man is Atreus' son Agamemnon, widely powerful,
> at the same time a good king and a strong spearfighter,[29]
> once my kinsman, slut that I am. Did this ever happen?"

The fate Hektor wishes on Paris is the fate Helen calls down upon herself: "'I wish bitter death had been what I wanted.'" Other traditions characterized Helen's elopement with Paris as a rape and an abduction; it was in this vein that Nestor called for the Achaeans to put aside all thoughts of home and to "avenge Helen's longing to escape and her lamentations."[30] Yet another tradition held that Helen never came to Troy but spent the war in Egypt, while men unwittingly fought over a ghostly cloud of her image.[31] Nestor's wishful thinking apart, the *Iliad* consistently, if sympathetically, portrays Helen as the remorseful agent of her own disastrous decision. "'Did this ever happen?'" are her wondering words.

Priam's query as to the identity of the unknown regal warrior who turns out to be Agamemnon marks the beginning of an extended scene conventionally referred to as the Teichoskopia, or "Viewing from the Walls." From the battlements of his city, with fair Helen beside him, the old king looks over the array of warriors gathered below and, pointing out one hero after another, asks who each is. His query and Helen's response afford the opportunity for a series of vivid character sketches. That Priam in this tenth year of the war could be ignorant of the identity of Atreus' son Agamemnon, lord of men and commander in chief of the Achaeans, is obviously implausible. Like the Catalogue of Ships, the entire sequence has been relocated from an earlier account of the beginning of the war, to serve as a theatrical prelude to the first scene of actual fighting:

> Next again the old man asked her, seeing Odysseus:
> "Tell me of this one also, dear child; what man can he be,
> shorter in truth by a head than Atreus' son Agamemnon,
> but broader, it would seem, in the chest and across the shoulders."

Helen's identification of Odysseus, son of Laertes, a man raised "'to know every manner of shiftiness and crafty counsels,'" is unexpectedly supplemented by Priam's counselor, Antenor, who stands nearby:

> In his turn Antenor of the good counsel answered her:
> "Surely this word you have spoken, my lady, can be no falsehood.
> Once in the days before now brilliant Odysseus came here
> with warlike Menelaos, and their embassy was for your sake.
> To both of these I gave in my halls kind entertainment
> and I learned the natural way of both, and their close counsels.
> Now when these were set before the Trojans assembled
> and stood up, Menelaos was bigger by his broad shoulders
> but Odysseus was the more lordly when both were seated.

Now before all when both of them spun their speech and their
   counsels,
Menelaos indeed spoke rapidly, in few words
but exceedingly lucid, since he was no long speaker
nor one who wasted his words though he was only a young man.
But when that other drove to his feet, resourceful Odysseus,
he would just stand and stare down, eyes fixed on the ground
   beneath him,
nor would he gesture with the staff backward and forward, but
   hold it
clutched hard in front of him, like any man who knows nothing.
Yes, you would call him a sullen man, and a fool likewise.
But when he let the great voice go from his chest, and the words
   came
drifting down like the winter snows, then no other mortal
man beside could stand up against Odysseus. Then we
wondered less beholding Odysseus' outward appearance."

Amid much else, Antenor's justly famous characterization of one of the most enduring heroes in all mythology drops a casual reference to what had evidently been an attempt by both parties to avoid the war. "'Their embassy was for your sake,'" he says in passing to Helen. That Odysseus is spoken of by the Trojans with open admiration, and even Menelaos with approbation, suggests the possibility of an optimistic outcome; what, one wonders, went wrong?[32]

This civilized interlude is interrupted by the appearance of the herald Idaios summoning Priam to seal the oaths so that the duel for Helen can begin. Priam, "shuddering," sets out and makes a striking arrival, striding between the two armies. The oath taken by both parties to abide by the duel's outcome is performed in a solemn ceremony, with prayers, libations, and sacrifice. Agamemnon, cutting the hairs from the heads of the lambs of sacrifice, himself offers a prayer to Zeus:

"If it should be that Alexandros slays Menelaos,
let him keep Helen for himself, and all her possessions,
and we in our seafaring ships shall take our way homeward.
But if the fair-haired Menelaos kills Alexandros,
then let the Trojans give back Helen and all her possessions,
and pay also a price to the Argives which will be fitting,
which among people yet to come shall be as a standard.
Then if Priam and the sons of Priam are yet unwilling
after Alexandros has fallen to pay me the penalty,
I myself shall fight hereafter for the sake of the ransom,
here remaining, until I have won to the end of my quarrel."[33]

The oaths cut, Priam hastily remounts his chariot and heads back to Troy, because, as he says, he "'cannot look with these eyes on the sight of my dear son / fighting.'" As the leaders and princes make the last preparations for the duel, the rank and file murmur a startling, ambiguous prayer of their own:

"Father Zeus, watching over us from Ida, most high, most
    honoured,
whichever man has made what has happened happen to both sides,
grant that he be killed and go down to the house of Hades.
Let the friendship and the sworn faith be true for the rest of us."

Strikingly, no man at Troy prays for his own side to win. Achaean and Trojan are indifferent to the outcome—so long as it brings the war to an end.

The duel itself comes and goes in a relative flash of a mere forty lines. Paris hurls a spear and strikes Menelaos' shield; Menelaos strikes the shield of Paris. Menelaos then strikes at Paris' helmet with his silver nail-studded sword, causing it to shatter into pieces and drop from his hand. In desperation, he also drops his warrior's posture and starts to brawl, grabbing Paris' helmet and dragging him toward the Achaeans, causing the chinstrap to throttle Paris' soft throat. Here Menelaos would have "won glory forever" had Aphrodite, Paris' patron goddess, not intervened. Invisible to the mortal onlookers, she breaks his chinstrap to free him, then whisks Paris away, shrouded in thick mist, and drops him in his own bedchamber.[34] Next setting out to look for Helen, she finds her on the tower with other women. Disguising herself as an old wool dresser whom Helen had known in Sparta, the goddess tugs at her robe and addresses her:

> "Come with me: Alexandros sends for you to come home to him.
> He is in his chamber now, in the bed with its circled pattern,
> shining in his raiment and his own beauty; you would not think
> that he came from fighting against a man; you would think he was
>   going
> rather to a dance, or rested and had been dancing lately."

Looking closely at her, Helen recognizes "the round, sweet throat of the goddess" and in a flash of anger offers the goddess an astonishing challenge:

> "Go yourself and sit beside him, abandon the gods' way,
> turn your feet back never again to the path of Olympos
> but stay with him forever, and suffer for him, and look after him
> until he makes you his wedded wife, or makes you his slave girl.
> Not I. I am not going to him. It would be too shameful.
> I will not serve his bed, since the Trojan women hereafter
> would laugh at me, all, and my heart even now is confused with
>   sorrows."

No other of the *Iliad*'s characters so directly confronts any of the deities who toy with their lives. With her woman's instinct, Helen sees through everything, not only Aphrodite's feeble disguise but her most secret motives. The goddess's description of Paris, with its jarring emphasis on his beauty and his bed, is transparent to Helen: the goddess of desire herself desires Paris and is pimping Helen to him as her surrogate.

In Greek mythology, Helen's origins are bizarre. The best-known story tells of the rape of her mother, Leda, by Zeus in the guise of a swan, the fruit of this coupling being an egg, from which was hatched Helen; in other versions her mother, suggestively, is Nemesis, also united with Zeus "under harsh compulsion."[35] The *Iliad* frequently acknowledges Helen as being "descended from Zeus" but ignores the exact role he plays in her parentage. An Indo-European reconstruction of her name, *Swelénā*, from a word stem associated with burning and sun glare, suggests that she was the shining Daughter of the Sun.[36] In later Greek mythology and cult, she has intriguing associations with trees, birds, and eggs, suggestive of a fertility goddess who lost her divinity over time, while retaining her essential attributes.[37] Aphrodite's origins are found in Ishtar-Astarte, the Phoenician queen of heaven and divine prostitute, whose cult was brought to Greece by way of the island of Cyprus (or Kypros); "Kypris" is one of Aphrodite's Iliadic epithets.[38] Helen's thralldom to lust and desire, whether taken metaphorically or as a literal servitude forced upon her by Aphrodite's spell, is used in the *Iliad* to render one of the most complex and convincing of all its many characters.[39]

Aphrodite's response to Helen's challenge is to lash out in anger:

"Wretched girl, do not tease me lest in anger I forsake you
and grow to hate you as much as now I terribly love you,
lest I encompass you in hard hate, caught between both sides,
Danaans and Trojans alike, and you wretchedly perish."

Bereft of desirability, as Helen herself knows, she would not stand a chance within Troy's walls, or without. Submitting in anger and humiliation to Aphrodite, Helen follows her to Paris' chamber, where the goddess herself, with menacing solicitude, pulls up a chair for her by Paris' bed. "'So you came back from fighting,'" says Helen to her lord "in derision." "'Oh, how I wish you had died there / beaten down by the stronger man, who was once my husband.'" "'Lady, censure my heart no more in bitter reprovals,'" Paris responds unconcernedly, and, distracted by his desire, he draws Helen to his bed. Aphrodite's bestowal of Helen on Paris is undoubtedly inspired by the story of the first fateful seduction, when Paris came to Sparta—yet another scene belonging to the early phase of the war but restated here for dramatic effect.[40]

Back on the plain of Troy, Menelaos still rages, searching for Paris, whom he last saw in his very hands.

> Yet could none of the Trojans nor any renowned companion
> show Alexandros then to warlike Menelaos.
> These would not have hidden him for love, if any had seen him,
> since he was hated among them all as dark death is hated.

Who won the duel? Although neither man was killed in accordance with the terms the solemn oath had projected, the advantage, as Agamemnon declares before the assembly, is clearly to Menelaos. But the unorthodox situation causes a quandary, not only on earth but on Olympos, where the gods are sitting in council and Zeus ponders what to do next:

> "Let us consider then how these things shall be accomplished,
> whether again to stir up grim warfare and the terrible
> fighting, or cast down love and make them friends with each other.
> If somehow this way could be sweet and pleasing to all of us,
> the city of lord Priam might still be a place men dwell in,
> and Menelaos could take away with him Helen of Argos."

At this moment, Zeus' pledge to Thetis and Achilles seems to have slipped his mind; there is no question but that the war must be resumed if Achilles is to be missed, and therefore honored, by his Achaean companions. Such lapses in the *Iliad*'s memory are most usually attributed to the hazards of a long, traditional oral composition. It may also be that such lapses were forgiven by their ancient audiences and that dramatic value counted more than consistency. At any rate, here and now, Achaeans and Trojans stand at a crossroad; the possibility looms that they can all go home.

But Zeus' suggestion that the whole business be wrapped up bloodlessly is viciously struck down by Hera, whose appetite for this war never, ever flags. Angrily, she evokes "'the sweat that I have sweated in toil, and my horses worn out / gathering my people, and bringing evil to Priam and his children.'" Zeus' response is that of a very weary husband: reluctantly, against his own inclination, he gives in. His speech to Hera and hers again to him bear some of the most tragic import in the epic:

Deeply troubled, Zeus who gathers the clouds answered her:
"Dear lady, what can be all the great evils done to you
by Priam and the sons of Priam, that you are thus furious
forever to bring down the strong-founded city of Ilion?
If you could walk through the gates and through the towering
    ramparts
and eat Priam and the children of Priam raw, and the other
Trojans, then, then only might you glut at last your anger.
Do as you please then. Never let this quarrel hereafter
be between you and me a bitterness for both of us.
And put away in your thoughts this other thing that I tell you:
whenever I in turn am eager to lay waste some city,
as I please, one in which are dwelling men who are dear to you,
you shall not stand in the way of my anger, but let me do it,
since I was willing to grant you this with my heart unwilling.

For of all the cities beneath the sun and the starry heaven
dwelt in by men who live upon earth, there has never been one
honoured nearer to my heart than sacred Ilion
and Priam, and the people of Priam of the strong ash spear.
Never yet has my altar gone without fair sacrifice,
the libation and the savour, since this is our portion of honour."
    Then the goddess the ox-eyed lady Hera answered:
"Of all cities there are three that are dearest to my own heart:
Argos and Sparta and Mycenae of the wide ways. All these,
whenever they become hateful to your heart, sack utterly.
I will not stand up for these against you, nor yet begrudge you."

Once this agreement has been reached, events unfold swiftly: Athene
is given orders "'to visit horrible war again on Achaeans and Trojans,'"
and to do so in a way that makes the Trojans the offenders. Like a falling
star, she flashes to earth in a blaze of light and then, in the likeness of a
man, insinuates herself among the Trojans. Her patsy is the Trojan Pandaros, son of Lykaon. Sidling up to him, she speaks "winged words"
describing the glory and gratitude he will win from the Trojans, the gifts
he will receive from Paris, if he lets fly an arrow at Menelaos: "So spoke
Athene, and persuaded the fool's heart in him." The arrow Pandaros
shoots flies true but is deflected from its intended mark by Athene herself, true to her role as a double agent. Driven into Menelaos' belt buckle,
the arrow harmlessly grazes his skin, while drawing blood.

"'Dear brother, it was your death I sealed in the oaths of friendship, /
setting you alone before the Achaeans to fight with the Trojans,'" groans
Agamemnon, unmanned at the sight of his brother's blood. In his loving
solicitude, he makes here, perhaps, his most sympathetic appearance
in the epic. Vacillating between self-recrimination and anger, Agamemnon calls for the Trojan people to pay a great penalty for this outrage
"'with their own heads, and with their women, and with their children.'"
The war machinery starts to grind again; as the Trojans approach,

Agamemnon rallies and positions his troops: "The Achaeans again put on their armour, and remembered their warcraft."⁴¹ Shortly afterward, the first man in the epic is killed, a Trojan named Echepolos, who falls at the hands of Antilochos. And so the truce, with all the promise it held, is shattered, and the war is on. There will be a few future acts of friendship between individual warriors, and one more solemn attempt to end the war, made by an assembly of Trojans desperate to save their city, but this also will be futile.

The proud drumroll represented by the Catalogue of Ships' magnificent display of men and nations dies away here—specifically, it dies with the deal cut between Zeus and Hera. Zeus will sacrifice the Trojans, whom he loves beyond all other peoples, and Hera will sacrifice the Achaean cities she holds most dear in order to glut her hatred. Both gods have agreed to an understanding that will break their own hearts. The unwitting, unwilling victims of this pact are all that grand host, the thousands of lives paraded in such pomp and magnificence by both Catalogues. "'O son of Atreus, blessed, child of fortune and favour / many are these beneath your sway, these sons of the Achaeans,'" Priam had exclaimed in wondering admiration, viewing from the battlement of his doomed city the glittering Achaean host.

For Homer's audience, the exchange on Olympos would have held particular, devastating import. The cities named by Hera as those she held most dear—"'Argos and Sparta and Mycenae of the wide ways'"—had been their own.⁴² As Greek populations descended from the refugees of these lost cities would have recognized, the self-defeating pact between the gods represented a bitter parable—the price of the war against Troy was their own defeat. Later traditions would spell out this conviction in more detail, but never with more devastating eloquence.

"'Father Zeus, watching over us from Ida, most high, most honoured, . . . Let the friendship and the sworn faith be true for the rest of us'"; ". . . the Trojans and Achaeans were joyful, / hoping now to be rid of all the sorrow of warfare." With deliberate, extended scenes, the *Iliad* establishes the hatred with which the war is held by both sides. *Lugrós, polúdakrus, dusēlegēs, ainós*—"baleful," "bringing many tears," "bringing much woe," "dread"—these are the epithets the *Iliad* uses of war.[43] Earlier, in vivid, dramatic detail, it established that the Achaeans are ready to flee for their homes. No one wants to be here; everyone regrets that the war ever started. Everyone wants a way out. The war seems to have gathered autonomous momentum, which, as the epic emphasizes, will end in mutual destruction.

> . . . on that day many men of the Achaeans and Trojans
> lay sprawled in the dust face downward beside one another.

These are the last, pointed words of *Iliad*, Book Four, summing up the renewal of fighting on the day that could have ended in peace. To echo Helen's uncomprehending despair: " 'Did this ever happen?' "

Enemy Lines

There the screaming and the shouts of triumph rose up together
of men killing and men killed, and the ground ran blood.

—*Iliad* 4.450–51

An epic of war, the greater part of the *Iliad* is concerned with killing and dying, and the deaths of some 250 warriors are recorded, the majority in relentlessly inventive detail: "This man Meriones pursued and overtaking him / struck in the right buttock, and the spearhead drove straight / on and passing under the bone went into the bladder. . . . He dropped, screaming, to his knees, and death was a mist about him." "Next he killed Astynoös and Hypeiron, shepherd of the people, / striking one with the bronze-heeled spear above the nipple, / and cutting the other beside the shoulder through the collar-bone / with the great sword, so that neck and back were hewn free of the shoulder." "He spoke, and threw; and Pallas Athene guided the weapon / to the nose next to the eye, and it cut on through the white teeth / and the bronze weariless shore all the way through the tongue's base / so that the spearhead came out underneath the jawbone."

Narrated, as it were, in the heat of battle, the swift, graphic descriptions of wounding and killing are endowed with just sufficiently realistic detail to render even the more far-fetched scenes believable; Homer "knew where the major organs were," as one medical authority has stated.

"He did not know what their function was."[1] For a civilian audience, however, they suffice to evoke convincingly the carnage of the battlefield. More to the point, notwithstanding the anatomical improbabilities, these deaths are clearly *intended* to be realistic.

More important, the deaths are also clearly intended to be pathetic, and on this point the *Iliad* parts company with conventional heroic saga. Fighting, battling, wounding, inflicting death are not merely the central tropes of heroic narrative, they are by and large what heroic narrative is about, as can be illustrated by the following fairly typical, fairly random examples:

The forty warriors rushed to the fight,
Began the fight against the heathen.
They came in a flood then,
They were covered in blood.
They scattered cries here.
They brandished their pikes here.
The face of the earth was covered with blood. . . .

—*Epic of Manas*

Or:

Each strained at the other from the saddle
Till the eight hoofs of their horses were mingled.
But neither was victorious.
They unsheathed their glittering swords from their covers,
Seven and eight times they dealt each other blows
Over their bladders,
But neither was victorious.
They made haste, they struck each other on their belts,
They dealt each other blows behind and before. . . .

—*Dzhangariada*[2]

In distinct contrast to these impersonal slugging matches, the *Iliad*'s "poetry of combat," as it has been called, takes pains to personalize its heroic deaths. The slain warriors of the *Iliad* are mostly obscure fellows who have received no previous mention in the epic, but who are evoked—brought to life—at the moment they are killed by some small personalizing detail: "Meriones in turn killed Phereklos, son of Harmonides, / the smith, who understood how to make with his hand all intricate / things. . . ." "Meges in turn killed Pedaios, the son of Antenor, / who, bastard though he was, was nursed by lovely Theano / with close care, as for her own children, to pleasure her husband. . . ." "Diomedes of the great war cry cut down Axylos, / Teuthras' son, who had been a dweller in strong-founded Arisbe, / a man rich in substance and a friend to all humanity / since in his house by the wayside he entertained all comers."

The vanquishing warrior may carry the action, but the audience's emotional attention is diverted to the fallen foe. This personalizing quality ensures that most of the *Iliad*'s deaths are perceived—perhaps only fleetingly—to be regrettable. Although the winning of glory in combat is the aim of the conventional hero of combat poetry, in the *Iliad* glory is usurped by sympathy for the human being, possessed of a family and life story, who has been extinguished. Fully three times as many Trojans die as Achaeans in this Greek epic, so the *Iliad* is dense with the descriptions of enemy warriors who die pathetically. This remarkable point is worth emphasizing: subtly, but with unflagging consistency, the *Iliad* ensures that the enemy is humanized and that the deaths of enemy Trojans are depicted as lamentable. The *Iliad* is insistent on keeping to the fore the price of glory.

The *Iliad*'s wounded warriors also tend to die. There are no instances in which a mortally wounded hero fights on to prevail over the weakness of his flesh; no god reattaches a hero's severed limb or miraculously restores a shattered skull. Nor are we ever shown the enduring wounds of war, the maimed soldiers who somehow survived a heroic onslaught at the cost of a limb, or an eye, or other diminishment. This may simply be a reflection of the medical realities of Homer's Dark Age, when, undoubt-edly, wounded soldiers did in fact tend to die. The inevitability of death after wounding may, then, be a historical, not a poetic, truth, but in any event the mortality of the Homeric warrior is never compromised.[3]

In a few exceptional cases, chosen warriors receive magical deliver-ance from certain death by divine intervention, as, for example, Paris was plucked out of combat with Menelaos by his patron goddess, Aph-rodite. The most striking instances of such deliverance involve the Tro-jan Aineias, who, for example, is also rescued, in Book Five, by Aphrodite, his divine mother, from the hands of Diomedes, the son of Tydeus and one of the most important Achaean heroes:

> Tydeus' son in his hand caught
> up a stone, a huge thing which no two men could carry
> such as men are now, but by himself he lightly hefted it.
> He threw, and caught Aineias in the hip, in the place where the
>   hip-bone
> turns inside the thigh, the place men call the cup-socket.
> It smashed the cup-socket and broke the tendons both sides of it,
> and the rugged stone tore the skin backward, so that the fighter
> dropping to one knee stayed leaning on the ground with his heavy
> hand, and a covering of black night came over both eyes.
>   Now in this place Aineias lord of men might have perished
> had not Aphrodite, Zeus' daughter, been quick to perceive him.

The facts of Aineias' parentage by Aphrodite and his mortal father, Anchises, is emphatically established by Aineias himself later in the epic, when he relates in exhaustive detail his genealogy to Achilles, as one demigod bragging to another. More important than Aineias' half-divine birth, however, is the extraordinary prophecy he bears to "'be the sur-vivor'" of the house of Priam when Ilion eventually falls. His descendants, so the ancient prophecy runs, will inherit the Troad; it was in deference to this tradition that the Romans claimed Trojan Aineias as their founder—a tradition that has recently received new consideration in view of DNA findings that indicate that the Etruscans, the first rulers of Rome, originated from Anatolia.[4]

Altogether, Aineias is rescued four times from certain death in the *Iliad,* twice in Book Five from Diomedes and twice in Book Twenty from Achilles[5]—far more than any other hero. If, as it seems, the tradition of his survival was already well established, these many close calls should perhaps be seen as the epic's playful sparring with its audiences' expectations: Aineias the legendary survivor appears to be doomed—"[Aineias] dropping to one knee stayed leaning on the ground with his heavy / hand, and a covering of black night came over both eyes"—the terrible darkening of vision is one of the *Iliad*'s most common descriptions of death. At the last moment, however, the epic relents and Aphrodite appears to protect her fated son, and the audience can smile with relief, and perhaps amusement.[6]

The few demigods, such as Aineias, who receive miraculous rescue are saved only by the direct intervention of a patron divinity, not by any special ingredient of their own semidivine nature. The flesh of the demigods is wholly vulnerable, the blood is the blood of mortals, the pain of injury that of ordinary mortal men, as is the inevitability of death. Nothing the men have inherited from their divine parents is itself protective; what saves them is the physical removal from the danger of the battlefield. The vividly evoked vulnerability of demigods such as Aineias will also have bearing upon the nature, and limitations, of the epic's most outstanding demigod—Achilles.

Diomedes' rampage is the most important feature of the epic's first major engagement, and it sweeps unflaggingly through Book Five: Book Five belongs to Diomedes. This is his *aristeía,* or display of prowess (from the verb *aristeúein,* "to be the best or the bravest"). The son of the hero Tydeus, one of the heroes of old from the generation before that at Troy and a member of the legendary seven who attacked Thebes, Diomedes is securely placed within the epic tradition's inner circle of heroes. The exploits of his father, Tydeus, are often recalled in the *Iliad,* by both gods and men, and Athene's aid to Diomedes is predicated on her affection for his father: "'Such a helper was I who stood then beside him,'" says the goddess to her protégé; "'Now beside you also I stand and ever watch over you, / and urge you to fight confidently with the Trojans.'" In earlier lore, Diomedes appears to have originally been a tribal hero, or even a god, associated with Aetolia, north of the Corinthian Gulf; in the *Iliad,* however, he is the king of Argos.[7] Embedded in Diomedes' family history are a number of telling incidents that suggest that the dramatic swath of slaughter he cuts through the enemy ranks in Book Five may be an extension of an inherited brutality. A great-uncle of his was "Agrios," meaning "fierce" or "savage," while his father almost won the gift of immortality from the gods but lost this opportunity by an act of peculiar savagery: "Tydeus the son of Oineus in the Theban war was wounded by Melanippus the son of Astacus," relates an ancient scholiast, or commentator, on the *Iliad:* "Amphiaraus killed Melanippus and brought back his head, which Tydeus split open and gobbled his brain in a passion. When Athena, who was bringing Tydeus immortality, saw the horror, she turned away from him."[8]

Cults honoring Diomedes throughout the Greek world are inevitably associated with horses, an association upheld in the *Iliad,* and in at least one instance with human sacrifice.[9] Out of these old, disturbing traditions, the *Iliad*'s Diomedes has been considerably refined, and while a courageous and effective warrior, he is also gracious and well spoken, both on the field and off. He is integral to the larger story of the siege and capture of Troy that takes place beyond the parameters of the *Iliad.*

As Diomedes blazes through the enemy forces, he twice—remarkably—transgresses into the divine realm. When Aphrodite, "the lady of Kypros," rescues her son Aineias, Diomedes' response displays a dangerous lack of awe; swinging his sword at her, he catches the goddess on her hand, causing *ichōr,* "that which runs in the veins of the blessed divinities" instead of blood, to flow. Shrieking, Aphrodite retreats to Olympos, as Diomedes shouts a warning after her:

"Give way, daughter of Zeus, from the fighting and the terror. It is not then enough that you lead astray women without warcraft? Yet, if still you must haunt the fighting, I think that now you will shiver even when you hear some other talking of battles."

Diomedes' dim view of the goddess of love and desire is humorously shared by the more warrior-like goddesses, Athene and Hera, who scornfully mock the Kyprian's tearful return to Olympos. Smiling indulgently at Athene, Zeus gently scolds Aphrodite for straying beyond the bedroom into the battlefield. It is left to her mother, Dione, to comfort the shaken goddess and to treat her wound. Taking her daughter's arm, she "stroked away . . . the ichor, / so that the arm was made whole again and the strong pains rested."

Athene herself plays a direct role in Diomedes' second assault on a god. Having obtained permission from Zeus to interfere in the fray, she and Hera, letting forth a shrieking war cry, swoop from Olympos to earth in their divine chariot. Parking horses and chariot on the Trojan plain, the two set forth "in little steps like shivering / doves, in their eagerness to stand by the men of Argos"—this image of the bloodthirsty divinities shivering in excitement as they mince toward their prey is inexpressibly sinister. On arrival, Athene immediately accosts Diomedes and directs him to charge straight for Ares, the very god of war, who, fighting for the Trojans, is hewing his own havoc on the field. Shoving Diomedes' henchman out of the way, Athene climbs beside him in his chariot, causing it to groan under her Olympian weight, and, taking up the whip and the reins, drives straight for Ares. The war god's response is to stab at Diomedes with his spear, but, easily, Athene brushes him aside, and it is Diomedes who "drove forward / with the bronze spear; and Pallas Athene, leaning in on it, / drove it into the depth of the belly where the war belt girt him." Bellowing with pain and dripping immortal ichor, Ares, like Aphrodite before him, makes his way speedily to Olympos to complain loudly to Zeus, but here he is met with blistering contempt. "'Do not sit beside me and whine, you double-faced liar,'" says Zeus. "'To me you are most hateful of all gods who hold Olympos.'" Nonetheless, it is not fitting that Ares, immortal as he is, remain wounded, and at Zeus' behest Paiëon, the god of healing (whose traits were later assumed by Apollo), administers medicinal herbs, and the god of war is healed.[10]

The remarkable accumulation of the variety of woundings and rescues in this first of the *Iliad*'s extended scenes of battle helps establish the parameters of mortal conflict on the heroic field of war. There are the minor characters who live to die at a greater hero's hands; there are those whom the gods choose to rescue, at least for the day, from certain death; there are the demigods who are rescued and healed by divine intervention. And then there are the gods themselves, who, like the mortals who so entertain them, throw themselves energetically into the fray, inflict and suffer wounds, bleed, feel pain and even fear. The remarkable *aristeia* of Diomedes shows that not only gods but men can cause divine ichor to flow; conversely, a divine touch can heal mortal and immortal wounds alike. This occasional blurring of boundaries between human and divine spheres serves to harden rather than obscure the essential, unassailable differences between god and man. Notwithstanding all the varieties of wounds and wounding, a single, salient fact remains, as Apollo reminds Diomedes: "never the same is / the breed of gods, who are immortal, and men who walk on the ground." The gods can play at war, but mortal heroes—healed or wounded, rescued or abandoned—must eventually die.

Death: the *Iliad* is ever mindful that war is about men killing or men killed. In the entire epic, no warrior, whether hero or obscure man of the ranks, dies happily or well. No reward awaits the soldier's valor; no heaven will receive him. The *Iliad*'s words and phrases for the process of death make clear that this is something baneful: dark night covers the dying warrior, hateful darkness claims him; he is robbed of sweet life, his soul goes down to Hades bewailing its fate.[11] Again and again, relentlessly, the *Iliad* hammers this fact: The death of any warrior is tragic and full of horror. Even in war, death is regrettable.

Diomedes' *aristeía* overruns the boundaries of Book Five, continuing into Book Six, where his martial success serves to inspire his Achaean companions to battle fever. Amid the ensuing wave of slaughter, Menelaos captures a Trojan warrior, Adrestos, alive. At Menelaos' knees, the captive begs for his life to be spared in exchange for a ransom from his father. Moved, Menelaos is on the point of sparing him when his brother, Agamemnon, comes "on the run" to dissuade him:

> "Dear brother, o Menelaos, are you concerned so tenderly
> with these people? Did you in your house get the best of treatment
> from the Trojans? No, let not one of them go free of sudden
> death and our hands; not the young man child that the mother
>   carries
> still in her body, not even he, but let all of Ilion's
> people perish, utterly blotted out and unmourned for."
>   The hero spoke like this, and bent the heart of his brother
> since he urged justice.[12] Menelaos shoved with his hand Adrestos
> the warrior back from him, and powerful Agamemnon
> stabbed him in the side and, as he writhed over, Atreides,
> setting his heel upon the midriff, wrenched out the ash spear.
>   Nestor in a great voice cried out to the men of Argos:
> "O beloved Danaan fighters, henchmen of Ares,
> let no man any more hang back with his eye on the plunder
> designing to take all the spoil he can gather back to the vessels;
> let us kill the men now, and afterwards at your leisure
> all along the plain you can plunder the perished corpses."

It is no surprise, perhaps, that Agamemnon should reject an offer of ransom; nor that his actions should be enthusiastically endorsed by zealous Nestor. Nestor's suggestion that plunder be gained by stripping the dead corpses, rather than by taking ransom, is a potent reminder that the war at Troy is principally about the acquisition of possessions. The terms of Menelaos' duel with Paris were that if Menelaos won, the Trojans would give back not only Helen but "Helen and all her possessions." There has been no evidence to this point in the epic that heroes fight for anything as insubstantial as glory.

The onslaught of Diomedes, aided by Athene, has made nonsense of the pledge Zeus gave Thetis to honor Achilles—" 'to help the Trojans, / and pin the Achaeans back against the ships and the water, / dying.'" With the Trojans in near rout, the Trojan prince Helenos urges on his brother Hektor a course of action that will have momentous consequences for the epic: Hektor will return to the city and instruct their mother, Hekabe, and the other women to make an offering to the city's cult statue of Athene, promising the goddess rich gifts " 'if only she will have pity / on the town of Troy, and the Trojan wives, and their innocent children.'"

Obediently, Hektor strides away to the city, his shield—a Mycenaean relic, to judge from its description—across his back: "against his ankles as against his neck clashed the dark ox-hide, / the rim running round the edge of the great shield massive in the middle."[13] If the ensuing scene between Hektor and the women of Troy was as famous in Homer's time as it has become today, then the lengthy interlude that now intervenes between his departure and arrival, retarding the anticipated scene, may have been a tactic to increase audience expectation. As it is, as Hektor recedes, Glaukos "sprung of Hippolochos" and Diomedes emerge as if from nowhere to encounter each other in the space between the two armies.

" 'Who among mortal men are you, good friend?' " Diomedes inquires, adding unconvincingly that if he is " 'some one of the immortals come down from the bright sky, / know that I will not fight against any god of the heaven.'"

"'High-hearted son of Tydeus, why ask of my generation?'" Glaukos responds.

"As is the generation of leaves, so is that of humanity.
The wind scatters the leaves on the ground, but the live timber
burgeons with leaves again in the season of spring returning.
So one generation of men will grow while another
dies. Yet if you wish to learn all this and be certain
of my genealogy: there are plenty of men who know it.
There is a city, Ephyre, in the corner of horse-pasturing
Argos . . ."

The famous opening lines of Glaukos' speech are one of the *Iliad*'s more obvious debts to Eastern literature, and a close counterpart can be found, to choose one example from the Hebrew Bible, in the book of Psalms: "Man's days are like grass, like the blossom of the field, so he blooms. For the wind passes over it and it is not there."[14] (On the other hand, similar words of the later Ecclesiasticus are probably inspired by Homer: "As with the leafage flourishing on a dense tree—it drops, and puts forth others—so with the generation of flesh and blood).[15]

The story of Glaukos' forebears forms a long, dense digression. At the heart of his tale is the saga of Bellerophontes "'the blameless,'" who was falsely accused of trying to seduce the wife of a political rival, Proitos, whose advances he had in fact spurned. Reluctant to have him killed outright, Proitos instead sent Bellerophontes to Lykia, in southwest Asia Minor, bearing "'murderous symbols, / which he inscribed in a folding tablet, enough to destroy life,'" which Bellerophontes was instructed to show to Proitos' father-in-law. These "murderous symbols" are the *Iliad*'s only reference to writing and are thought to refer either to some memory of the Linear B pictograph script or to Hittite cuneiform. A folding tablet of wood such as Glaukos describes has been discovered in the wreck of a Bronze Age ship dating to the fourteenth century B.C., off the southern coast of Turkey.[16]

The point of this digression is the revelation that Glaukos' forebear migrated from Greece to Lykia, the land of a Trojan ally, and that in this complicated story Diomedes, who has been patiently standing on the battlefield listening, recognizes that he and the enemy before him are descended from men who were guest friends, men who had honored the sacred laws of hospitality to strangers. "Gladdened," Diomedes drives his spear into the ground and extends his hand in friendship: " 'See now, you are my guest friend from far in the time of our fathers. . . . Let us avoid each other's spears, even in the close fighting.' "

Elsewhere in the epic, an exchange of genealogies between heroes establishes bragging rights as much as identity. Here, however, it serves the unheroic function of suggesting that if a hero tells his biography long enough, a common story may be found. Some of the very little that can be safely surmised of the Dark Age populations, and audiences, of Homer's time is the fact that their forebears had traveled—from land to land and from people to people. Guest friendships—always a potent concept in Greek culture—had surely been formed along the way and would have been retained in long family memory. This function of genealogical recitations still persists today. In her memoir of coming of age in Somalia, Ayaan Hirsi Ali describes how "Somali children must memorize their lineage. . . . Whenever a Somali meets a stranger, they ask each other, 'Who are you?' They trace back their separate ancestries until they find a common forefather."[17]

The interlude between Glaukos and Diomedes concludes, and abruptly the *Iliad* has us back with Hektor, at the very gates of Troy. Immediately he is besieged by the Trojan women, asking "after their sons, after their brothers and neighbours, / their husbands; and he told them to pray to the immortals, / all, in turn; but there were sorrows in store for many."

Hektor's arrival marks the second time the *Iliad* has opened up the civilian world inside the walls of Troy. The first occasion mostly served to introduce Helen, at which time, during the optimistic lull preceding the duel between Paris and Menelaos that was intended to end the war, there was a sense of something close to peace: from the walls of Troy, Priam and Helen had looked down on the men of both camps lolling in the grass, their armor piled beside them. Now Troy is again at war, and from the walls where Helen watched her husbands prepare for battle, the city's desperate women have been forced to watch the devastation of their men; "but there were sorrows in store for many," and this despite their pleas to every god in heaven.

Turning from them, Hektor enters the palace of Priam, with its smooth-stone cloister walks and sleeping chambers—fifty in all for his many sons and twelve for his daughters, where, in pointed comparison with Paris and Helen, each son sleeps "beside his own wedded wife," each son-in-law beside "his own modest wife." In the wonderful calm of these smooth-stone cloisters, Hektor meets his mother, Hekabe, and one of his sisters, the lovely Laodike. Resisting their pleas to take a rest, Hektor charges his mother with the task of making an offering to the statue of Athene, repeating the injunction given to him by Helenos. He himself will look for Paris and, once again, drag him out to battle:

"So go yourself to the temple of the spoiler Athene,
while I go in search of Paris, to call him, if he will listen
to anything I tell him. How I wish at this moment the earth might
open beneath him. The Olympian let him live, a great sorrow
to the Trojans, and high-hearted Priam, and all of his children.
If only I could see him gone down to the house of the Death God,
then I could say my heart had forgotten its joyless affliction."

Just as Glaukos' exchange with Diomedes established that friendship is not confined to allies, so Hektor's relationship with Paris establishes that hatred is not confined to the enemy. When Hektor leaves, the women select an elaborate robe and with tearful supplication one of them lays their offering on the knees of Athene's statue, praying for pity upon "'the town of Troy, and the Trojan wives, and their innocent children.' / She spoke in prayer, but Pallas Athene turned her head from her."

Hektor finds his brother Paris in his chamber, "busy with his splendid armour," where Helen is sitting with her women; this, it appears, is how Paris and Helen spend most of their days. "'Strange man!'" Hektor rebukes him. "'The people are dying around the city and around the steep wall / as they fight hard; and it is for you that this war with its clamour / has flared up about our city.'" Compliant, almost cheerfully so, as is his way, Paris allows that Helen had just been "'winning me over / and urging me into the fight.'"[18] Turning from her women, Helen herself addresses Hektor, "in words of endearment" and also with characteristic words of self-revilement.

This second meeting with Helen and Paris essentially repeats many of the elements of the first. Then as now their relationship is most starkly defined by Helen's loathing of her Trojan husband and herself. Yet the repetition is strategic. The sad, bitter union between these two agents of the war is reestablished here in order to set at best advantage one of the *Iliad*'s most memorable scenes—the meeting of Hektor with his own wife, Andromache, and their son.

Hektor had returned to Troy, it will be recalled, only to enjoin his mother and the Trojan women to supplicate Athene. Now, spontaneously, he decides to look for his own wife. When he does not find her at home, he asks their housekeeper of her whereabouts and is told that, hearing the Trojans were falling back, Andromache had gone to the wall "'like a woman / gone mad, and a nurse attending her carries the baby.'" Hektor, believing he has missed his wife, returns the way he had come and is nearing the Skaian Gates, "whereby he would issue into the plain." Suddenly Andromache comes running to meet him—a few steps more and Hektor would have been out the gate and one of the most celebrated scenes in literature would not have happened.

She came to him there, and beside her went an attendant carrying
the boy in the fold of her bosom, a little child, only a baby,
Hektor's son, the admired, beautiful as a star shining,
whom Hektor called Skamandrios, but all of the others
Astyanax—lord of the city; since Hektor alone saved Ilion.
Hektor smiled in silence as he looked on his son, but she,
Andromache, stood close beside him, letting her tears fall,
and clung to his hand and called him by name and spoke to him:
   "Dearest,
your own great strength will be your death, and you have no pity
on your little son, nor on me, ill-starred, who soon must be your
   widow;
for presently the Achaeans, gathering together,
will set upon you and kill you; and for me it would be far better
to sink into the earth when I have lost you, for there is no other
consolation for me after you have gone to your destiny—
only grief."

Andromache is already a casualty of the war. Her father, Eëtion, was
killed by Achilles along with her seven brothers; her mother, who had
been captured and ransomed by Achilles, died shortly afterward, perhaps of grief.

"Hektor, thus you are father to me, and my honoured mother,
you are my brother, and you it is who are my young husband.
Please take pity upon me then, stay here on the rampart,
that you may not leave your child an orphan, your wife a widow,
but draw your people up by the fig tree, there where the city
is openest to attack, and where the wall may be mounted. . . ."
   Then tall Hektor of the shining helm answered her: "All these
things are in my mind also, lady; yet I would feel deep shame
before the Trojans, and the Trojan women with trailing garments,

if like a coward I were to shrink aside from the fighting;
and the spirit will not let me, since I have learned to be valiant
and to fight always among the foremost ranks of the Trojans,
winning for my own self great glory, and for my father.
For I know this thing well in my heart, and my mind knows it:
there will come a day when sacred Ilion shall perish,
and Priam, and the people of Priam of the strong ash spear.
But it is not so much the pain to come of the Trojans
that troubles me, not even of Priam the king nor Hekabe,
not the thought of my brothers who in their numbers and valour
shall drop in the dust under the hands of men who hate them,
as troubles me the thought of you, when some bronze-armoured
Achaean leads you off, taking away your day of liberty,
in tears; and in Argos you must work at the loom of another,
and carry water from the spring Messeis or Hypereia,
all unwilling, but strong will be the necessity upon you;
and some day seeing you shedding tears a man will say of you:
'This is the wife of Hektor, who was ever the bravest fighter
of the Trojans, breakers of horses, in the days when they fought
    about Ilion.'
So will one speak of you; and for you it will be yet a fresh grief,
to be widowed of such a man who could fight off the day of your
    slavery.
But may I be dead and the piled earth hide me under before I
hear you crying and know by this that they drag you captive."

    So speaking glorious Hektor held out his arms to his baby,
who shrank back to his fair-girdled nurse's bosom
screaming, and frightened at the aspect of his own father,
terrified as he saw the bronze and the crest with its horse-hair,
nodding dreadfully, as he thought, from the peak of the helmet.
Then his beloved father laughed out, and his honoured mother,
and at once glorious Hektor lifted from his head the helmet

and laid it in all its shining upon the ground. Then taking
up his dear son he tossed him about in his arms, and kissed him.

With the baby in his arms, Hektor prays aloud to Zeus that his son
will thrive and grow great and come to rule over Ilion, that the Trojans
will say of him "'He is better by far than his father.'" Listening to her
husband's prayer, Andromache smiles through her tears, and Hektor,
pitying her, strokes her hand and takes his leave.

"Hektor of the shining helm": this was not, as it turns out, a heroic
attribute. Unheroic, too, is Hektor's unique prayer that his son be called
"better by far than his father," a father's instinctive inversion of the conventional dictate that sons are inferior to the heroic generation that pre-
ceded them. Much in this scene has been inverted. It is Andromache
who, with her naïve and pitiful plea, gives military directives, begging
her husband to "'stay here on the rampart, . . . draw your people up by
the fig tree, there where the city / is openest to attack'": the Hellenistic
commentator Aristarchus wanted to excise these lines on the grounds
that "the words are inappropriate to Andromache, since she sets herself
up against Hektor in generalship."[19] On the other hand, it is Hektor the
warrior who disarms to toss and kiss his child.

The actions that most memorialize Hektor, here and later, are emphatically unheroic, and commentators over the years have sourly remarked
upon the discrepancy between his outstanding reputation as a warrior
and, relative to other heroes, his modest accomplishments—and even
weaknesses—on the battlefield; but it is precisely these inconsistencies
that render him one of the most believable and sympathetic figures
in the *Iliad*. Perhaps not a warrior by nature—"'I have learned to be
valiant'"—the husband and father shoulders the burden that has fallen
unfairly upon him and fights the war he hates for a cause he disowns out
of honor and duty.[20]

Andromache's anxious identification of Achaean heroes from the
ramparts mirrors Helen's nostalgic identification of her former kinsmen

to Priam, from the same rampart. Both women, Homer makes clear, will earn a cruel renown in future ages: "'we shall be made into things of song for men of the future,'" says Helen bitterly of herself and Paris at one point, during Hektor's visit with them. "'"This is the wife of Hektor, who was ever the bravest fighter / of the Trojans, breakers of horses, in the days when they fought about Ilion." / So will one speak of you,'" Hektor tells Andromache.

The eventual fate of Andromache and Astyanax was told in one of the epics of the Trojan Cycle, the *Little Iliad*, attributed to the poet Lesches, from Lesbos, which related events following the downfall of Troy: "But great-hearted Achilles' glorious son led Hektor's wife back to the hollow ships," one ancient testimonial of the lost epic reads; "her child he took from the bosom of his lovely-haired nurse and, holding him by the foot, flung him from the battlement, and crimson death and stern fate took him at his fall. . . ."[21] The fate of Astyanax is thought to have been well established in pre-Homeric myth. Vase paintings from as early as the late eighth century B.C. depict his death, and by the sixth century B.C. it had become a popular motif, along with other events depicting the terrible aftermath of the fall of Troy.[22] It is likely, then, that audiences of Homer's time listened to the scene between his parents with foreknowledge that Andromache would be enslaved and Astyanax killed. Notwithstanding its terrible scenes of wounding and dying on the field of war, the *Iliad* hints that there are fates—Andromache's—that may be worse than death.[23]

In structural terms, the scene between Hektor and Andromache is wholly irrelevant to the *Iliad*. It does not advance the epic story in any substantive way, and it adds nothing at all to the main narrative arc, which is the story of Achilles' wrath and alienation, and their aftermath. Strictly regarded, it is as wild a digression as the meeting between Glaukos and Diomedes. And yet it is one of the handful of scenes without which the *Iliad* could not have been the *Iliad*. It casts a shadow behind, on events that have already occurred, as well as on everything that is to come. Nestor's rally of the Achaeans in Book Two, urging no man to go home "until after he has lain in bed with the wife of a Trojan" is exposed in all its brutality. The little, compressed biographies that pathetically accompany each fallen man are made suddenly more vivid. Even Glaukos' celebrated words—"'So one generation of men will grow while another / dies'"—have a new and tragic import.

"'No, let not one of them go free of sudden / death and our hands,'" Agamemnon urged, as Menelaos was poised to spare the life of a supplicant; "'not the young man child that the mother carries / still in her body, not even he.'" The single scene before the Skaian Gates makes it impossible to contemplate with any joy the spectacle of Priam's towers burning. Simply put, the Trojans are no longer the enemy of this Greek epic. And if the Trojans are not the enemy—who is?

Land of My Fathers

Toward dusk of the third day, following the cremation of their dead from the previous days' battles, the Achaeans embark upon a task of sudden urgency. Beside the remains of their burned-out funeral pyre, they build a fort "with towered ramparts, to be a defence for themselves and their vessels," surrounded by a deep, wide ditch, filled with sharp stakes.

The building of the fortification is embarked upon without discussion or prelude, and it is unclear what prompted this precaution, but it signals a slow yet inexorable turn in the fortunes of the Greeks and in the action of the epic. A little earlier, Zeus had addressed an assembly of the Olympians and in forceful, threatening language prohibited any god from interfering in the war: henceforth the two mortal armies will face each other on a level field. And although numerically inferior, the Trojans, "caught in necessity, for their wives and their children," will gain the upper hand. Thus, at last, does Zeus take decisive action to honor his pledge to Thetis, for fight as they will, the Achaeans cannot win without Achilles.

Slowly, in a series of battles fought by individual heroes, the momentum shifts toward the Trojans. By nightfall the Greeks are on the run, driven back to their very ships. Standing "on clean ground, where there showed a space not cumbered with corpses," Hektor excitedly gives his men their orders for the night and for the following dawn that will surely bring success. Succumbing to the heady taste of imminent victory, this most careful of heroes drops his reserve to cry in dangerous exaltation:

"Oh, if I only
could be as this in all my days immortal and ageless
and be held in honour as Athene and Apollo are honoured
as surely as this oncoming day brings evil to the Argives."

High on Olympos, however, where the gods have been watching this turn in the tide of battle, Zeus has already pronounced what he knows will be the inevitable outcome of the ensuing events: Hektor will prevail in battle until the time that " 'there stirs by the ships the swift-footed son of Peleus,' " the father of gods and men had stated, " 'on that day when they shall fight by the sterns of the beached ships / in the narrow place of necessity over fallen Patroklos. / This is the way it is fated to be.' " The remainder of the epic is similarly punctuated with blunt summaries of the events ahead, ensuring that the audience feels the weight of the impending tragedies. Now, despite what Achaeans or Trojans might in their innocence believe, the audience knows what Zeus knows: Achilles' comrade Patroklos will die, Achilles will "stir," and Hektor will at that time be stopped from fighting.

Oblivious that he labors under outcomes already determined by fate, Hektor orders his men to keep a vigil through the night, fearful that the panicked enemy might flee in their ships under cover of darkness. As the men settle down for their long duty, the multitude of their watch fires across the dark plain mirrors the stars in the night sky above Ilion.

As the Trojans while away the night in high spirits, "Panic, companion of cold Terror," takes hold of the Achaeans, and of all the Achaeans the most stricken is the son of Atreus. Calling an emergency assembly, Agamemnon stands before his men in tears. Groaning aloud, he concedes that Zeus has deceived him: there is no victory for the Achaeans anywhere on the horizon. He then broaches his solution: the army should " 'run away with our ships to the beloved land of our fathers.' " A stunned silence follows this suggestion, broken at length by Diomedes. Displaying admirable restraint, he takes issue with his leader, concluding his remarks with a stinging observation: "'The son of devious-devising Kronos has given you / gifts in two ways: with the sceptre he gave you honour beyond all, / but he did not give you a heart, and of all power this is the greatest.'"

In a pattern repeated in the epic, the Achaeans are once again assembled in time of crisis, making public rebuke of their king. Once again Nestor steps forward, now offering a cautious rebuke to Diomedes, along with the suggestion that Agamemnon convene an emergency council of the princes: "'Here is the night that will break our army, or else will preserve it,'" he grimly concludes.

With sentries set, the lords file into Agamemnon's shelter, where, away from the rank and file, Nestor speaks more bluntly. Things have gone badly from the day that Agamemnon took Briseis from Achilles by force; Achilles must be placated: "'let us / even now think how we can make this good and persuade him / with words of supplication and with the gifts of friendship.'"

Agamemnon's response to Nestor's words is unqualified acquiescence and relief; he has been led onto terrain he understands. "Gifts"—of course, Achilles will be won back with gifts. With almost abject eagerness, Agamemnon enumerates the personal treasure he is willing to surrender: seven unfired tripods, ten talents' weight of gold,[1] prizewinning horses, seven women from Lesbos "'who in their beauty surpassed the races of women,'" and Briseis, the "prize" who caused the costly rift with his best warrior and whose bed Agamemnon now swears he never entered. All of this, as well as future prizes from plunder still to come, and, as a crowning offer, Achilles' choice of one of Agamemnon's own three daughters to be his wife, along with a glittering dowry.

"'All this I will bring to pass for him,'" Agamemnon concludes, and then demonstrates that his ordeal has wrought no real change in his character: "'And let him yield place to me, inasmuch as I am the kinglier.'"

The ensuing Embassy to Achilles—the account of the small delegation of chosen men bearing Agamemnon's offer of gifts—is one of the most remarkable and innovative scenes in the *Iliad*. Briefly, the carefully appointed delegates—Odysseus and Aias, led by a previously unmentioned character called Phoinix—make their way along the beach to Achilles' tent, bearing the fate of the entire Achaean army in their diplomatic hands.

In the camp of the Myrmidons, the delegation comes abruptly upon Achilles, "delighting his heart in a lyre, clear-sounding, / splendid and carefully wrought, with a bridge of silver upon it" and taken from spoils won during the sack of Andromache's city. With this lyre, Achilles is pleasuring his heart—*áeide d' ára kléa andrōn*—"singing of men's fame." *Kléa* is the plural of *kléos*, meaning "rumor," "report," "news." The reports made about a hero constitute his renown, his fame and glory. Desire to win *kléos* motivates a hero to fight rather than to flee, for he knows that the report of his actions will outlive him. The great heroes—the "men of old"—are the subject of songs that commemorate their deeds. Yet, Achilles, the hero of the *Iliad*, is now found, after a considerable absence, contentedly playing the role of a bard—a singer of the glorious deeds of other men, not the performer of his own.[2]

Alone, watching in ambiguous silence, is Achilles' closest companion, Patroklos, the son of Menoitios. As the Embassy enters, both men spring to their feet in surprise, and Achilles offers an unexpectedly gracious and encouraging greeting: "'Welcome. You are my friends who have come, and greatly I need you, / who even to this my anger are dearest of all the Achaeans.'"

Achilles orders a meal for his guests, and Patroklos serves. The moment seems propitious. Aias looks at Phoinix and nods, and Odysseus takes the cue and with his legendary eloquence lays out the terms of Agamemnon's offer. Golden treasures, horses, women, even "'seven citadels, strongly settled'" of Agamemnon's own kingdom—Odysseus faithfully recites the list, along with a private and strategic offering of his own:

"But if the son of Atreus is too much hated in your heart,
himself and his gifts, at least take pity on all the other
Achaeans, who are afflicted along the host, and will honour you
as a god."

But Achilles is not moved, and in a scorching speech he rejects out of hand all offers of reconciliation. The Embassy stalls, and to the horror of his old comrades it seems disaster for the Achaeans is assured.

What does Achilles want? The withdrawal of an angry hero from his people is a standard motif in both folktale and epic—a motif that presupposes, however, the angered hero's eventual appeasement and return. The failure of the Embassy to appease Achilles, then, represents a shocking, dramatic break with tradition. Achilles, moreover, not only rejects the Embassy but, as will be seen, goes further, challenging the very premise of the heroic way of life, which is to say the heroic way of war that epic traditionally extols. The Embassy's many innovative elements suggest that this scene came late in the *Iliad*'s evolution and is the work of its last poet—of Homer.[3] Certainly it is in the Embassy that the *Iliad* most overtly declares that it is undertaking something new and not simply telling another *kléos andrōn,* or story of old. Intrinsic to the *Iliad*'s vision is Achilles, and indeed, it is his character that is the catalyst of the epic's bold new direction.

In plain genealogy, Achilles is, of course, the son of a goddess, the sea nymph Thetis, and a mortal man, Peleus. In heroic society, all warriors are defined by their patrimony; Achilles is Pēleídēs—son of Peleus, whose biography and career can be pieced together from the usual collection of fragments of lost epics, references in other poetry, as well as compilations of traditional genealogy and mythology made by later writers of antiquity.[4]

From these variegated sources we learn that Peleus was the son of Aiakos, the ruler of the island of Aigina, off the coast of Attica. On killing his half brother—accounts vary as to whether this was by accident or not—Peleus fled north, taking sanctuary with the king of Iolkos, in Thessaly.[5] Henceforth Aiakos' son Peleus is associated only with this northern frontier region, specifically with Mount Pelion, and with his small kingdom, Phthia, where he is king over the Myrmidons.[6] Tradition also relates how when the king of the important Thessalian city of Iolkos and his wife later wronged Peleus, he "single-handed, without an army, took Iolkos"; this is the sole unambiguously martial feat attributed to him.[7] Peleus also makes respectable appearances in a number of heroic sagas: he is among the Argonauts, with Jason, for example (another tale with Thessalian origins), as well as a high-profile participant in the Kalydonian Boar Hunt, a saga relating the attempt by numerous heroes to hunt the monstrous boar that had been sent by a vengeful goddess to devastate the land of Kalydon.

Various themes cluster around Peleus, the most consistent and striking being those of murder and purification, exile and sanctuary. Peleus himself, as was seen, came as an exile to Thessaly, where he was purified for the murder of his half brother. Later he accidentally killed a companion in the Kalydonian Boar Hunt and was purified again. To his kingdom, as the *Iliad* relates, come other exiles, who are received and purified by him in turn, the most important of these being Menoitios' son Patroklos, Achilles' closest friend (and, in some accounts, his cousin): "'just as we grew up together in your house,'" Patroklos recalls to Achilles, later in the epic,

> "when Menoitios brought me there from Opous, when I was little,
> and into your house, by reason of a baneful manslaying,
> on that day when I killed the son of Amphidamas. I was
> a child only, nor intended it, but was angered over a dice game.
> There the rider Peleus took me into his own house,
> and brought me carefully up, and named me to be your henchman."

Also received by Peleus were an otherwise obscure Myrmidon warrior called Epeigeus and, most significantly, Phoinix, a faithful family retainer and the third man in the Embassy to Achilles. Having come close to killing his father, who had placed a curse on him never to have sons of his own, Phoinix had fled to Phthia, where Peleus received him and " 'gave me his love, even as a father loves his own son / who is a single child brought up among many possessions.' "

Peleus, then, stands in a somewhat similar relation to troubled men as Thetis does to troubled gods: in the *Iliad*, Thetis is credited with saving Dionysos, Hephaistos, and of course, most famously, Zeus. Importantly, however, Peleus is harboring outlaws, and the congregation of so many fugitives from justice on the wild frontier of Thessaly is striking and suggestive.[8]

The manner in which Peleus won the hand of the immortal Thetis is described in various, not wholly incompatible traditions, the most famous being that he was told "to seize her and hold her fast in spite of her shape-shifting," to quote the vivid account of Apollodorus (writing in the second century B.C.): "he watched his chance and carried her off, and though she turned, now into fire, now into water, and now into a beast, he did not let her go till he saw that she had resumed her former shape." [9] The theme of a mortal man who wins a fey, or supernatural maiden, by holding her throughout her changeable forms is widely familiar in fairy and folktales. Such mystical marriages are usually resolved when the maiden eventually forsakes the world of men and returns to her own kin, whether they be swans or seals or, in Thetis' case, deities of the sea.[10] Significantly, although the *Iliad* implies that Peleus and Thetis lived together in the past, it is clear that they are now apart, Peleus living forlornly in Phthia and Thetis with her sisters and father, Nereus, "the sea's ancient."

In other accounts of this unequal marriage, Thetis is not captured but married off by a directive from Zeus. Usually this is prompted by his discovery of Thetis' unique destiny to bear a son greater than his father;

as has been seen, this is the tradition to which the *Iliad* alludes.[11] In the *Iliad*, the unhappy outcome of this forced union is made unambiguously clear: "'I had to endure mortal marriage / though much against my will,'" Thetis laments, and her keening brokenheartedness for the marriage and the mortal son the marriage produced is her most characteristic trait in the epic.[12]

Why, if it was necessary to marry this ill-fated goddess to a mortal, did the gods choose Peleus above all other men? According to one tradition, Zeus, in his role as defender of the rights of hospitality, chose Peleus to reward him for resisting the illicit advances of his host's lustful wife.[13] The righteousness of Peleus is further underscored by his ancestry: Peleus' father, Aiakos, was said to be wisest of mortals, even rendering judgment among the gods, and in later tradition he appears in the Underworld as one of the three judges of the dead.[14]

This specific reward for his righteousness apart, Peleus seems, from early tradition, to have been renowned for enjoying the exceptional love and blessings of the gods. In the *Iliad*, this love is spoken of on two occasions, once by Hera, who refers to him as "'one dear to the hearts of the immortals,'" and once by Achilles, who recalls the many "'shining gifts'" the gods gave his father. Hesiod gives a long, striking account of Peleus' good fortune, and from this, one suspects that Peleus was once a byword for his god-bestowed blessings: "he came to Phthia, mother of sheep, / bringing [much] wealth from spacious Iolcus, / Peleus,] Aeacus' son, dear to the immortal gods. / The spirit of all [the people] who saw him was astonished at how] he had sacked the well-founded [city], and how he had fulfilled / a lovely marriage], and they all of them said this speech: 'Three times blessed, son of Aeacus, and four times happy, Peleus.'"[15]

Yet while a nexus of traditions speaks of Peleus' good fortune, in the *Iliad* he is most memorably recalled as a forlorn object of pity, "'on the door-sill of sorrowful old age,'" and it is in this pathetic light that Achilles himself perceives his famous father. The striking disjunction between

Peleus' early legendary good fortune and later abandonment suggests that the characterizations preserved in both the *Iliad* and other traditions are mutually incomplete and that some other story, now lost, included him in an account of heroes whose fabled prosperity turned to fabled adversity.[16]

Starkly contrasting with the unhappy ending of their famous marriage is the tradition of the actual wedding of Peleus and his divine bride, one of the favorite set pieces in early art as well as literature.[17] The *Cypria* gave an account of the wedding: how "the gods gathered on Pelion to feast, and brought gifts for Peleus," and, as Hera notes in the *Iliad*, "'you all / went, you gods, to the wedding.'" Yet the origins of much tragedy and heartbreak lay in these joyous celebrations, for, as the *Cypria* also recounted, it was at the wedding of Peleus and Thetis that "Zeus confers . . . about the Trojan War. As the gods are feasting at the wedding of Peleus, strife appears and causes a dispute about beauty among Athena, Hera, and Aphrodite."[18] This rivalry led to the famous beauty contest between the goddesses, of which the Trojan prince Paris was selected, inexplicably, to be the judge; his reward for awarding the crown to Aphrodite was Helen, the wife of Greek Menelaos, and this event, as Zeus had planned, was the cause of the Trojan War.

Various traditions describe the desperate tactics deployed by Thetis to rescue her mortal offspring from his mortal fate. A lost work attributed to Hesiod told of how "Thetis cast the children she bore to Peleus into a cauldron of water since she wanted to find out whether they were mortal. . . . And after many had been destroyed Peleus became annoyed and prevented Achilles from being cast into the cauldron." In other accounts, Thetis secretly places the young Achilles in a fire at night to temper him; when Peleus intervenes, the spell is broken.[19] The best-known story tells of how Thetis dipped Achilles in the river Styx to render him immortal but, holding him by his heel to do so, left his "Achilles' heel" vulnerable.[20]

The theme of tempering a child to make him invulnerable or immortal belongs, as do so many of the themes pertaining to Peleus and his household, to the world of folklore or fairy tale, rather than to heroic epic. Greek mythology tells of two other similar cases of such maternal "magic": the goddess Demeter attempts to render a protégé immortal by placing him in a fire; and the hero Meleager, a participant in the Kalydonian Boar Hunt, is similarly tempered by fire but eventually killed by his mother, who one day burns the log that represents her son's life.[21] Significantly, Meleager will be evoked, in a story of great length and detail, as an example to Achilles in the Embassy scene.

While other traditions speak of Peleus and Thetis' multiple (if destroyed) offspring, the *Iliad* knows of only one—their single, wholly mortal son Achilles.[22] His name may possibly appear in the Linear B tablets, as *a-ki-re-u*, in a context that suggests a common name,[23] while attempts to determine the meaning of his name have drawn different conclusions. Its components—*áchos laós*—have been variously interpreted to mean either "grief/pain to the people" or "fear to the fighting men"; the latter has strong parallels in Germanic and Celtic languages.[24]

In the *Iliad*, the epithets most commonly associated with Achilles among his companions are "shining, godlike" and "swift-footed"; the epithet used by Thetis, however, is *minunthádios*—"lasting but a short time," "of persons, short-lived":[25] "'Why did I raise you? . . . since indeed your lifetime is to be short, of no length'"; "'Now give honour to my son short-lived beyond all other / mortals.'" To this inexorable, not-to-be-prayed-away fact, Thetis obsessively again and again returns. She can negotiate with Zeus for her son's honor, but not for his life. For the immortal mother, her son's fame, his prowess, his legendary feats count for nothing in the face of the fact that she knows that she will endure to see him die; an immortal goddess, she knows her grief will be everlasting. The keening of Thetis is one of the most consistent themes in the *Iliad*. She first appears as if shrouded in a mist of tears and at every appearance thereafter seems to be prostrate, paralyzed with grief for the event that she knows must come.

It is a striking fact that in this epic dedicated to a heroic world essentially defined by father-son dynamics, the voice of Peleus is virtually not heard, as similarly the *Iliad* does not make even glancing reference to the heroic deeds attributed to him by other traditions. Unlike Nestor, the *Iliad*'s most conspicuous aged hero, Peleus is not around to recall continually the accomplishments of his youth. The only recollection anyone in the *Iliad* seems to have of Peleus is of his saying farewell to Achilles as he sets out for Troy.[26] Yet while Peleus has been edited out of the epic, so to speak, Achilles' emotional bonds are nonetheless unambiguously with his mortal father and not his divine, ever-present mother: the climax of the entire *Iliad* is in fact predicated on this filial bond. The nature of Achilles' relationship to his mother is immediately apparent, from the moment in Book One when he retreats to the lonely shore to cry a favor: being divine, she is both magically ubiquitous, arising from the sea whenever he calls, and has access to valuable resources, such as the ear of Zeus. Achilles' relationship to his father, by contrast, is subtly revealed only in the course of the epic; but the clues to his regard first surface in the Embassy scene.

Peleus, whether because he was "annoyed" at the murder of his other children or because he believed that his only son would benefit from a particular, if eccentric, upbringing, is presented in all known traditions as handing the young Achilles over to the righteous centaur Cheiron to raise amid the wild animals of the Pelion Mountains. Although the *Iliad* characteristically suppresses such far-fetched, outlandish stories, it allows this tradition to stand. Achilles' tutelage under Cheiron is mentioned pointedly in the *Iliad:* at the height of battle, an appeal is made to Achilles' friend Patroklos to lend his medicinal art to a wounded warrior, "'which they say you have been told of by Achilles, / since Cheiron, most righteous of the Centaurs, told him about them.'"[27] A lost poem attributed (wrongly) to Hesiod called the *Precepts of Cheiron* was devoted to the instruction that this good centaur imparted to Achilles, an indication of the popularity and strength of this particular tradition; from the pitiful few surviving fragments, however, these precepts seem to have been bland stuff ("Whenever you come home, make a beautiful sacrifice to the eternally living gods. . . .").[28] Emerging from all this is the fact that Achilles, the most effective killer at Troy, is also the most adept in the art of healing.[29]

The manner in which Achilles came to Troy is also decidedly unheroic. Hesiod relates how all other Achaeans came to Troy because they were formerly suitors of Helen and took an oath to her father that they would come to her aid if she were ever abducted; Homer does not refer to this oath overtly, but the fact that their united cause is Helen, of course, is unambiguous in the *Iliad*. Achilles, however, was too young to have been one of the suitors. In this all-important respect, he again stands apart from his comrades.[30] Why, then, if Achilles and his family have no personal stake in the war, are he and his considerable force of Myrmidons at Troy?

An early tradition tells of Thetis' knowledge that Achilles was destined to die at Troy—in folklore, creatures of the sea are often attributed prophetic powers.[31] Disguising her son as a girl, she hid him on the island of Skyros, amid the many women of King Lykomedes' court. One unforeseen result of this ploy was that the youthful Achilles impregnated one of the women, Deidameia, who later bore his son; the *Iliad* makes brief reference to this son's being raised on Skyros.[32] Later narratives pick up the tale: Odysseus and Diomedes arrive on Skyros to seek out the young man who is destined to be the war's greatest warrior. Hidden amid the bales of beautiful clothing that the two bring as gifts are various armaments, and when one of the "girls," ignoring the other finery, grasps these, they know they have found their man.[33] The fact that Achilles was not immediately recognizable as a young man is intended to be a tribute to his striking beauty. Other Achillean trivia: his name among the women was "Pyrrha," supposedly a reference to his red-gold hair (from *purrós*, "flame-colored"), while modern scholarship, after considerable sober study, has declared that the son of Peleus was not quite eighteen when he went to Troy.[34]

Where now does this mass of information take us? What bearing does all this have on Achilles in the *Iliad* and, specifically, on the Embassy scene of Book Nine? First, it tells us that Achilles' origins lie not only on the fringes of the Greek world, in remote Thessaly, but also outside epic tradition. In contrast to a hero like Diomedes, whose father, Tydeus, was well established in such epic narratives as the war at Thebes, Achilles and his parents come from the world of folklore, their histories embedded in tales of magical and supernatural events, as opposed to narratives dedicated to heroic, warlike accomplishments. This in turn partly accounts for Peleus' striking absence in the *Iliad;* Peleus, great hero though he is, does not authentically belong to this tradition, does not share these heroic mores, and the community of heroes in the *Iliad* knows him only as the father of Achilles. In this way, as befits his unique destiny, Achilles is in fact proved to be greater than his father; alone of the heroes at Troy, it is he who defines his sire.

Folklore heroes, it has been said, "tend to stand out as lonely wanderers, as folk from far away or from nowhere."[35] The aloofness of Achilles from the rest of the Achaeans, his essential isolation, is another attribute of his parents' legacy.[36] But most poignantly, and most useful to Homer's vision, the hero of this war epic, is not, in his essence, a military figure. Famously vulnerable and unnaturally defined by his mortality, raised to know the arts of healing, a figure not of men but of the wild beasts of the mountains, Achilles does not belong in the warrior company at Troy. He did not cross the wine-dark sea for the common cause, nor did he come for glory. Achilles came to Troy because he was tricked into doing so.

It appears, then, that this distinctive Thessalian folk hero, with his magic arts and mystical birth, was swept from his folktale moorings and appropriated into the evolving story of the siege and sack of Troy; his inclusion suggests that he was a charismatic figure even before he was brought to epic. Most probably, his entry came at a relatively late stage. Alone of the *Iliad*'s major heroes, Achilles dies before Troy is taken, for instance, indicating that his role was not an essential element in the overarching story of its siege and capture. His distinctive characterization also reveals a number of typically late features: no one in the *Iliad* speaks as idiosyncratically as Achilles, with less use of traditional expressions, for example, and no one makes more frequent use of similes, which generally belong to the later stages of the epic.[37]

In the mythic background of Achilles, a great poet could discern exciting possibilities: Here was a peerless warrior with a life unrelated to war, a loner and an outsider who could see in the collective military endeavor nothing that pertained to himself, the most poignantly mortal of all heroes whose business was the daily hazard of war. Here was a hero with both the nature and the stature to think and speak as an individual, to stand apart and challenge heroic convention. In the hyperstated mortality of Achilles lay the origins of something potentially greater even than epic—and that was tragedy.

Above all, Achilles afforded Homer, the tradition's last poet, the means by which the epic could convincingly be taken into a new direction. Through Achilles, the ancient story of the Trojan War would not culminate as an epic extolling martial glory but as a dark portrayal of the cost of war, even to its greatest and most glorified hero. And it is in the Embassy scene that Homer gives his hero the freest rein; and so, with an eye to these complex antecedents, we rejoin the delegation.

Achilles' rejection of Agamemnon's offer is immediate, decisive, and unambiguous: "'without consideration for you I must make my answer,'" he tells the Embassy spokesman Odysseus; "'that you may not / come one after another, and sit by me, and speak softly. / For as I detest the doorways of Death, I detest that man, who / hides one thing in the depths of his heart, and speaks forth another.'"

With angry authority, Achilles unfurls for his companions the dark tale of his warrior life. Great hero though he is, worshipped, as more than one Achaean will tell him, like a god among them, his existence is joyless and his war work thankless; his life always at hazard, he has lain " 'the many nights unsleeping, / such as I wore through the bloody days of the fighting, / striving with warriors for the sake of these men's women.' " By contrast, Agamemnon, waiting by his ships, has piled up the plunder that other men, like Achilles, brought to him—yet it is Agamemnon who has taken the bride of his heart: " 'Yet why must the Argives fight with the Trojans? / And why was it the son of Atreus assembled and led here / these people? Was it not for the sake of lovely-haired Helen? / Are the sons of Atreus alone among mortal men the ones / who love their wives?' " Three days' sailing will bring one to Phthia—his home. Here aged Peleus lives, amid all his own possessions, and it is to home, to Phthia, to Peleus, that Achilles will now return. This is the sudden prospect against which Agamemnon's glittering gifts and all the honor they imply are now weighed and found resoundingly, unnegotiably wanting:

"I hate his gifts. I hold him light as the strip of a splinter. . . .

                       . . . For not
worth the value of my life are all the possessions they fable
were won for Ilion, that strong-founded citadel, in the old days
when there was peace, before the coming of the sons of the
    Achaeans. . . .

                                   Of possessions
cattle and fat sheep are things to be had for the lifting,
and tripods can be won, and the tawny high heads of horses,
but a man's life cannot come back again, it cannot be lifted
nor captured again by force, once it has crossed the teeth's barrier.
For my mother Thetis the goddess of the silver feet tells me
I carry two sorts of destiny toward the day of my death. Either,
if I stay here and fight beside the city of the Trojans,
my return home is gone, but my glory shall be everlasting;

but if I return home to the beloved land of my fathers,
the excellence of my glory is gone, but there will be a long life
left for me, and my end in death will not come to me quickly.
And this would be my counsel to others also, to sail back
home again, since no longer shall you find any term set
on the sheer city of Ilion, since Zeus of the wide brows has strongly
held his own hand over it, and its people are made bold.

   Do you go back therefore to the great men of the Achaeans,
and take them this message, since such is the privilege of the
   princes:
that they think out in their minds some other scheme that is better,
which might rescue their ships, and the people of the Achaeans
who man the hollow ships, since this plan will not work for them
which they thought of by reason of my anger. Let Phoinix
remain here with us and sleep here, so that tomorrow
he may come with us in our ships to the beloved land of our fathers,
if he will; but I will never use force to hold him."

   So he spoke, and all of them stayed stricken to silence
in amazement at his words.

Life is more precious than glory; this is the unheroic truth disclosed
by the greatest warrior at Troy. More extraordinary than its subversion
of a conventional story line—the anticipated and triumphant return of
the gift-laden hero—is the *Iliad*'s very deliberate confrontation with the
core tenets of its own tradition. That glory, honor, and fame are more
important than life is a heroic convention so old it can be traced securely
to Indo-European tradition; integral to this heroic view is the belief that
glory—*kléos*—is achieved through heroic poetry, in other words, through
epic.[38] But with his unimagined speech, Achilles hijacks the *Iliad*, taking this particular epic onto thrilling new ground.[39]

   The magnitude of Achilles' words is dramatically underscored by the
reaction of aged Phoinix, the third member of the Embassy party, who

"in a stormburst of tears" embarks upon a lengthy, digressive speech jumbling personal emotion with a heroic, cautionary tale. "'How then shall I, dear child, be left in this place behind you / all alone?'" he begins, and by addressing this most fearsome of man slayers as "'dear child,'" he establishes his position as a long-serving family retainer, who was sent to Troy by Peleus himself as a guardian of the young Achilles. Phoinix, it will be recalled, had first come to Phthia many years earlier, when he fled his own country after almost killing his father. Awarded care of Peleus' single child, Phoinix became nurse and mentor to Achilles:

> "I made you all that you are now,
> and loved you out of my heart, for you would not go with another
> out to any feast, nor taste any food in your own halls
> until I had set you on my knees, and cut little pieces
> from the meat, and given you all you wished, and held the wine
>   for you.
> And many times you soaked the shirt that was on my body
> with wine you would spit up in the troublesomeness of your
>   childhood.
> So I have suffered much through you, and have had much trouble,
> thinking always how the gods would not bring to birth any children
> of my own; so that it was you, godlike Achilles, I made
> my own child, so that some day you might keep hard affliction
>   from me.
> Then, Achilles, beat down your great anger."

Phoinix's long reminiscence of Achilles' childhood is in itself strikingly antiheroic. Epic as a genre has "difficulty in dealing with the infancy and youth patterns" of its heroes, since this material is inherently unsuitable to heroic tales.[40] The usual remedy is to attribute to the young hero precocious feats in his childhood; the infant Herakles, for instance, strangled snakes in his crib. The deeds of the young Achilles while under

Cheiron's tutelage in the mountains, where he reportedly slew wild beasts and outran deer, could surely have furnished the necessary material.[41] Instead Homer deliberately supplanted tales of daring for a baby-sitter's recollection of young Achilles' spewing up his wine.

Phoinix appears to have been invented by Homer for this scene.[42] Broadly, he serves as a paternal figure in the place of the ever-absent Peleus, possessed of the kind of reminiscences expected from a father. Thus Phoinix—and Homer who has determinedly created him—humanizes Achilles at the precise moment the great warrior appears most pitiless; the young demigod was once a wholly human child, and not even Thetis, whose preoccupation with Achilles' death seems to preclude all other aspects of her maternal relationship, provides such memorable, touching details of Achilles as he was before he came to Troy.

This naturalistic prelude contrasts jarringly with the long, discursive tale that Phoinix next relates, a parable regarding a hero of old who, like Achilles, was angry with his people and who, like Achilles, rejected gifts of appeasement. It is a story from "the old days, the deeds that we hear of / from the great men, when the swelling anger descended upon them. / The heroes would take gifts; they would listen, and be persuaded."

In Phoinix's parable, the hero Meleager kills his maternal uncle, incurring his mother's curse. Angered by his mother's act, Meleager remains resolutely inside his city, Kalydon, when it is besieged by an enemy people. A series of delegations arrive to beg him to come to his city's defense—chiefs, priests, his parents, including the offending mother, and his comrades, all to no avail. Finally his wife, Kleopatra, successfully intervenes, and Meleager enters the fray and succeeds in turning the tide of battle. By returning so late in the day, however, he does not get the gifts the delegations had first offered:

> "Listen, then; do not have such a thought in your mind; let not
> the spirit within you turn you that way, dear friend. It would be
> worse

to defend the ships after they are burning. No, with gifts promised
go forth. The Achaeans will honour you as they would an immortal.
But if without gifts you go into the fighting where men perish,
your honour will no longer be as great, though you drive back the
     battle."

For all its great length and vividness, Phoinix's long parable is a clumsy
effort. Its climactic warning against the potential loss of gifts would seem
to be pointless given Achilles' own emphatic, adamantine rejection of
any consideration of them. In fact, the parable is wholly pointless, for
later in the epic Achilles will be swamped with gifts of honor, presented
to him in the most public and gratifying manner possible. Indeed, the
meaning of this interlude with Phoinix and his long speech seems to be
precisely that he and it are inappropriate to Achilles' circumstances:
Achilles is not, for all Phoinix's emotion, his "'own child'" who will "'some
day . . . keep hard affliction from me.'" Peleus is Achilles' father, not Phoinix, and the filial duty of caring for his real father in old age, as will be
seen, hangs very heavy on Achilles' heart. In all respects, in fact, Phoinix's tender memories and extended plea relentlessly mangle the most
defining touchstones of Achilles' tragic life. Having fled from his own
hated father, Phoinix came to Peleus, who "'gave me his love, even as a
father loves his own son / who is a single child brought up among many
possessions'"; but it is Achilles who is the single child and who has just
declared he would like to return to his father to enjoy these many possessions. Peleus was one of the heroes at the Kalydonian Boar Hunt—it
is one of his best-known feats—yet in Phoinix's rendition of the story of
Meleager and the hunt, he never mentions Peleus—so much for heroic
deeds' winning everlasting glory.[43]

   In his long-winded discursiveness, in his insistence on "'the old days
also, the deeds that we hear of / from the great men,'" Phoinix is like no
one else so much as Nestor. Stuck in his time warp, faithfully invoking
the old traditions, Phoinix does not, for all his passion and tears, address

a single syllable to Achilles' most striking assertion—that the war is not worth the value of his life. The speech that no warrior before has uttered—a speech that indeed negates the warrior's heroic code—receives in exchange only a conventional appeal to heroes of old. Perhaps for another hero, perhaps in another epic, such a time-honored tactic would have been persuasive, but this is Achilles, and this is the *Iliad*, and this is perhaps Homer's declaration that the old heroic values enshrouded in their formless prolixity are no longer relevant. With his outright rejection of conventional gifts, conventional appeals, and, above all, the conventional heroic code, Achilles has crossed into new territory, where stories of what moved the men of old—*kléa andrōn*—have no force.

Among the many idiosyncratic features of Achilles' language are his unique words, his use of striking similes, of violent words and invective, and his "tendency to invoke distant places":[44]

"I for my part did not come here for the sake of the Trojan
spearmen to fight against them, since to me they have done nothing.
Never yet have they driven away my cattle or my horses,
never in Phthia where the soil is rich and men grow great did they
spoil my harvest, since indeed there is much that lies between us,
the shadowy mountains and the echoing sea."

"Tomorrow, when I have sacrificed to Zeus and to all gods,
and loaded well my ships, and rowed out on to the salt water,
you will see, if you have a mind to it and if it concerns you,
my ships in the dawn at sea on the Hellespont where the fish
    swarm
and my men manning them with good will to row. If the glorious
shaker of the earth should grant us a favouring passage
on the third day thereafter we might raise generous Phthia."

The distant place Achilles most consistently evokes is his own home, Phthia; Phthia, related to *phthíō*, "waste away, decay, wane dwindle";[45] Phthia, where the soil is rich and men grow great, is also the Waste Land, and it is here that his heroic father is languishing, his *kléos*, or glory, if one is to judge by its absence in the *Iliad*, already dwindled. Phthia is where Achilles now chooses to bury himself for the rest of what he hopes will be a long and undistinguished life.[46]

The choice of two destinies—to die at Troy and win everlasting glory or to return to live a long life in the Waste Land, where glory withers away—is, as far as can be judged from the material that has survived, also unique to the Embassy. Elsewhere, even in the *Iliad*, Achilles shows no awareness of this prophecy, and it would seem to be another feature that was invented by Homer for this remarkable scene. The prophecy serves to ensure that Homer's audience—if not Phoinix and the Embassy delegates— do not overlook the considered, passionate decision of this now-reluctant warrior. While Achilles is still enraged with Agamemnon, it is no longer wrath that drives him homeward, but the determination to live.

"'Phoinix my father, aged, illustrious, such honour is a thing / I need not. I think I am honoured already in Zeus' ordinance'" is Achilles' response to Phoinix's shrill urging that he accept gifts:

"These men will carry back the message; you stay here and sleep here
in a soft bed, and we shall decide tomorrow, as dawn shows,
whether to go back home again or else to remain here."
He spoke, and, saying nothing, nodded with his brows to Patroklos
to make up a neat bed for Phoinix, so the others might presently
think of going home from his shelter.

Odysseus and Aias take the hint, and it remains for Aias, the least eloquent of the delegation, to speak in parting with a soldier's blunt words. "'He is hard, and does not remember that friends' affection / wherein we honoured him by the ships, far beyond all others,'" Aias says, ostensibly addressing himself to Odysseus. "'Pitiless.'"

And it is Achilles the companion-in-arms, the comrade, whom Aias' straight-talking words now fatally touch; more to the point, while Homer can challenge and interpret his tradition innovatively, he cannot credibly thwart its entire story—his legendary hero cannot simply exit Troy. "'Son of Telamon, seed of Zeus, Aias, lord of the people: / all that you have said seems spoken after my own mind,'" Achilles begins, and with no thought for the high words that he just expressed about life and mortality, he reverts to the traditional theme, his wrath toward Agamemnon. Now he offers a vaguely stated compromise:

"Do you then go back to him, and take him this message:
that I shall not think again of the bloody fighting
until such time as the son of wise Priam, Hektor the brilliant,
comes all the way to the ships of the Myrmidons, and their
    shelters."

Significantly, when the defeated delegation returns to the Achaean camp, Odysseus, in debriefing Agamemnon and his anxious comrades, makes no mention at all of Achilles' final position, reporting instead only that Achilles has said he is going home; it is as if Homer were determined to emphasize, unambiguously and unforgettably, that this was Achilles' first choice: "'And he himself has threatened that tomorrow as dawn shows / he will drag down his strong-benched, oarswept ships to the water. / He said it would be his counsel to others also, to sail back / home again.'"

For centuries, scholars have debated the Embassy scene and what exactly it was that Achilles really wanted. Should he have accepted the gifts, or was he right to reject them? Since Achilles' refusal to be appeased marks the beginning of his tragedy, the usual conclusion is that he made the wrong decision and he will learn his lesson. But the point of the Embassy scene was to establish that Achilles had three options, not two, and it is the third that will break his heart. Achilles' tragic error did not lie in his acceptance or rejection of Agamemnon's gifts; his tragic error was that he did not follow where his thoughts always seem to tend—to Phthia beyond the sea; to Peleus, his father; to home.

In God We Trust

From a peak on Mount Ida overlooking the plain of Troy, Zeus, the father of gods and men, sits in splendid isolation, "rejoicing in the pride of his strength . . . , watching the flash of the bronze, and men killing and men killed." Hitherto the gods have been busily embroiled in the activities of the field, but now the epic pulls back to unfold a more chilling divine perspective, which is war as pure spectacle.

Dawn has broken on the twenty-fifth day of the *Iliad,* and the longest day in the epic. Night does not come until well into Book Eighteen, and the intervening narrative encompasses the epic's bloodiest, most unrelieved, and ultimately most momentous fighting.[1] The harsh injunction that Zeus laid upon the other gods in Book Eight to keep clear of the battle is still in force: "'And any one I perceive against the gods' will attempting / to go among the Trojans and help them, or among the Danaans, / he shall go whipped against his dignity back to Olympos.'" Absent divine interference—and Achilles, who remains in his shelter, where the Embassy left him—the momentum of the war continues in favor of the Trojans, as Zeus intends.

A cascade of similes drawn from the broadest sweep of life conveys the extent of slaughter in the now all-encompassing universe of battle. The Achaeans and Trojans square off "like two lines of reapers who, facing each other, / drive their course all down the field of wheat or of barley / for a man blessed in substance." Although hard-pressed, the Achaean lines stand firm, "held evenly as the scales which a careful widow / holds, taking it by the balance beam, and weighs her wool evenly / at either end, working to win a pitiful wage for her children." The infinite ways of wounding and of dying are paraded in pitiless detail. Pierced by a spear, a warrior's "heart was panting still and beating to shake the butt end / of the spear." An arrow driven into his bladder, a fallen warrior, in the hands of his companions, "gasped out his life, then lay like a worm extended / along the ground."

Outstanding performances by the most important Achaean heroes punctuate the long sweep of battle narrative and provide dramatic tension by delaying the inevitable arrival of Hektor and the Trojans at the Achaean ships, in accordance with Zeus' earlier prediction. The most startling *aristeía* belongs to Agamemnon, in his most warrior-like moment in the epic. Having donned his armor, he takes up his splendid shield with its ten circles of bronze, studded with pale tin and dark cobalt, in the middle of which is "the blank-eyed face of the Gorgon / with her stare of horror, and Fear was inscribed upon it, and Terror."

The arming of Agamemnon, one of four elaborate arming scenes in the epic, is the prelude to what is one of the most unsavory series of slaughters in the war: "Agamemnon stabbed straight at his face as he came on in fury / with the sharp spear, nor did the helm's bronze-heavy edge hold it, / but the spearhead passed through this and the bone, and the inward / brain was all spattered forth"; "as a lion seizes the innocent young of the running / deer, and easily crunches and breaks them caught in the strong teeth / when he has invaded their lair, and rips out the soft heart from them, . . . so there was no one of the Trojans who could save these two / from death"; "Hippolochos sprang away, but Atreides killed him dismounted, / cutting away his arms with a sword-stroke, free of the shoulder, / and sent him spinning like a log down the battle."

Briefly, the Trojans are routed and flee toward their city while Agamemnon "followed them always, screaming, / Atreus' son, his invincible hands spattered with bloody filth." This is less a portrait, in the grand manner, of a warrior gripped by battle fury than of a man unhinged. At length, Agamemnon's bloody rant is ended by a wound to his arm, the effects of which are described in pointedly unheroic terms: pain breaks upon the son of Atreus, as when "the sharp sorrow of pain descends on a woman in labour, / the bitterness that the hard spirits of childbirth bring on."

One by one, the Achaeans' best warriors limp off the field, and it is now the Trojan warriors who shine. The dramatic, thrilling climax of this long sequence is the triumphant arrival of the Trojans at the very gates of the Achaean camp. Beneath the high walls of the palisade that shelters the beached Achaean ships, Hektor, at the head of a pack of Trojans, heaves up a massive stone and hurls it at the gates. Groaning and splintering, the gates give way under the impact, and Hektor bursts in, "with dark face like sudden night," shining "with the ghastly / glitter of bronze . . . ; and his eyes flashed fire."

Zeus is not the only god watching this spectacle. From his own lookout on a forested summit on the island of Samothrace, Poseidon regards the plight of the Achaeans with pity. Poseidon—Zeus' younger brother, lord of the sea and shaker of the earth—is an implacable enemy of the Trojans, and along with the other immortals he bristles under his brother's injunction to keep out of the fray. But Samothrace is in sight of Mount Ida, where Zeus is ensconced, and from this convenient vantage Poseidon is able to see not only the whole of the Trojan plain but also the strategic moment when Zeus turns his attention elsewhere.

Seizing this moment in impulsive defiance, Poseidon descends the mountain in three long strides; the fourth brings him to his golden, glittering house in the depths of the sea, where he harnesses "his bronze-shod horses, / flying-footed, with long manes streaming of gold." Driving these across the waves, "about him the sea beasts came up / from their deep places and played in his path, and acknowledged their master, / and the sea stood apart before him, rejoicing. The horses winged on / delicately, and the bronze axle beneath was not wetted." Reaching the field of battle, Poseidon, in disguise, whirls through the demoralized Achaeans, inspiring them. The action of Book Thirteen is largely devoted to the brief respite the Achaeans win with Poseidon at their side.

Soaring above the many memorable images—of the god of the sea in all his sweeping, glittering, exuberant glory, of the Achaeans weeping with weariness, of the mutilated and the dying—is the single transfixing moment when Zeus looks away from the plain of Troy, and

> turned his eyes shining
> far away, looking out over the land of the Thracian riders
> and the Mysians who fight at close quarters, and the proud
>   Hippomolgoi,
> drinkers of milk, and the Abioi, most righteous of all men.
> He did not at all now turn his shining eyes upon Troy land . . .

Zeus is bored with events on the Trojan plain. His attention has drifted; there are other mortals to watch, the Mysians, for example, who, it seems, are also fighters, or the Hippomolgoi, nomadic Scythian "Mare-milkers."[2] His initial interest had been held by his vigilant concern that other gods stay out of the fray and that Hektor reach the ships; but with these events past, as he believes, his attention simply wanders.

As an epic, the *Iliad*, by definition, narrates "the deeds of heroic or legendary figures"—in other words, the actions and events of men, and the emotional weight of the poem is borne by its mortal heroes and its few, but potent, heroines. Yet there is no action in the *Iliad* that does not have divine prompting. The epic opens with the "plan of Zeus," pitting Achilles against Agamemnon, and other divine initiatives follow quickly: the plague sent by Apollo, the delusive dream sent by Zeus to Agamemnon, and the crisis to which the Achaeans have now arrived, with Hektor and the Trojans at their gates, in accordance with Zeus' strategy to honor his pledge to Thetis. In this manner, it is possible to reduce the entire story of the *Iliad* to a series of divine actions.[3]

The *Iliad*, moreover, is not only the definitive telling of the icono-graphic Trojan War but also the most important seminal religious text of ancient Greece. "Homer and Hesiod are the poets who composed theogonies," wrote Herodotus in his *Histories*, in the mid-fifth cen-tury B.C., "and described the gods for the Greeks, giving them all their appropriate titles, offices, and powers."[4] While Hesiod's *Theogony*—literally, "the generations of the gods"—is a poetic list of deities, includ-ing the many outlandish creatures from the murky age before the establishment of Zeus, Homer's pantheon comprised convincingly real-ized characters. Compelling enough to survive millennia of changing religious and artistic mores, the *Iliad*'s portraits of the Olympian divin-ities drew from a variety of sources, in Greece and abroad, as well as Homer's genius for characterization. The names of Zeus, Hera, Poseidon, Ares, and Dionysos appear in the Linear B tablets among a list of deities receiving offerings of honey, olive oil, perfume, gold vessels, wine, grains, animals, and human slaves: "to Zeus"; "to the Poseidon sanctuary"; "to the Zeus sanctuary"; "for Zeus, Hera, Drimios the son of Zeus . . ." This last, otherwise unknown son of Zeus is edited out by passing generations, along with the Great Mistress, the Divine Mother, and the cult to the Winds, all similarly lost. Nor is it known if the familiar names that do appear in the tablets correspond with the deities of Homer. The tablets refer to a "spreading of the bed" in a ceremony for Poseidon, for example, which seems to imply some kind of marriage, or fertility rite, difficult to correlate with the Poseidon who appears in epic as lord of the sea and earthquakes.[5]

The *Iliad*'s epithet for Zeus' wife and sister, Hera—*bo-ōpis*, literally "cow-eyed" or "ox-eyed," sometimes translated less literally as "having large, dark, soft eyes"—may derive from an Indo-European tradition asso-ciating the Sky God with cows and bulls: in Greek mythology specifically, Zeus couples with various partners while either he or they are in bovine form.[6] The origins of Ares, god of war, are writ large in his name—*arē*, *áros*—"ruin," "damage."[7] Despite the centrality of war in both myth and history, shrines and cult centers to Ares were rare in Greece. "'Do not sit beside me and whine, you double-faced liar'" were Zeus' dark words to his son at the end of Book Five. "'To me you are most hateful of all gods who hold Olympos.'" Shunned in heaven as well as on earth, Ares is credited in the *Iliad* with not a single act of dignity; he is even disgraced by the goddess Athene in the physical contests in which, as the god of war, he ought to have been supreme.

The prototype of Athene may possibly lie in Mycenaean depictions of helmeted and shield-bearing goddesses, and warrior goddesses, such as Ishtar and Anat, are also found in the Near East.[8] Traditionally the protectress of favored heroes and especially cities, Athene is warlike, but rarely savage;[9] the goddess's vanquishing of Ares, in Book Five, is proof of her contempt toward this truly brutal bully. Athene is also the goddess of handiwork and craftsmanship, both male and female, and her patronage of domestic work such as weaving is further evidence of her essentially civilized sympathies; Athene is above all a friend to mankind. In the poetry of Hesiod, she is born full-grown from Zeus' own head, owl-eyed and wearing armor.[10] She is the closest to Zeus of all his many children, distinguished by her *mētis*, or "skill in counsel, . . . astuteness, shrewdness." She is *glaukōpis*, "bright-eyed," like the wise-seeming, all-discerning owl.[11]

Appropriately, the lineage of the Father of Gods and men is of all the gods the most secure: He is *Zeus pater*—Zeus the father—*Diespiter* in Indo-European, eventually becoming the Latin *Jupiter*.[12] His name means "the Bright One" and has cognates in a variety of Indo-European languages with words for "day" and "sky";[13] the God of the Bright Sky, he later appropriates the attributes of a storm god, analogous to the Hittite Weather God.[14] Echoes of his original nature reverberate throughout the *Iliad*. "'Father of the shining bolt, dark-misted,'" Athene addresses him. He sits on the loftiest summits, close to the sky; he is "Zeus who delights in the thunder" and "Zeus who gathers the clouds." Such epithets and associations are very old; Zeus the cloud-gatherer may have inherited an

Ugaritic epithet for Ba'al, the "cloud-gatherer or cloud-rider."[15] God of the sky, he is the all-seeing god, privy to all activities of men below.

The individual deities in the *Iliad* are characterized not only by their unique attributes—power, wisdom, warfare—but also by their well-drawn personalities. Athene may "represent" wisdom, but there is nothing abstract about her compelling characterization. The contradictory range of attributes assigned to her—warfare and weaving—survive intact into later centuries because they work so well within the vivid personality created by Homer. Characterized in wholly human terms, the Olympians indulge in the pleasures, troubles, and pursuits of man. They can be wounded, scolded, punished, thwarted; they are loving, indulgent, petty, and jealous; they are just like man—except that the consequences of their actions are never terminal. They will survive their travails because unlike mortals they are one and all *athánatos kaì agérōs*—"deathless and unaging."

The epic tradition anointed Olympos, a 9,570-foot-high peak of a remote Macedonian range, to be the gods' home. Here, above the world of men, they live lives of untroubled ease and luxury in their splendid houses crafted by Hephaistos. Yet, as the *Iliad* makes clear, notwithstanding the attractions of their abode above the clouds, the gods cannot tear themselves from the world of men. This is not only because mortals provide the savory burnt offerings and sacrifice they find so gratifying but because the lives and deeds of men are objects of endless fascination to them. The war at Troy provides the gods with excitement and stimulation. Seemingly, they cannot get their fill of watching it, arguing about it, and participating in it; the Trojan War is the best show playing.

Deceptively, the actions of the gods blend perfectly with those of men. When Hera and Athene descend to fight for the Achaeans, and Apollo and Ares for the Trojans, for example, the gods are wholly assimilated into the ranks of mortals. They come as allies, distinguished from the diverse peoples gathered to fight at Troy only by the type of assistance—immeasurably greater—that they are able to render. Their aspirations, even their pride and anger, are in accord with those of their mortal comrades. It is this commonality of emotional and moral character, as much as the physical human disguises they so often assume, that allows the gods of the *Iliad* to infiltrate the company and confidence of mortal men.

No testimonials of any kind survive to tell us whether an audience of Homer's time was scandalized or entertained by such an irreverent depiction of divinity; the survival of the *Iliad* itself can be taken as evidence of a kind that audiences at some level "approved." Some later audiences, however, did not. Three and a half centuries after Homer, Plato famously banned the works of Homer from his ideal republic on the grounds that shameful "stories about gods warring, fighting, or plotting against one another" were unsuitable material for the training of young souls as just citizens.[16] But others, perceiving that the nature of the Homeric gods tempered the nature of Homeric man, were more generous.

"I feel indeed," wrote "Longinus," in his first-century-A.D. treatise *On the Sublime*, "that in recording as he does the wounding of the gods, their quarrels, vengeance, tears, imprisonment, and all their manifold passions Homer has done his best to make the men in the *Iliad* gods and the gods men."[17]

Of all the antics performed by the gods in the *Iliad*, few are as mischievous, memorable, and ultimately disconcerting as those depicted in the extended scene in Book Fourteen traditionally known as *Diòs apátē*, or "the deception of Zeus."[18] The scene begins when Hera observes that Poseidon, unnoticed by Zeus, whose attention has drifted, has managed to deploy himself among the Achaeans. Supportive of Poseidon's championing of the Achaeans, Hera decides to help his efforts with a scheme of her own to "beguile the brain in Zeus":

And to her mind this thing appeared to be the best counsel,
to array herself in loveliness, and go down to Ida,
and perhaps he might be taken with desire to lie in love with her
next her skin, and she might be able to drift an innocent
warm sleep across his eyelids, and seal his crafty perceptions.
She went into her chamber, which her beloved son Hephaistos
had built for her, and closed the leaves in the door-posts snugly
with a secret door-bar, and no other of the gods could open it.
There entering she drew shut the leaves of the shining door, then
first from her adorable body washed away all stains
with ambrosia, and next anointed herself with ambrosial
sweet olive oil, which stood there in its fragrance beside her,
and from which, stirred in the house of Zeus by the golden
    pavement,
a fragrance was shaken forever forth, on earth and in heaven.
When with this she had anointed her delicate body
and combed her hair, next with her hands she arranged the shining
and lovely and ambrosial curls along her immortal
head, and dressed in an ambrosial robe that Athene
had made her carefully, smooth, and with many figures upon it,
and pinned it across her breast with a golden brooch, and circled
her waist about with a zone that floated a hundred tassels,
and in the lobes of her carefully pierced ears she put rings
with triple drops in mulberry clusters, radiant with beauty,
and, lovely among goddesses, she veiled her head downward
with a sweet fresh veil that glimmered pale like the sunlight.
Underneath her shining feet she bound on the fair sandals.[19]

Like a mortal hero, Hera is arming for battle and her detailed head-to-toe preparations, reversing the usual feet-first heroic formula, suggest a kind of tongue-in-cheek arming scene: "First he placed along his legs the fair greaves. . . . Over his powerful head he set the well-fashioned helmet."

Armed like a warrior, Hera sets forth to conquer a hated adversary—her husband. And like a strategizing general, she solicits allies. For her plan to succeed, she needs both the seductive charms of Aphrodite and the complicity of Sleep. To both of these deities, Hera spins a story, "with false lying purpose," about needing their help to reconcile discord that has arisen between the sea gods Okeanos and his wife, Tethys.[20] From Aphrodite, Hera extracts the loan of the goddess's charm, apparently an amulet, on which "are figured all beguilements, and loveliness / is figured upon it, and passion of sex is there, and the whispered / endearment that steals the heart away even from the thoughtful." From Sleep, bribed by the promise of marriage to one of the Graces, Hera extracts a pledge to descend upon Zeus after she has seduced him.

Her attack meticulously prepared, Hera now drifts casually past her lord, where he sits alone on towering Ida. "Zeus who gathers the clouds saw her, / and when he saw her desire was a mist about his close heart," and, as planned, he suggests they lie together. Answering him again "with false lying purpose," Hera protests that they cannot do so on the peaks of Ida in the open where " 'everything can be seen.' "

> Then in turn Zeus who gathers the clouds answered her:
> "Hera, do not fear that any mortal or any god
> will see, so close shall be the golden cloud that I gather
> about us. Not even Helios can look at us through it,
> although beyond all others his light has the sharpest vision."
> So speaking, the son of Kronos caught his wife in his arms. There
> underneath them the divine earth broke into young, fresh
> grass, and into dewy clover, crocus and hyacinth
> so thick and soft it held the hard ground deep away from them.
> There they lay down together and drew about them a golden

wonderful cloud, and from it the glimmering dew descended.
So the father slept unshaken on the peak of Gargaron
with his wife in his arms, when sleep and passion had stilled him.

The length of this sequence and the luxurious pace at which it is unfolded suggest that it was a set piece, undoubtedly famous in its own day; one of its jokes is the utilitarian use Zeus makes of his trademark cloud gathering. Similar stories about the trickery of the gods are found in Hesiod and the Homeric Hymns, while in the *Odyssey* the poet Demodokos sings a lengthy story "about the love of Ares and sweet-garlanded Aphrodite," who are caught in adultery.[21]

As a piece of pure entertainment, the Deception serves the dramatic function of breaking what would otherwise have been a long, unrelieved battle narrative. The scene begins while fierce fighting is under way, and when Zeus awakens, he opens his eyes to see Hektor, who had been almost killed by a boulder hurled by Aias, "lying in the plain, his companions sitting / around him, he dazed at the heart and breathing painfully, / vomiting blood," with carnage all around. While Zeus slept, Poseidon has done much damage to the Trojans. At face value, then, the Deception is simply an amusing interlude within a long, grim sequence.

But it is its very function *as* an interlude that is most disconcerting. Men are fighting for their lives, suffering mutilating wounds, and dying—and Zeus the father, distracted, is heedless of them.

Of greater interest than the nature of the gods per se is the nature of their relationship with mortal men. The Olympians of the *Iliad* know everything about the mortals they look down upon; Zeus himself is *euruópa*, "far-seeing," a direct legacy of his origins as the all-seeing God of the Bright Sky, to whose celestial vantage the events on earth are laid bare.[22] Rarely indolent, usually zestful and opinionated, the extended family of Zeus aggressively engages with the mortal world. In disguise, the Olympians move, speak, and act freely among men, partaking of the human experience. There is nothing about the men and women at Troy that the gods do not know, even to foreknowledge of their individual fates.

By contrast, despite the busy flow of divine activity that drums through their lives, the Homeric heroes and heroines know very little about their gods. Few could claim to know what a god looks like, as most encounters take place with the deity in disguise. There are exceptions: Helen famously recognizes Aphrodite, despite her masquerade as an old servant woman, by the "round, sweet throat of the goddess / and her desirable breasts and her eyes that were full of shining." Likewise, Poseidon's disguise as the seer Kalchas is betrayed by his footprints: "'this is not Kalchas, the bird interpreter of the gods,'" Aias the son of Oïleus says to Telamonian Aias, "'for I knew / easily as he went away the form of his feet, the legs' form / from behind him. Gods, though gods, are conspicuous.'"

By and large, however, the men at Troy fight in a kind of fog of existential ignorance, never knowing where or who the gods are or what divine activities and plans already under way may affect their own actions. Nor do they know what they must do for their supplications and prayers to be received. A very few incidents appear to suggest that Zeus, at least, punishes the wicked, which, if true, would furnish some minimal guidance for gaining his favor and avoiding his wrath. Menelaos, for example, rants at the Trojans for taking Helen away: "'wretched dogs, and your hearts knew no fear / at all of the hard anger of Zeus loud-thundering, / the guest's god, who some day will utterly sack your steep city.'" On closer look, however, in this and other such cases, it is clear that punishment is to be meted out by Zeus only in his capacity as patron of a specific institution: he is *Zeus Orkios*, "Zeus who upholds oaths," or *Zeus Xenia*, the god of guest friendship.[23] Zeus' loyalty, then, is in fact to himself in his particular cultic aspects, not to a principle of overarching justice.

If no clear principles sway the gods, how can mortals fathom their divine will? Seers, the interpreters of omens and dreams like Kalchas, on occasion provide guidance by clarifying a particular god's wishes, as

Kalchas does so effectively at the outset of the epic, divining the cause of Apollo's plague. But the *Iliad* also takes pains to demonstrate that omens can be problematic, as is seen in a critical, extended exchange between Hektor and the wise Poulydamas. As the two men stand on the edge of the Achaeans' defensive ditch, deliberating whether to cross it, an immense eagle appears overhead, carrying a "gigantic snake, blood-coloured, / alive still and breathing." Writhing upward, this monstrosity bites its captor, causing the eagle to drop it to the ground, where it lands conspicuously on the field of battle. Turning to Hektor, Poulydamas cautions his brother not to venture against the Achaeans in the face of this evil portent:

> Looking darkly at him tall Hektor of the shining helm answered:
> "Poulydamas, these things that you argue please me no longer.
> Your mind knows how to contrive a saying better than this one.
> But if in all seriousness this is your true argument, then
> it is the very gods who ruined the brain within you,
> you who are telling me to forget the counsels of thunderous
> Zeus, in which he himself nodded his head to me and assented.
> But you: you tell me to put my trust in birds, who spread
> wide their wings. . . .
> One bird sign is best: to fight in defence of our country."

The incident contains a menacing, tragic irony. Zeus had indeed earlier sent his personal messenger, Iris, to declare to Hektor that "'Zeus guarantees power to you / to kill men, till you make your way to the strong-benched vessels, / until the sun goes down and the blessed darkness comes over.'" Day is far from over when the baneful snake drops with a thud at the feet of the Trojans. The snake is an omen to be heeded, clearly, but on the other hand Hektor's directives came from Zeus. Nonetheless, as the epic audience knows, it is Poulydamas, not pious, trusting, "Zeus-loved" Hektor, who reads the situation correctly; Hektor's delusion will destroy him.

The dual perspective of gods and men is a hallmark of Homeric epic and the basis of much of the *Iliad*'s pathos. Sometimes this is played out as a kind of split-screen drama, like the Deception, unfolding actions that take place simultaneously on Olympos and on earth. Sometimes this epic perspective has a darker function, disclosing the fundamental ignorance in which even the most heroic mortals must operate. When Hektor pounds on the gates of the Achaean palisade, he believes that victory is within his grasp—after long years of suffering and effort, salvation appears to be within reach; his city is surely saved, he can return to his home, to his wife and child—but we, the epic's audience, know what Zeus knows, that Hektor's glory is transient, is in fact only a means to an end, the end being the honor of Achilles, Hektor's enemy. Similarly, Agamemnon rises from sleep inspired by a dream that assures him Troy is his for the taking; but we, the audience, know what Zeus knows, that this was a false dream sent by the father of gods and men to lure the Achaeans into a trap, in which many will die.

More tragic than such episodes of outright delusion is the men's pervasive, entrenched, fatalistic acceptance that the gods are tricky. "'This time Menelaos with Athene's help has beaten me,'" says Paris languidly, following his inconclusive duel with Menelaos; "'another time I shall beat him. We have gods on our side also.'" "'Zeus son of Kronos has caught me badly in bitter futility,'" Agamemnon groans shortly before he dispatches the Embassy to Achilles. "'He is hard: who before this time promised me and consented / that I might sack strong-walled Ilion and sail homeward. / Now he has devised a vile deception.'" Most terrible of all is Hektor's simple insight of what will be his final battle: "'Athene has tricked me.'"

Equipped as they may be with this grim knowledge, men and women, heroes and civilians have little recourse but to pray to the gods and carry on. That the gods have power to save them is made explicit not so much by the few miraculous rescues—such as of Paris and Aineias—as by those cases when death could have been, but was not, forestalled; as when, on this longest day in the *Iliad,* Zeus looks down and recognizes that his own son, Sarpedon of Lykia, born of a mortal woman, will shortly be killed. "'Ah me,'" Zeus sighs to Hera. "'The heart in my breast is balanced between two ways as I ponder, / whether I should snatch him out of the sorrowful battle / and set him down still alive in the rich country of Lykia, / or beat him under at the hands of the son of Menoitios.'" Beside him, Hera bristles:

> "Majesty, son of Kronos, what sort of thing have you spoken?
> Do you wish to bring back a man who is mortal, one long since
> doomed by his destiny, from ill-sounding death and release him?
> Do it, then; but not all the rest of us gods shall approve you.
> And put away in your thoughts this other thing I tell you;
> if you bring Sarpedon back to his home, still living,
> think how then some other one of the gods might also
> wish to carry his own son out of the strong encounter;
> since around the great city of Priam are fighting many
> sons of the immortals."

Zeus is chastised in this manner on more than one occasion. Always, regretfully, he backs down, and the contested event takes its fated course. Here, as elsewhere, the implication is that Zeus is stronger than Fate and could change even destined outcomes, if he chose to; maintenance of peace among his undying peers on Olympos, however, outweighs concerns for transient mortals on the earth below. As Apollo, the god least well disposed to humans, puts it most bluntly, he will not fight with another god "'for the sake of insignificant / mortals, who are as leaves are, and now flourish and grow warm / with life, and feed on what the ground gives, but then again / fade away and are dead.'"

The plain of Troy, then, like any field of war, is dense with the prayers of doomed and frightened men and their womenfolk, who do not know if a god is near, or even listening: "'. . . have pity / on the town of Troy, and the Trojan wives, and their innocent children,'" the women of Troy pray, "but Pallas Athene turned her head"; "'Zeus, and you other immortals, grant that this boy, who is my son, / may be as I am,'" Hektor prays to Zeus, but Homer's audience knows that his young son will be killed. Some of the epic's most heartbreaking futile prayers still lie ahead.

Unsolicited and unsummoned, the gods crowd the plain of Troy, thrilled by the great game of mortal warfare, jostling to rally, rescue, or menace embattled heroes. Their presence in the epic is usually diverting; the inspiration for their presence, however, surely lies in history as much as poetry—a reflection of the soldier's very real need to believe, in the face of all evidence to the contrary, that he is not abandoned on the field of war. How powerful this need can be is illustrated by an extraordinary story that arose at the very outset of the First World War, in 1914. Harrowed by intense days of artillery battle, the British forces had also endured a grueling thirty-six-hour-long forced march to the south of the Belgian town of Mons. Titanic thunderclouds, illuminated by lurching searchlights, loomed over the field of battle. The German cavalry, almost upon them, slowed to await the arrival of their artillery.

"We were surrounded by Germans at the time and we were out to the last round," recalled Private John Ewings of the Royal Inniskilling Fusiliers.

> We had only one round left in our rifles. I got down on my knees. I had the rifle ready to blow my own brains out. And, I'm shaking, my whole nerves are shaking just thinking about it. And I got down on my knees and I looked up to the sky, you know what you do when you are going to pray, . . . and there was like what we thought a [clap] of thunder. I just looked up and the clouds parted—this big cloud parted—and this man came out with a flaming sword.[24]

The Angel of Mons would eventually be recalled by many soldiers in many forms—as St. George, as one of a line of angelic bowmen, as the archers of Agincourt returned to fight for their countrymen, as a ghostly cavalry charging from the clouds. Careful investigative studies, however, have not been able to discover a single contemporary account of the phenomenon. Attestations like that of Private Ewings all arose after the fact, fueled by the power of suggestion and the stricken need to believe that almighty powers intervened on the harrowing field of war. The story of the Angel of Mons was eventually traced to a short work of fiction masquerading as journalism entitled "The bowmen," by one Arthur Machen. This is perhaps beside the point. What matters is that the myth was absorbed and multiplied in desperate earnest by untold numbers of both military and even civilian Britons, whom the early horror of war had induced to look beyond the Church of England.

The antidote to this wishful fantasy that the soldier never really stands alone can be found in a few grim verses of the same era. A. E. Housman's "Epitaph on an Army of Mercenaries" is a commemoration of the rank and file who did their job in a universe in which prayers could be expected to go unanswered:

> These, in the day when heaven was falling,
>   The hour when earth's foundations fled,
> Followed their mercenary calling
>   And took their wages and are dead.
>
> Their shoulders held the sky suspended;
>   They stood, and earth's foundations stay;
> What God abandoned, these defended,
>   And saved the sum of things for pay.[25]

The *Iliad*'s few miraculous deliverances notwithstanding, by and large its warriors battle for their lives on a dark plain that, as they know and accept, the gods may well abandon. Like all soldiers', their heroism is forged from those twin facts—their knowledge and their battle.

Man Down

Back at the Achaean camp, now under siege by Hektor and the Trojans, the wounded are returning from the field. Standing on the stern of one of his ships is Achilles, who, Zeus-like, looks "out over the sheer war work and the sorrowful onrush." He has not, it appears, yet returned to Phthia. Despite the cavalcade of events that has transpired on earth and in heaven since his last appearance, and the multitude of strong heroes who have died, only two weeks have passed since Achilles withdrew himself and his men from the war. But, from the lofty vantage of his beached ship, it appears he has been closely watching.

Embedded in the tumultuous events and deaths of this longest day of the Trojan War, which begins in Book Eleven and will end with Book Eighteen, is the episode upon which the *Iliad* turns, and which was categorically predicted by Zeus to Hera, as early as Book Eight:

"For Hektor the huge will not sooner be stayed from his fighting
until there stirs by the ships the swift-footed son of Peleus
on that day when they shall fight by the sterns of the beached ships
in the narrow place of necessity over fallen Patroklos.
This is the way it is fated to be."

The extended sequence that will culminate with the fall of Patroklos is broken into several widely separated segments. It begins, however, with Achilles on the lookout of his ship's stern, from where he observes the returning soldiers, including a warrior whom he does not recognize. Calling to his companion-in-arms, Patroklos, he dispatches him to find out what has happened. Patroklos "heard it from inside the shelter, and came out / like the war god, and this was the beginning of his evil."

Obedient to Achilles, Patroklos sets out on his commission in Book Eleven; he does not return to Achilles until Book Sixteen. Between departure and return, Patroklos is detained by two parties, and during these delays the epic narrative cuts back to the ongoing battle. Poseidon's defiant interference in the fray, the Deception of Zeus, the breach of the Achaean defenses, the Trojan setback while Zeus slumbers—all occur while Patroklos dallies in the tents of his companions. A casual audience could be forgiven for losing track of Patroklos' mission, and of Patroklos himself, amid these other dramatic episodes. This risk is offset in part by the several prophecies that relentlessly forecast the course of events that will lead to Patroklos' imminent death; and the audience has been warned that this is "the beginning of his evil."

Hastening on his mission of inquiry through the Achaean camp, Patroklos first comes to the tent of Nestor, where he is warmly greeted and offered hospitality. "'No chair, aged sir,'" Patroklos declines when asked to sit down. "'Honoured, and quick to blame, is the man who sent me to find out / who was this wounded man you were bringing. Now I myself / know, and I see it is Machaon, the shepherd of the people. / Now I go back as messenger to Achilles, to tell him.'"

Nestor's response is sarcastic: "'Now why is Achilles being so sorry for the sons of the Achaeans?'" he asks, and embarks upon a list of the heroes who have been injured. "'Meanwhile Achilles / brave as he is cares nothing for the Danaans nor pities them. / Is he going to wait then till the running ships by the water / are burned with consuming fire . . . ?'" As often, Nestor's aged helplessness inspires memories of earlier youthful prowess. A long digression follows, involving the division of spoils of a long-ago raid that had once brought him, the young Nestor, much glory. Then, abruptly, the old man suddenly concludes his reminiscence and wheels around to Patroklos:

"That was I, among men, if it ever happened. But Achilles
will enjoy his own valour in loneliness, though I think
he will weep much, too late, when his people are perished
    from him.
Dear child, surely this was what Menoitios told you
that day when he sent you out from Phthia to Agamemnon."

Years ago, Nestor had come to Phthia with Odysseus "'assembling
fighting men'" for the war that was just beginning at Troy across the sea.
The two recruiters had found Peleus in his courtyard making sacrifice,
with Achilles, Patroklos, and Patroklos' father, Menoitios; and when the
two fathers took leave of their sons, each had given parting words of
advice. Peleus had enjoined Achilles "'to be always best in battle and pre-
eminent beyond all others,'" and Menoitios had told Patroklos "'to speak
solid words'" to his stronger, younger companion, to "'give him good
counsel, / and point his way.'"

"'This is what the old man told you, you have forgotten,'" Nestor now
admonishes. "'Yet even / now you might speak to wise Achilles, he might
be persuaded.'" In the event that Patroklos cannot persuade Achilles to
relent, Nestor suggests a fateful alternative:

"Let him send you out, at least, and the rest of the Myrmidon
    people
follow you, and you may be a light given to the Danaans.
And let him give you his splendid armour to wear to the fighting,
if perhaps the Trojans might think you are he, and give way
from their attack, and the fighting sons of the Achaeans get wind
again after hard work."

To this solemn directive, Patroklos gives no response, although
Nestor's words "stirred the feeling" in his breast. Departing, he makes

directly for the ships and Achilles but is delayed again, this time by the appearance of a wounded companion, Eurypylos, who is dripping sweat and blood as he limps out of battle. "'No longer, illustrious Patroklos, can the Achaeans / defend themselves,'" Eurypylos replies bluntly in answer to Patroklos' query as to how they are faring, and he asks Patroklos to attend to his wound with medicines, "'good ones, which they say you have been told of by Achilles, / since Cheiron, most righteous of the Centaurs, told him about them.'"

Anxious though he is to return to Achilles, Patroklos is moved by pity for his friend, and with an arm about him helps the wounded warrior to his shelter. And here he stays, throughout all of Books Twelve and Thirteen and the Deception of Zeus in Book Fourteen, which results in Poseidon's rallying of the Achaeans.

When Zeus awakes from his cloud-enshrouded sleep, he sees the Trojans in rout and instantly perceives he has been deceived. "'Hopeless one,'" he growls at Hera, who lies beside him, "'it was your evil design, your treachery, Hera, / that stayed brilliant Hektor from battle.'" After issuing threats such as lashing her, or hanging her from heaven with anvils on her feet, Zeus pronounces an adamantine directive: Hektor will return to battle, fortified by Apollo, and the Achaeans will be driven back in panic. Achilles will send out Patroklos, and glorious Hektor will cut him down, and eventually the Achaeans will capture Ilion.

Zeus' resumption of power turns the tide of battle again to the Trojans, driving the Achaeans once again back to their ships; and it is thus, with the Achaeans in full rout, that the narrative rejoins Patroklos. In the tent of Eurypylos, he makes the determination to "'go in haste to Achilles, to stir him into the fighting. / Who knows if, with God helping, I might trouble his spirit / by entreaty, since the persuasion of a friend is a strong thing.'" Nestor's words evidently struck home. Shortly, Patroklos, delayed by loyalty and pity, returns at last to Achilles' tent. And this really is the beginning of his evil.

Who is Patroklos? In the *Iliad*, he is wholly defined by his relationship to Achilles; he is Achilles' *therápōn*, or "comrade," "comrade-at-arms," "follower," "retainer," or "henchman." A *therápōn* attends his royal master by greeting guests and serving wine, assisting in sacrifices, acting as a messenger to other chiefs, driving a chariot, and fighting by his commander's side; Patroklos' epithets *hippeús*, "fighting from a chariot," and *hippokéleuthos*, "horse-driving," reflect this last duty.[1] Accordingly, Patroklos helped greet the Embassy, saw to the accommodation of Phoinix, and, at Achilles' bidding, sprinted off to find out news about Machaon and his wound. A *therápōn* is a nonkinsman of noble but dependent status to his lord—an "esquire, not servant" as one old dictionary worriedly emphasizes, fearful one might imagine that Patroklos was not a gentleman.[2] As important, he is also Achilles' *phílos hetaîros*, his own, his dear, his beloved companion.[3]

Although central to the dramatic action of the *Iliad*, outside of the *Iliad* Patroklos has a remarkably slight presence, suggesting that he was mostly developed by Homer for the specific role he plays in this epic. An ancient commentator reports that "Hesiod says that Patroclus' father Menoetius was Peleus' brother, so that accordingly they were each other's first cousins."[4] No mention of the familial relationship is made in the *Iliad*, which is rather wholly focused on the relationship between the two men as comrades-in-arms. In the *Iliad*, Patroklos enters Achilles' life when he flees from Opous in Lokris, in east-central Greece, following a childhood misdeed (the accidental murder of a playmate), with his father, to Phthia.[5] This accident apart, nothing is said of the life—or existence—of Patroklos prior to his inclusion in Achilles' orbit, by the *Iliad* or any other tradition.

The name of Patroklos, who in the *Iliad* stands closest to Achilles of all his companions, is suspiciously reminiscent of the name of the person closest to Meleager, who figured so prominently in Phoinix's wildly scattered parable in the Embassy scene. In that rambling paradigm, it will be remembered, Meleager, whom Phoinix intended to stand as an example to Achilles, was finally moved to rejoin his companions in battle by the entreaties of his wife, Kleopatra. Kleo-patra, Patro-kleos—both names mean "renown of the father"[6]—and it may be that the old folktale of Meleager was Homer's inspiration for both the name of Achilles' closest friend and the role he plays as mediator between the angry hero and his community. The implications of this resemblance will shortly be seen.

The adventures of paired or inseparable heroes are a favorite theme of myth and legend. In Greek mythology, to choose one example, we find Theseus, slayer of the Minotaur, closely paired in a number of exploits with Peirithoös of Thessaly.[7] A more ancient and striking parallel, long noted, is found in the Akkadian epic of Gilgamesh, dating to at least 1700 B.C. The emotional heart of this saga of the deeds of Gilgamesh, king of Uruk (now in Iraq), is his close friendship with the wild man Enkidu, whose death drives the grieving Gilgamesh to the limits of mortal existence.[8]

Achilles and Patroklos perform no heroic deeds together. In fact, Achilles' *therápōn* has no life at all outside his death, and he performs no deed except the grand, last mission that will kill him. Homer worked hard to ensure that this outline of a figure whose single, simple role is so transparent be invested with as much humanity as his poetic art could muster in short compass: the death of Patroklos simply *must* be pathetic, *must* stir emotion, or the whole grand scheme of the *Iliad* fails. Consequently, man and god give rare tribute to the character of Achilles' doomed *therápōn;* Patroklos "'was gentle, and understood how to be kindly toward all men,'" according to a companion. Zeus himself knows Patroklos as "'strong and gentle.'"

> Meanwhile Patroklos came to the shepherd of the people, Achilles,
> and stood by him and wept warm tears, like a spring dark-running
> that down the face of a rock impassable drips its dim water;
> and swift-footed brilliant Achilles looked on him in pity,

and spoke to him aloud and addressed him in winged words:
  "Why then
are you crying like some poor little girl, Patroklos,
who runs after her mother and begs to be picked up and carried,
and clings to her dress, and holds her back when she tries to hurry,
and gazes tearfully into her face, until she is picked up?
You are like such a one, Patroklos, dropping these soft tears.
Could you have some news to tell, for me or the Myrmidons?
Have you, and nobody else, received some message from Phthia?
Yet they tell me Aktor's son Menoitios lives still
and Aiakos' son Peleus lives still among the Myrmidons.
If either of these died we should take it hard. Or is it
the Argives you are mourning over, and how they are dying
against the hollow ships by reason of their own arrogance?
Tell me, do not hide it in your mind, and so we shall both know."

"Groaning heavily," Patroklos replies by listing the heroes who have been wounded; then, cursing Achilles as pitiless, he makes the request that Nestor urged—to send him out with Achilles' men, disguised in Achilles' armor:

So he spoke supplicating in his great innocence; this was
his own death and evil destruction he was entreating.

Patroklos, for all his good intentions, has bungled his mission. Faithfully, he echoed the latter part of Nestor's speech—but he forgot its major point: Nestor intended for Patroklos to persuade *Achilles* to return to battle, and only if this entreaty failed was he to request that he, Patroklos, return in Achilles' armor. This blunder represents Patroklos' second missed cue. Previously, in the Embassy, Phoinix's obscure parable of Meleager offered one clear lesson: an entreaty by the person closest to the angry hero—spelled out for emphasis as Kleo-patra—could induce him back to battle. Achilles stormed past the parable without consideration; but so, too, more fatefully, did Patroklos, who, as the *Iliad* took pains to point out, was standing by, watching and listening. In the Embassy, Patroklos did not hear the hint; now he registers Nestor's hints but embraces the wrong one.

"Deeply troubled," Achilles answers Patroklos, briefly defending his anger against Agamemnon. Nonetheless, swiftly and without altercation, he accedes to Patroklos' request. Directing him to draw his "'glorious armour'" about his shoulders, Achilles gives Patroklos command of the Myrmidons, and last stern injunctions:

"When you have driven [the Trojans] from the ships, come back;
    although later
the thunderous lord of Hera might grant you the winning of glory,
you must not set your mind on fighting the Trojans, whose delight
is in battle, without me. So you will diminish my honour.
You must not, in the pride and fury of fighting, go on
slaughtering the Trojans, and lead the way against Ilion,
for fear some one of the everlasting gods on Olympos
might crush you. Apollo who works from afar loves these people
dearly. You must turn back once you bring the light of salvation
to the ships, and let the others go on fighting in the flat land.
Father Zeus, Athene and Apollo—if only
not one of all the Trojans could escape destruction, not one
of the Argives, but you and I could emerge from the slaughter
so that we two alone could break Troy's hallowed coronal."

No one speaks like Achilles. The astounding vision—the annihilation of enemy and ally alike, with the survival only of the two companions—reveals not only Achilles' closeness to Patroklos but also how wholly disassociated he believes himself to be from anything to do with this war. Also manifest within his stern, thrice-repeated injunctions are his deepest fears—that he lose honor, that Patroklos not return to him alive. While they talk, the storm of battle has risen around Aias, who had been defending the ships with almost single-handed courage. Under a barrage of spears, this solitary and stalwart warrior at last retreats. The Trojans fling firebrands at Achilles' ship and the flames stream over it:

> Achilles
> struck his hands against both his thighs, and called to Patroklos:
> "Rise up, illustrious Patroklos, rider of horses.
> I see how the ravening fire goes roaring over our vessels.
> They must not get our ships so we cannot run away in them.
> Get on your armour; faster; I will muster our people."

Events have taken a bewildering turn: Patroklos had come intending to arouse Achilles, but it is Achilles who now rouses Patroklos. It is he who will muster the Myrmidons. Achilles had pledged not to return "'until that time came / when the fighting with all its clamour came up to my own ships.'" Now the fighting and the flames have surely arrived; if Patroklos had not offered himself, might it not be Achilles setting forth?

As Achilles musters his men, the legendary Myrmidons, Patroklos arms himself in the borrowed armor. The scene is typical of the three other great arming scenes in the epic, belonging respectively to Paris, to Agamemnon, and, most magnificently, and yet to come, to Achilles. Together, the four scenes demonstrate how traditional set pieces such as arming can be adapted, and in this case personalized for each hero.[9] First, Patroklos puts on his greaves with their silver fastenings, then the corselet, "starry and elaborate of swift-footed Aiakides," then the sword and the great shield:

> Over his mighty head he set the well-fashioned helmet
> with the horse-hair crest, and the plumes nodded terribly above it.

He took up two powerful spears that fitted his hand's grip,
only he did not take the spear of blameless Aiakides,
huge, heavy, thick, which no one else of all the Achaeans
could handle, but Achilles alone knew how to wield it;
the Pelian ash spear which Cheiron had brought to his father
from high on Pelion to be death for fighters.

Patroklos may be clad, head to foot, in Achilles' armor, but he cannot wield Achilles' spear. Used here eloquently to signify how out of his depth Patroklos is, the spear is one of three remarkable gifts to Peleus that were in turn handed down to his son. The *Cypria* relates how "at the wedding of Peleus and Thetis the gods gathered on Pelion to feast, and brought gifts for Peleus, and Chiron cut down a fine ash and gave him it for a spear. They say that Athena planed it and Hephaestus fashioned it."[10] The other gifts were a pair of horses, Xanthos and Balios, born of the mare Podarge and the West Wind, "swift and immortal / horses the gods had given as shining gifts to Peleus"; and the armor, described as *ámbrota*, or "armour of non-dying, invincible armour,"[11] which "the gods gave Peleus, a glorious present, for that day they drove [Thetis] to the marriage bed of a mortal."

In folklore and saga, gifts from fairies or higher powers to a mortal prince are usually magical. A magic spear would return to its master when hurled; magic horses would convey him safely out of battle; and magic armor would make the hero invulnerable.[12] Typically, Homer has suppressed all such outlandish protection; no hero fighting at Troy has any charm or power to escape death.[13] Nonetheless, as will shortly be revealed, remnants of the original attributes of each of Peleus' divine gifts are discernible in the *Iliad*, although transformed and turned by Homer to tragic effect.

At Patroklos' bidding, Automedon, Achilles' charioteer, harnesses the immortal horses,

Xanthos and Balios, who tore with the winds' speed,
horses stormy Podarge once conceived of the west wind
and bore, as she grazed in the meadow beside the swirl of the
    Ocean.
In the traces beside these he put unfaulted Pedasos
whom Achilles brought back once when he stormed Eëtion's city.
He, mortal as he was, ran beside the immortal horses.
    But Achilles went meanwhile to the Myrmidons, and
        arrayed them
all in their war gear along the shelters. And they, as wolves
who tear flesh raw, in whose hearts the battle fury is tireless,
who have brought down a great horned stag in the mountains, and
        then feed
on him, till the jowls of every wolf run blood, and then go
all in a pack to drink from a spring of dark-running water,
lapping with their lean tongues along the black edge of the surface
and belching up the clotted blood; in the heart of each one
is a spirit untremulous, but their bellies are full and groaning;
as such the lords of the Myrmidons and their men of counsel
around the brave henchman of swift-footed Aiakides
swarmed, and among them was standing warlike Achilles
and urged on the fighting men with their shields, and the horses.

Many images have been used to convey the mayhem and bloodshed
of war, but for sheer chilling glamour, few can match this mustering of
the Myrmidons, wolf-hungry for battle, with the immortal horses straining at their traces. "Fifty were the fast-running ships wherein Achilles /
beloved of Zeus had led his men to Troy, and in each one / were fifty men."
The origins of the Myrmidons are obscure and the usual explanation of
their name is highly unsatisfactory. According to Hesiod, Aiakos, Achilles' grandfather and a mortal son of Zeus, found himself to be the only

human on the desolate island of Aigina; lonely, he prayed to his father for companions, and Zeus transformed the island's ants—*múrmēkes*—into humans, who became the Myrmidons.[14] Later writers theorized they were so called for their antlike habits, such as living in caves and digging up soil.[15] Attempts to correlate either explanation with the warrior tribe of Achilles remain mostly unconvincing—ants are industrious and have exemplary social organization; they are fierce and ravenous and fight in a "pack"; Aigina's defining central mountain is conical and looks like an anthill, and so forth.[16] It is difficult not to view these explanations as a whimsical folk etymology confronted with an old and mysterious name. In the apocryphal Acts of Andrew (dating to the third century A.D.), there is a "city of the cannibals," which is identified as Myrmidon; it is possible that this account taps into some more ancient, and savage, lost tradition.[17]

In the *Iliad*, the Myrmidons are simply the twenty-five hundred men from Phthia under the command of Achilles. That they are distinct from Phthians per se is made clear: during Achilles' absence, one finds "the Phthians" fighting alongside Lokrians and Epeians, trying to hold Hektor from the ships, and somewhat later a "Medon" is named as their leader. The boundaries of the kingdom of Peleus and Achilles are never securely delineated; Phthia is evidently a large area, possibly encompassing several tribes.[18] This telling vagueness suggests that the Myrmidons are defined less by geography—a small region inside Phthia, for instance—than by status and function. They are an elite guard, a Delta Force. The comparison to wolves is also suggestive; well attested in Indo-European culture is the war band—a fraternity of "foot-loose young men," unmarried and unsettled, who "live on the margins of society and follow their leader wherever he takes them, generally on raiding and looting expeditions" and who "consciously adopted a wolfish identity."[19] The Myrmidons are banded around Achilles; they are loyal to no other agent or cause, certainly not to Agamemnon, as is clear from Patroklos' address to them before they charge to battle:

"Myrmidons, companions of Peleus' son, Achilles,
be men now, dear friends, remember your furious valour;
we must bring honour to Peleus' son, far the greatest of the Argives
by the ships, we, even the henchmen who fight beside him,
so Atreus' son wide-ruling Agamemnon may recognize
his madness, that he did no honour to the best of the Achaeans."

As the Myrmidons muster, Achilles retreats to his shelter and from an elaborately decorated chest draws forth a goblet, "nor did any other / man drink the shining wine from it nor did Achilles / pour from it to any other god, but only Zeus father." This ritual goblet is tucked away beside the clothes his anxious mother had packed for him when he left on campaign, his "tunics / and mantles to hold the wind from a man." Standing in the compound outside his shelter, Achilles lifts the filled goblet and prays to Zeus:

"As one time before when I prayed to you, you listened
and did me honour, and smote strongly the host of the Achaeans,
so one more time bring to pass the wish that I pray for.
For see, I myself am staying where the ships are assembled,
but I send out my companion and many Myrmidons with him
to fight. Let glory, Zeus of the wide brows, go forth with him.
Make brave the heart inside his breast, so that even Hektor
will find out whether our henchman knows how to fight his battles
by himself, or whether his hands rage invincible only
those times when I myself go into the grind of the war god.
But when he has beaten back from the ships their clamorous onset,
then let him come back to me and the running ships, unwounded,
with all his armour and with the companions who fight close beside
    him."
So he spoke in prayer, and Zeus of the counsels heard him.
The father granted him one prayer, and denied him the other.

That Patroklos should beat back the fighting assault on the vessels
he allowed, but refused to let him come back safe out of the
    fighting.

The appearance of Patroklos at the head of the Myrmidons, as "they fell
upon the Trojans in a pack," has the desired effect; immediately the Trojans are shaken and "each man looked about him for a way to escape the
sheer death." As they flee, Patroklos and his men quench the fire around
the ships. Book Sixteen is Patroklos' *aristeía*. Not only do he and the
Myrmidons wreak havoc on the terrified Trojans, but their very appearance, as Nestor had hoped, inspires the exhausted and embattled Achaeans, and, rallying, they fall upon the Trojans "as wolves make havoc
among lambs." At some point that the epic does not disclose, Patroklos
is recognized for himself, despite the borrowed armor; for a brief period,
then, Achilles is not missed. Patroklos will kill a total of fifty-four Trojans, a casualty list that compares impressively with, for example, the
twenty of Diomedes' dazzling *aristeía*.[20] Soon Patroklos catches up with
what will be his most illustrious victim, Sarpedon, son of Zeus—and his
own destiny presses closer.

"'Ah me,'" sighs Zeus, watching, "'that it is destined that the dearest
of men, Sarpedon, / must go down under the hands of Menoitios' son
Patroklos'"; and (as quoted in the previous chapter) he debates whether
to spare his son against destiny, snatching him out of battle and setting him down in his native land—the desperate fantasy of many a
fighting man—or allow him to die. "'What sort of thing have you spoken?'" is Hera's unfeeling response. "'Think how then some other one of
the gods might also / wish to carry his own son out of the strong encounter; / since around the great city of Priam are fighting many / sons of the
immortals.'" Hera's retort and Zeus' submission terminate any hope
of rescue for Sarpedon and also, by extension, for Achilles, the most
prominent of all the sons of the immortals by Priam's city. Hera
continues:

"No, but if he is dear to you, and your heart mourns for him,
then let him be, and let him go down in the strong encounter
underneath the hands of Patroklos, the son of Menoitios;
but after the soul and the years of his life have left him, then send
Death to carry him away, and Sleep, who is painless,
until they come with him to the countryside of broad Lykia
where his brothers and countrymen shall give him due burial
with tomb and gravestone. Such is the privilege of those who have
     perished."
     She spoke, nor did the father of gods and men disobey her;
yet he wept tears of blood that fell to the ground, for the sake
of his beloved son, whom now Patroklos was presently
to kill, by generous Troy and far from the land of his fathers.

As the two advance, Patroklos throws his spear and hits Sarpedon's
therápōn; in his turn, Sarpedon casts at Patroklos and misses, "but the
spear fixed in the right shoulder of Pedasos / the horse, who screamed
as he blew his life away, and went down"—Pedasos, who, mortal as he
was, ran beside the immortal horses. Every action now presages Patroklos'
own fate.

When at length Sarpedon is hit, he falls "as when an oak goes down
or a white poplar, / or like a towering pine tree which in the mountains
the carpenters / have hewn down with their whetted axes to make a ship-
timber," for ships like those that sailed to Troy. Dying, "raging," Sarpedon
"called aloud to his beloved companion" begging him to ensure that his
body is not dishonored, nor his armor stripped from him; his is the first
of what will be three dying speeches in the epic. His companion Glaukos
hears him and, praying to Apollo for strength, rallies his companions,
and a battle erupts over the body, and armor, of Sarpedon.

So they swarmed over the dead man, nor did Zeus ever
turn the glaring of his eyes from the strong encounter,

but kept gazing forever upon them, in spirit reflective,
and pondered hard over many ways for the death of Patroklos;
whether this was now the time, in this strong encounter,
when there over godlike Sarpedon glorious Hektor
should kill him with the bronze, and strip the armour away from
   his shoulders,
or whether to increase the steep work of fighting for more men.

Zeus decides upon two strategies: he will allow Patroklos one more triumphant assault, and, as Hera had suggested, he instructs Apollo to aid Sleep and Death in bearing Sarpedon's body to his home.[21] The body is whisked away, and the mortal remains of Sarpedon are gone. He and his companion and kinsman Glaukos are the most prominent of the Trojans' many allies, and Sarpedon's death is the most significant casualty to befall the Trojan side. Together the two warriors have given the epic some of its most reflective moments, such as Glaukos' speech on the generations of men in Book Six. In Book Twelve, toward the beginning of this longest day, it had been Sarpedon who uttered to Glaukos the simple statement that later ages would adopt as defining the Homeric warrior's rationale for war:

"Man, supposing you and I, escaping this battle,
would be able to live on forever, ageless, immortal,
so neither would I myself go on fighting in the foremost
nor would I urge you into the fighting where men win glory.
But now, seeing that the spirits of death stand close about us
in their thousands, no man can turn aside nor escape them,
let us go on and win glory for ourselves, or yield it to others."[22]

In short, the death of Sarpedon is an important landmark in the epic. A fully realized character, he will be missed. The grieving, loyal companion he leaves behind, the extraordinary attention he receives from

Zeus, and the fight over his fallen body and armor are all motifs that will shortly be repeated as the *Iliad* moves relentlessly toward its tragic climax.[23]

Immediately following the gentle disposition of Sarpedon's body, the action returns abruptly to Patroklos. His onslaught has been an unmitigated success; the Trojans have been driven back, and the ships are saved. By the terms of Achilles' orders, he should now return to the Achaean camp; but, "besotted" with blind fury, he rages on: "Then who was it you slaughtered first, who was the last one, / Patroklos, as the gods called you to your death?"

At the very threshold of Troy, Patroklos attempts to mount the angled walls; three times he tries, and three times he is batted down by the city's menacing guardian, Apollo, who strides the ramparts and cries out to him "in the voice of danger: / 'Give way, illustrious Patroklos: it is not destined / that the city of the proud Trojans shall fall before your spear / not even at the hand of Achilles, who is far better than you are.'"

Patroklos is allowed one last victory, over Hektor's charioteer and half brother, but as the sun sinks, his destiny claims him in the suddenly huge and terrifying apparition of Apollo:

> . . . there, Patroklos, the end of your life was shown forth,
> since Phoibos came against you there in the strong encounter
> dangerously, nor did Patroklos see him as he moved through
> the battle, and shrouded in a deep mist came in against him
> and stood behind him, and struck his back and his broad shoulders
> with a flat stroke of the hand so that his eyes spun. Phoibos
> Apollo now struck away from his head the helmet
> four-horned and hollow-eyed, and under the feet of the horses
> it rolled clattering, and the plumes above it were defiled
> by blood and dust. Before this time it had not been permitted
> to defile in the dust this great helmet crested in horse-hair;
> rather it guarded the head and the gracious brow of a godlike

man, Achilles; but now Zeus gave it over to Hektor
to wear on his head, Hektor whose own death was close to him.
And in his hands was splintered all the huge, great, heavy,
iron-shod, far-shadowing spear, and away from his shoulders
dropped to the ground the shield with its shield sling and its tassels.
The lord Apollo, son of Zeus, broke the corselet upon him.
Disaster caught his wits, and his shining body went nerveless.
He stood stupidly, and from close behind his back a Dardanian
man hit him between the shoulders with a sharp javelin:
Euphorbos, son of Panthoös, who surpassed all men of his own age
with the throwing spear, and in horsemanship and the speed of his
    feet. He
had already brought down twenty men from their horses
since first coming, with his chariot and his learning in warfare.
He first hit you with a thrown spear, o rider Patroklos,
nor broke you, but ran away again, snatching out the ash spear
from your body, and lost himself in the crowd, not enduring
to face Patroklos, naked as he was, in close combat.
Now Patroklos, broken by the spear and the god's blow, tried
to shun death and shrink back into the swarm of his own
    companions.
But Hektor, when he saw high-hearted Patroklos trying
to get away, saw how he was wounded with the sharp javelin,
came close against him across the ranks, and with the spear
    stabbed him
in the depth of the belly and drove the bronze clean through.
    He fell,
thunderously, to the horror of all the Achaean people.

Of the many deaths the *Iliad* records, no other resembles that of
Patroklos. Nowhere is the pitiful vulnerability of a mortal so exploited
as it is by the savage malevolence of Apollo's blow and the hounding of

the wounded man as he tries to shun death among his companions. The horror of this extraordinary scene is reinforced by the resonance of two disparate, submerged traditions. One of these concerns that magic armor, worn by the folktale predecessors of Achilles, whose fairy-tale function had undoubtedly been to render its wearer invulnerable. As has been said, Homer severely repressed any hint that the armor given by the gods to Peleus had supernatural properties, yet he allows one aspect of this ancient motif to surface here, turning it to electrifying effect—Patroklos must be stripped of the armor before he can be killed. Thus Apollo's savage blow strikes off his helmet and breaks the corselet upon him.[24] Patroklos is killed—slaughtered—naked.

"To select a victim, to adorn it, and to drive it towards the enemies to be killed by them" in time of crisis—such is the ancient rite of substitution.[25] Patroklos has been made a scapegoat, a ritual substitute for his king, in whose distinctive armor—and in whose stead—he is driven to his death; Patroklos has become the literal alter ego of Achilles, his second self.[26] The stunning blow that Apollo deals him, the stab between the shoulder blades and the final death stroke—these are more the actions of ritual slaughter, than of battle.

Broken by the most malevolent of gods, and subsequently by two opportunistic mortals, Patroklos, dying, must endure Hektor's hollow vaunt over him. Exalting, Hektor imagines—very wrongly, as we know—how Achilles must have instructed Patroklos to return with his bloodied tunic: "'In some such / manner he spoke to you, and persuaded the fool's heart in you.'" Poor Hektor can have no idea how badly he reads the unfolding events.

And now, dying, you answered him, o rider Patroklos:
"Now is your time for big words, Hektor. Yours is the victory
given by Kronos' son, Zeus, and Apollo, who have subdued me
easily, since they themselves stripped the arms from my shoulders.
Even though twenty such as you had come in against me,

they would all have been broken beneath my spear, and have
    perished.
No, deadly destiny, with the son of Leto, has killed me,
and of men it was Euphorbos; you are only my third slayer.
And put away in your heart this other thing that I tell you.
You yourself are not one who shall live long, but now already
death and powerful destiny are standing beside you,
to go down under the hands of Aiakos' great son, Achilles."

    He spoke, and as he spoke the end of death closed in upon him,
and the soul fluttering free of his limbs went down into Death's house
mourning her destiny, leaving youth and manhood behind her.

Everything Hektor believes is false, just as everything Patroklos states
with his last breath is true. For all his prowess, Hektor is an ordinary
soldier, privy to no prophecies, blind to his own fate. Elated, drunk with
triumph, Hektor allows himself to entertain an impossible notion—that
perhaps Achilles, too, will fall to him.

    As Trojans and Achaeans previously swarmed over the body of Sarpe-
don, contending for his corpse and the prize of his armor, so now both
sides converge to fight for Patroklos. Menelaos strides forward and stands
over him, "as over a first-born calf the mother / cow stands lowing, she
who has known no children before this." This will be Menelaos' finest
hour in the epic, although soon, faced with the relentless onslaught of
ranks of Trojans, he is forced to make a temporary retreat. Safe among
his own companions, he looks around wildly for Aias: " 'This way, Aias,
we must make for fallen Patroklos / to try if we can carry back to Achilles the body / which is naked; Hektor of the shining helm has taken his
armour.' " At stake is the timeless credo "Leave no man behind." The
stakes are very high, as Hektor of the shining helm, the loving family
man and dutiful patriot, having stripped the remaining armor from
Patroklos, "dragged at him, meaning to cut his head from his shoulders

with the sharp bronze, / to haul off the body and give it to the dogs of Troy."[27]

Aias, always reliable, joins Menelaos in returning to Patroklos, and while the two heroes mount a second, pitched defense over the corpse, Hektor briefly withdraws so as to put on the plundered armor of Achilles. For all of Book Seventeen, throughout the remainder of this long day, the battle rages over the body of Patroklos, which is soon obscured in an eerie mist. Waves of grief are set in motion by his death, washing over god, man, and even Achilles' immortal horses, who stand apart from the fray in shock:

> ... still as stands a grave monument which is set over
> the mounded tomb of a dead man or lady, they stood there
> holding motionless in its place the fair-wrought chariot,
> leaning their heads along the ground, and warm tears were running
> earthward from underneath the lids of the mourning horses
> who longed for their charioteer, while their bright manes were
>   made dirty
> as they streamed down either side of the yoke from under the yoke
>   pad.[28]

As the day draws at last toward dusk, Antilochos, Achilles' other close companion, is dispatched to break the dreadful news to Achilles. Amid the din and confusion and the dusty mist that engulfs the toiling men, the fall of Patroklos has passed unnoticed for a few, and one of these few is Antilochos. Now he, too, learns the tragic news; he, too, like the immortal horses, stands stock-still in grief: "He stayed for a long time without a word, speechless, and his eyes / filled with tears, the springing voice was held still within him."

The shock waves of this one death reverberate through the heavens and across the plain, from Zeus to the horses of Achilles to Antilochos.

The audience holds its breath while the news is at last carried by Antilochos toward the ships. Simultaneously, with momentous effort, Menelaos and Meriones of Crete hoist the body of Patroklos over their shoulders and, covered by great Aias and his companion, attempt a slow, dangerous retreat.

At the ships, where he has been keeping an anxious watch, Achilles is gripped by a premonition, "thinking / over in his heart of things which had now been accomplished," and noting that the Achaeans are once again retreating in confusion. As his fears mount, Antilochos appears and breaks the dreaded news: "the black cloud of sorrow closed on Achilles. / In both hands he caught up the grimy dust, and poured it / over his head and face, and fouled his handsome countenance."

As he lies sprawled in the dust, Thetis, from the depths of the sea, hears her son's crying. Knowing what this forebodes, she, too, "cried shrill in turn." From the deep recesses of the ocean throng about her the shadowy multitude of her sister Nereïds, daughters of Nereus, the old man of the sea. Filling the "silvery cave" where Nereus dwells, they beat their breasts and wail, their threnody echoing that of the handmaids of Achilles and Patroklos. "'Hear me,'" Thetis wails to her sisters:

"Ah me, my sorrow, the bitterness in this best of child-bearing,
since I gave birth to a son who was without fault and powerful,
conspicuous among heroes; and he shot up like a young tree,
and I nurtured him, like a tree grown in the pride of the orchard.
I sent him away with the curved ships into the land of Ilion
to fight with the Trojans; but I shall never again receive him
won home again to his country and into the house of Peleus."

So profound and affecting is Thetis' grief that one could overlook the fact that she is mourning the wrong man; it is Patroklos who has died— not Achilles.

Homer's *Iliad* describes the events of a very few days in the last year of the Trojan War; these events do not encompass what was surely one of the most climactic moments of the entire Trojan War cycle—the death of Achilles. That the *Iliad* knew the body of tradition that did describe Achilles' death, however, is evident from its striking parallels with key scenes in the other epics. In the *Aethiopis*, Achilles avenges the Trojan ally Memnon for the death of his close friend Antilochos, whose role resembles that of Patroklos in the *Iliad*. Then, having slain Memnon,

> Achilles puts the Trojans to flight and chases them into the city, but is killed by Paris and Apollo. At the Scaean Gates he is shot by Alexander and Apollo in the ankle. A fierce battle develops over his body, in which Ajax kills Glaucus. He hands over Achilles' armor to be taken to the ships; as for the body, he takes it up and carries it towards the ships, with Odysseus fighting the Trojans off.
>
> Then they bury Antilochus, and lay out the body of Achilles. Thetis comes with the Muses and her sisters, and laments her son.[29]

A telling counterpart of the Iliadic scene of Thetis' mourning of Patroclos also occurs toward the end of Homer's second epic, the *Odyssey*. There the ghost of Agamemnon tells the ghost of Achilles that when he, Achilles, died, "'your mother, hearing the news, came out of the sea, with immortal / sea girls beside her. Immortal crying arose and spread over / the great sea'" (24.47–49).

For an audience of Homer's days, then, knowledgeable of the wider epic tradition, the *Iliad*'s account of the death of Patroklos would have directly evoked the death of his alter ego, Achilles. Above all, the extended scene of Patroklos' death, with its echoes of the traditional deaths of both Antilochos and Achilles—and Sarpedon's death, in turn, with its foreshadowing of the fate of Patroklos—did more than ensure that the *Iliad*'s audience was entertained with a subtle evocation of one of the most famous, possibly popular episodes of the Trojan war cycle.[30] As each death presages the next, the sense of dreadful, impending fate is heightened. The Embassy of Book Nine is memorable for Achilles' passionate declaration that nothing offered on earth is more precious than life. Now the *Iliad* has reached that point where the death of Achilles is forecast as confidently as was the death of Patroklos. Having calibrated the value of his wrath and his honor against his existence, Achilles has been ambushed by guilt and love, and regardless of whether the *Iliad* covers the event or not, unambiguously, he will shortly die. Thetis mourns now because this tragic fact is already as good as accomplished.

These background resonances are made explicit when Thetis comes to comfort her son. Rising from out of the sea with her grieving sisters, she comes to Achilles' shelter. Crying out, she cradles his head in her arms and, weeping, reminds him that all the things he prayed to Zeus for "are brought to accomplishment." He replies:

> ". . . there must be on your heart a numberless sorrow
> for your son's death, since you can never again receive him
> won home again to his country; since the spirit within does not
> drive me
> to go on living and be among men, except on condition
> that Hektor first be beaten down under my spear, lose his life
> and pay the price for stripping Patroklos, the son of Menoitios."
> Then in turn Thetis spoke to him, letting the tears fall:
> "Then I must lose you soon, my child, by what you are saying,
> since it is decreed your death must come soon after Hektor's."
> Then deeply disturbed Achilles of the swift feet answered her:
> "I must die soon, then; since I was not to stand by my companion
> when he was killed. And now, far away from the land of his fathers,
> he has perished, and lacked my fighting strength to defend him."[31]

The *Patrokleia* and the events of its immediate aftermath reflect some of the most masterful and sophisticated narrative structuring in the *Iliad*.

Sarpedon and Glaukos; Antilochos and Achilles; immortal armor that cannot save the man who wears it; divine horses who could run with the West Wind but are stilled with grief, and the screaming death of the mortal horse who dared to run with them; ancient sacrificial ritual and echoes from *Gilgamesh;* a grieving mother whose son still lives—all these motifs and themes dramatically darken the last hours and death of Patroklos. In turn, the layered resonances of the *therápōn*'s death foreshadow the event the *Iliad*'s audience will never see—the death of Achilles.

The creation of Patroklos established one of the memorable figures in epic and also forged a moral link between two ancient themes: a story of heroic wrath, in which the angered hero is propitiated to return to his community, and a story of retribution, in which the death of the hero's companion is avenged. Homer's innovation was to inexorably relate the one to the other. Achilles' wrath will never be appeased; rather it will be effaced by survivor's guilt.[32]

Phílos; hetaîros—"comrade," "buddy," "mate"—"my own," "my best," "my beloved companion." The terms that define the relationship between Patroklos and Achilles have no true counterparts in the civilian world but belong to the enduring terminology of war. "It's a closeness you never had before," as a veteran of the Vietnam War described his friend-in-arms. "It's closer than your mother and father, closest [*sic*] than your brother or your sister."[33] Today the "loss of a buddy," along with "fear of death," is recognized as one of the standard primary causes of war trauma. At the Walter Reed Army Medical Center, a grieving soldier returned from Iraq "walks the hospital campus in the bloodied combat boots of a friend he watched bleed to death."[34]

Magic armor and horses that carry the hero out of danger—Homer understood that this was pale stuff. The creation of Achilles' alter ego, his sacrificial second self, allowed Homer to unleash the emotions that will always most authentically memorialize war. In the concluding lines of his magisterial account of the Great War, John Keegan offers a summation that is true of all:

Men whom the trenches cast into intimacy entered into bonds of mutual dependency and sacrifice of self stronger than any of the friendships made in peace and better times. That is the ultimate mystery of the First World War. If we could understand its loves, as well as its hates, we would be nearer understanding the mystery of human life.[35]

No Hostages

"Now I shall go, to overtake that killer of a dear life,
Hektor; then I will accept my own death, at whatever
time Zeus wishes to bring it about, and the other immortals."
—*Iliad* 18.114–16

Achilles' stern resolve is declared to Thetis, and his grieving mother both accepts his decision and determines to make one last attempt to outmaneuver fate. Just as all the traditions outside the *Iliad* characterize her as being obsessed with protecting her son—attempting to render him invulnerable or immortal, disguising him as a woman among women—so she now embarks upon a last desperate strategy to forestall the death she well knows he is destined to die. New armor, divine armor, armor made by Hephaistos, the very smith of the gods—in this Thetis lays her faith of last resort. Achilles' own armor—the divine gift to Peleus—is now worn on Hektor's shoulders, and Achilles has no armor of his own.[1] "'Do not yet go into the grind of the war god, / not before with your own eyes you see me come back to you,'" Thetis implores her son. "'For I am coming to you at dawn and as the sun rises / bringing splendid armour to you from the lord Hephaistos.'"

Achilles consents, and Thetis speeds her way to Olympos. During the lengthy interlude before she is seen again, Achilles remains in the Achaean camp. Meanwhile, despite the valiant efforts of Aias and Menelaos, the battle for Patroklos' corpse still rages on the Trojan plain.

Hektor is on the verge of breaking the impasse, dragging at Patroklos' body, when Hera suddenly takes matters into her own hands and, "secretly / from Zeus and the other gods," dispatches Iris with instructions for Achilles.

"'Rise up, son of Peleus, most terrifying of all men,'" Iris greets Achilles, and brings him a fearful bulletin from the field of battle: the Trojans are trying to drag Patroklos into their city, and Hektor "'is urgent / to cut the head from the soft neck and set it on sharp stakes.'"

"'Divine Iris, what god sent you to me with a message?'" Achilles replies coolly. His reaction is a small but potent touch; no other mortal would address Zeus' messenger in so challenging a manner. On learning that Iris comes from Hera, Achilles becomes practical; the Trojans have his armor, and there is little he can do. "'Yes, we also know well how they hold your glorious armour,'" Iris replies. "'But go to the ditch, and show yourself as you are to the Trojans.'"

> So speaking Iris of the swift feet went away from him;
> but Achilles, the beloved of Zeus, rose up, and Athene
> swept about his powerful shoulders the fluttering aegis;
> and she, the divine among goddesses, about his head circled
> a golden cloud, and kindled from it a flame far-shining.
> As when a flare goes up into the high air from a city
> from an island far away, with enemies fighting about it
> who all day long are in the hateful division of Ares
> fighting from their own city, but as the sun goes down signal
> fires blaze out one after another, so that the glare goes
> pulsing high for men of the neighbouring islands to see it,
> in case they might come over in ships to beat off the enemy;
> so from the head of Achilles the blaze shot into the bright air.

As the fire plays around his head, Achilles cries aloud, and Athene cries with him in a voice like that "screamed out by a trumpet / by murderous attackers who beleaguer a city." Terrified, the Trojans retreat, and the Achaeans are at last able to retrieve Patroklos' torn body. Fire and the destruction of cities—the images accompanying Achilles' return signal the war's fateful new threshold. The end is now in sight—of Achilles' absence, and of Achilles himself, of Hektor and, with his death, the end of Ilion.[2] The toll the war has so far taken on Troy, its fragile state, is unexpectedly disclosed as the shaken Trojans debate among themselves how to contend with the catastrophic development represented by Achilles' return. Should they remain on the plain? Or retreat to "'the great walls / and the gateways'" of their city, as careful Poulydamas suggests? To this last suggestion, Hektor, however, is contemptuous:

> "Have you not all had your glut of being fenced in our outworks?
> There was a time when mortal men would speak of the city
> of Priam as a place with much gold and much bronze. But now
> the lovely treasures that lay away in our houses have vanished,
> and many possessions have been sold."

When Troy falls, then, the Achaean victors will gain little for their ten years of effort. Meanwhile, Hektor, made dangerously confident, perhaps, by the fact that he wears Achilles' divine, unaccustomed armor, is intolerant of any strategy for safety. Rather, at his direction the Trojans will spend another night on the plain, by their encampment, and will arm at dawn. He then continues with words that will come to haunt him:

> "If it is true that brilliant Achilles is risen beside their
> ships, then the worse for him if he tries it, since I for my part
> will not run from him out of the sorrowful battle, but rather
> stand fast, to see if he wins the great glory, or if I can win it."

While the Trojans prepare for the night, Achilles oversees the reception of Patroklos' body, which is gently washed in warm water and anointed with olive oil and its gashes filled with unguents; a thin, shroudlike sheet is then laid over it.³ "'I will not bury you till I bring to this place the armour / and the head of Hektor,'" Achilles vows to his dead companion. "'Before your burning pyre I shall behead twelve glorious / children of the Trojans, for my anger over your slaying.'"

All through the night of this longest, disastrous day, the Myrmidons mourn over Patroklos. And while they are mourning, Thetis reaches Olympos and Hephaistos' home, "imperishable, starry," and built of shining bronze. The god himself is at his forge, working on twenty tripods, each set on golden wheels "so that of their own motion they could wheel into the immortal gathering." Wheeled tripods from Cyprus are known from the ninth and eighth centuries B.C.;⁴ perhaps, in their day, such cutting-edge innovation inspired bemused speculation about divine technology and handiwork.

Thetis is greeted by the lame smith and his wife, Charis, one of the beautiful Graces, with exceptional warmth: "'She saved me,'" Hephaistos recalls of Thetis to his wife, "'when I suffered much at the time of my great fall / through the will of my own brazen-faced mother, who wanted / to hide me, for being lame.'"⁵ Cast from Olympos by Hera, his mother, who was ashamed of his lameness, Hephaistos had fallen into the sea where Eurynome, the daughter of Okeanos, and Thetis had caught him. "'With them I worked nine years as a smith, and wrought many intricate / things,'" Hephaistos says, and recalls the necklaces and cups and brooches and other trinkets he devised for them, "'working / there in the hollow of the cave, and the stream of Ocean around us / went on forever with its foam and its murmur.'"⁶

Although Hephaistos' name appears in the Linear B inscriptions, little can be gleaned of his origins or how he came into the Olympian pantheon. The story of his rescue and embrace by Thetis echoes a well-attested Indo-European association between a fire deity and nurturing spirits of the water, evocative perhaps of phosphorescence, the fiery light that seems to burn in the sea.⁷ The status of a metalworker in the ages we dub "Bronze" and "Iron" would obviously be very great, and there is evidence throughout the Eastern Mediterranean of cults and even kingships associated with the smith.[8] Also intriguing are the many examples in myth in which a smith is the nurturer—the forger—of a young god or hero, and epic stories from Tibet to the Caucasus to Ireland tell of the smith who makes safe a young hero, fostering him and serving as his guardian.[9] And it is as protector of young heroes that Hephaistos is approached by Thetis, seeking divine armor that will safeguard her son.

" 'So I must by all means / do everything to give recompense to lovely-haired Thetis / for my life,' " Hephaistos declares to his wife, and, taking his bellows off the fire, he makes touching efforts to prepare for his feminine guest: "with a sponge he wiped clean his forehead, and both hands, / and his massive neck and hairy chest, and put on a tunic, / and took up a heavy stick in his hand, and went to the doorway / limping." " 'We honour you and love you,' " he tells Thetis, taking her hand, and listens kindly to her weeping plea:

"Hephaistos, is there among all the goddesses on Olympos
one who in her heart has endured so many grim sorrows
as the griefs Zeus, son of Kronos, has given me beyond others?
Of all the other sisters of the sea he gave me to a mortal,
to Peleus, Aiakos' son, and I had to endure mortal marriage
though much against my will. And now he, broken by mournful
old age, lies away in his halls. Yet I have other troubles.
For since he has given me a son to bear and to raise up
conspicuous among heroes, and he shot up like a young tree,
I nurtured him, like a tree grown in the pride of the orchard.
I sent him away in the curved ships to the land of Ilion
to fight with the Trojans; but I shall never again receive him
won home again to his country and into the house of Peleus. . . .
Therefore now I come to your knees; so might you be willing
to give me for my short-lived son a shield and a helmet
and two beautiful greaves fitted with clasps for the ankles

and a corselet. What he had was lost with his steadfast companion
when the Trojans killed him. Now my son lies on the ground, heart
sorrowing."

Thetis' tearful plea represents the enduring prayer of all terrified mothers whose sons must go to war. Whether holding bake sales to raise
money for ceramic-plated body armor for their sons in Iraq[10] or pleading directly with the smith of the gods, the objective is the same—magic
armor that will protect my son.

Famously, Hephaistos has made armor for other heroes. In the *Iliad*,
Diomedes wears a coveted "'elaborate corselet that Hephaistos wrought
with much toil,'" for example, and in the *Aethiopis*, Memnon, who mirrors Achilles in so many important respects, appears "wearing armour
made by Hephaestus."[11] This is also not the first occasion in the *Iliad* on
which one god has begged a favor of another. The most significant divine
plea, of course, was also made by Thetis, when she beseeched Zeus to
uphold the honor of her son; to win that favor, she had felt compelled
to remind him, strenuously, of her past service to him and the debt he
owed her. Hera also asked favors of fellow gods, by way of preparation
for her seduction of Zeus; by lying she won from Aphrodite the loan of
her seductive zone, and by bribery she won from Sleep the promise of
his compliance in her scheme. But now Thetis' request of Hephaistos is
honored willingly and out of love. Thetis is greeted by the smith with
great tenderness, and his spontaneous recollection of the aid she once
gave him is sincere and even nostalgic. This brief flashback to the circumstances that bind the lame smith to Thetis is one of Homer's mas-
terstrokes. The smith's pitying, loving response to the nakedness of
Thetis' grief ensures that he will pour not merely his skill but his heart
into his work. Achilles' armor in the *Iliad* will be exceptional, surpassing
all other examples, such as "'men shall wonder at'"; it will represent not
merely the workmanship of the divine smith but his supreme, sublime
effort.

Hearing her the renowned smith of the strong arms answered her:
"Do not fear. Let not these things be a thought in your mind.
And I wish that I could hide him away from death and its sorrow
at that time when his hard fate comes upon him, as surely
as there shall be fine armour for him, such as another
man out of many men shall wonder at, when he looks on it."

"'I wish that I could hide him away from death'"—Hephaistos knows as well as Thetis does that this cannot be done. The smith of the gods can make tripods with magic wheels, a brazen house for every Olympian, gates of the sky "moving of themselves," even golden attendants "in appearance like living young women," capable of speech and intelligence—all such wonders he can work, but he cannot hide the son of Thetis from his fated death.

Back at his forge, with twenty self-propelled bellows blowing on the crucibles, Hephaistos casts bronze, tin, gold, and silver and with hammer and anvil begins his work. The first piece of armament he turns to is Achilles' shield. "Huge and heavy," it is composed of five overlapping folds of metal and has a "triple rim" for additional strength:

> . . . and upon it
> he elaborated many things in his skill and craftsmanship.
> He made the earth upon it, and the sky, and the sea's water,
> and the tireless sun, and the moon waxing into her fullness,
> and on it all the constellations that festoon the heavens. . . .
> On it he wrought in all their beauty two cities of mortal
> men. And there were marriages in one, and festivals.
> They were leading the brides along the city from their maiden
>   chambers
> under the flaring torches, and the loud bride song was arising. . . .
> But around the other city were lying two forces of armed men
> shining in their war gear. For one side counsel was divided

whether to storm and sack, or share between both sides the
  property
and all the possessions the lovely citadel held hard within it. . . .
  He made upon it a soft field, the pride of the tilled land,
wide and triple-ploughed, with many ploughmen upon it
who wheeled their teams at the turn and drove them in either
  direction. . . .
The earth darkened behind them and looked like earth that has
  been ploughed
though it was gold. Such was the wonder of the shield's forging.

For the Iron Age audiences of Homer's day, the description of the
shield of Achilles may have been enjoyed as a bravura piece that conjured
wonders of modern technology and art; Hephaistos' technique is that of
the ironworker after all, or blacksmith.[12] For later audiences, however,
the shield's allure comes less from art than from life—rare glimpses of
lives lived nearly three millennia ago. The elders sitting on benches of pol-
ished stone to adjudicate a dispute; those rich, thrice-turned fields; the
herdsmen playing pipes as they watch their sheep and "shambling cattle"—
all this parade of life has been preserved intact from the Iron Age.[13]

Descriptions of elaborate armor were evidently popular set pieces in
epic. Hesiod's *Shield of Heracles*, dating to around 600 B.C.,[14] is a lengthy
epic fragment dominated by the depiction of that hero's shield: "In the
middle was Fear, made of adamant, unspeakable, glaring backwards with
eyes shining like fire . . . upon it burned Tumult and Murder and Slaughter . . . upon it deadly Fate was dragging men by the feet through the
battle, holding one who was alive but freshly wounded, another who was
unwounded, another who had died."[15] Monsters, gods, terrors personi-
fied are the predominant motifs, along with themes manifestly borrowed
from Homer—a "servile dependence upon Homeric models," according
to one indignant editor of the work.[16] The Homeric model in this case

was not the shield of Achilles but the shield of Agamemnon, which, it will be recalled, was emblazoned with Fear and Terror and the "blank-eyed face of the Gorgon."[17]

The shield that Hephaistos makes for Achilles will be borne into war by the most formidable and man-slaughtering of all mortal heroes—"most terrifying of all men," as Achilles is called even by the gods; moreover, it will be carried by Achilles into the most climactic and significant *aristeía* of the epic. Yet for all that, Hephaistos eschews the motifs most predictably associated with warfare and furnishes the *Iliad* with its most memorable images of peace. Reapers in the field followed by children picking up cut swaths; a vineyard, with dark-clustered grapes and young men and girls carrying the fruit in woven baskets; a youth who sings to the accompaniment of a lyre; cattle and farmyards; lions stalking the herds; and "a meadow / large and in a lovely valley for the glimmering sheepflocks"; men and maidens in light, long robes dancing—in sum, the shield Hephaistos forges for Achilles carries all of life.

" 'And I wish that I could hide him away from death and its sorrow' ": from Hephaistos' inspired hammer emerge all those things that he knows he cannot give Achilles. Achilles' new shield, like his other divine gifts—the armor, the spear, and the horses he inherited from his father—once again serves less to protect him than to highlight his mortality. The new shield Achilles will bear before him into war underscores the enormity of all he is to lose—which is all of life.

Thetis delivers the armor to her son at dawn, setting it, clattering, on the ground before him, where its terrifying brilliance causes the Myrmidons to look away: "Only Achilles / looked, and as he looked the anger came harder upon him / and his eyes glittered terribly under his lids, like sunflare."

Running his hands over Hephaistos' immortal handiwork, Achilles "satisfie[s] his heart with looking" and then strides forth to make official his return to his army, and to the war. Proceeding along the shore, he calls his great cry, and from the ships and shelters Achaeans of every rank stream forth to meet him, stewards and helmsmen as well as warriors, some wounded and leaning on their spears; "and last of them came in the lord of men Agamemnon."

The epic action has returned to where it began, in an assembly in the Achaean camp, at a time of crisis that has taken many lives, and with Achilles assuming de facto command of the listening army. His "unsaying" of his anger is eloquent, unsqueamish, and succinct:

"Son of Atreus, was this after all the better way for
both, for you and me, that we, for all our hearts' sorrow,
quarrelled together for the sake of a girl in soul-perishing hatred?
I wish Artemis had killed her beside the ships with an arrow
on that day when I destroyed Lyrnessos and took her.
For thus not all these too many Achaeans would have bitten
the dust, by enemy hands, when I was away in my anger.
This way was better for the Trojans and Hektor; yet I think
the Achaeans will too long remember this quarrel between us.
Still, we will let all this be a thing of the past, though it hurts us,
and beat down by constraint the anger that rises inside us.
Now I am making an end of my anger. It does not become me
unrelentingly to rage on. Come, then! The more quickly
drive on the flowing-haired Achaeans into the fighting,
so that I may go up against the Trojans, and find out
if they still wish to sleep out beside the ships. I think rather
they will be glad to rest where they are, whoever among them
gets away with his life from the fury of our spears' onset."

He spoke, and the strong-greaved Achaeans were pleasured to
hear him
and how the great-hearted son of Peleus unsaid his anger.

Achilles' return, the unsaying of his wrath or anger, is one of the most dramatic moments of the *Iliad*, the culmination of the theme of wrath with which the epic had begun; it is also the fulfillment of a pattern common to many myths—the withdrawal of the hero from his community, the ensuing devastation, and his return. Phoinix's paradigmatic tale of Meleager is one obvious example of this pattern, as to some extent is the *Odyssey,* which is dedicated to the story of a lonely hero enduring devastating hardships to win his return home.[18]

Of more significance to Achilles, however, are those myths and stories describing the anger and withdrawal not of a hero but of a god. The Homeric "Hymn to Demeter" tells the story of the goddess Demeter's grief and wrath at the loss of her daughter, Persephone, who was abducted and carried to the Underworld. In bitterness and grief, Demeter retreats from the world; as she is the goddess of corn and of the harvest, her departure deprives mankind of her gifts, and a dreadful winter of devastation spreads over the earth. Eventually Persephone is retrieved by the worried gods, Demeter is appeased, and she returns to earth, bringing spring and the harvest with her.[19]

The word used to describe Demeter's baneful, cosmic wrath is *mēnis,* which is also the first word of the *Iliad:* "Wrath, sing goddess, of Peleus' son Achilles," runs the Greek text. Close studies of the use of this word, in Homer and elsewhere, have yielded tantalizing conclusions. *Mēnis* can be summarized as "enduring anger, justified by a desire for rightful vengeance, said especially of gods, of dead heroes, but also of humans, parents or suppliants, and particularly of Achilles in the *Iliad.*"[20]

Mēnis, then, is a charged word, more solemn and potent than its more mundane counterparts, *chólos,* or *kótos*—"anger," "rancor."[21] *Mēnis* "is a dangerous notion, which one must fear; a sacral, 'numinous' notion."[22] In the *Iliad,* it is used only of gods and of Achilles. Like Demeter, Achilles makes his wrath felt by the withdrawal of his considerable abilities. "Wrath, sing goddess, of Peleus' son Achilles, / and its devastation." The devastation comes not from what he does do but from what he does not.

As often with Achilles, the distant thunder of the fate he almost had and the god he almost was rumbles behind his words and actions. It is this word—this *mēnis*—that Achilles "unsays" before the assembly, and the renouncement of such anger—divine anger, cosmic anger—is clearly a momentous event. If sacrificial elements can be discerned in the death of Patroklos, it can now be seen that the sacrifice was effective; the death of Patroklos broke the baneful spell of wrath and has reunited the hero with his community.

Against this profound and consequential background, Agamemnon makes his now almost irrelevant appearance. He speaks to the assembly "from the place where he was sitting, and did not stand up among them," and in his confused first words it seems he has to shout for attention over the noise of an indifferent crowd: "'it is well to listen to the speaker, it is not becoming / to break in on him. This will be hard for him, though he be able. / How among the great murmur of people shall anyone listen / or speak either?'"

Unlike Achilles' forthright declaration of a mutual mistake, Agamemnon must obfuscate; he knows that his own people have faulted him for his treatment of Achilles—this much he allows—but his actions were not his own doing: "'yet I am not responsible / but Zeus is, and Destiny. . . . Yet what could I do? It is the god who accomplishes all things. / Delusion is the elder daughter of Zeus.'"

A long story ensues, illustrating that even Zeus is prey to *Átē*, or Delusion.[23] Then abruptly, comically, Agamemnon wraps up:

"So I in my time . . . could not forget Delusion, the way I was first
    deluded.
But since I was deluded and Zeus took my wits away from me,
    I am willing to make all good and give back gifts in abundance."

"'Son of Atreus,'" says Achilles, and Agamemnon's string of stately epithets has never sounded more ironic, "'most lordly and king of men, Agamemnon, / the gifts are yours to give if you wish, and as it is proper, / or to keep with yourself. But now let us remember our joy in warcraft, / immediately.'"

So much for the riches by which Agamemnon defines his authority. Agamemnon's offer also gives the lie to Phoinix's cautionary paradigm in the Embassy; there, it will be recalled, by way of moral example to Achilles, Phoinix had outlined the fate of Meleager, a hero of old, who, having earlier rejected all offers of reconciliation, was eventually compelled to return to fighting without gifts and without honor.[24] Dismissive as Achilles is of the gifts, or any talk of gifts, Agamemnon is insistent upon this transaction, and so the tired parade of wealth, cataloged twice before in the Embassy, is now carried forth and duly deposited in the assembly. Coming on the heels of Achilles' divine armor, the many cauldrons and talents of gold do not bedazzle as they once might. Now Agamemnon does arise and before the entire army swears the solemn oath, sanctified by sacrifice, that he "'never laid a hand on the girl Briseis / on pretext to go to bed with her, or for any other / reason, but she remained, not singled out, in my shelter'"; and so Agamemnon's unmanning before his army is perfected.

Briseis, who was last seen when led unwillingly from Achilles' shelter, now makes a startling reappearance. Confronted with Patroklos' torn body, she cries aloud and tears her face in mourning:

"Patroklos, far most pleasing to my heart in its sorrows,
I left you here alive when I went away from the shelter,
but now I come back, lord of the people, to find you have
    fallen.
So evil in my life takes over from evil forever.
The husband on whom my father and honoured mother
    bestowed me
I saw before my city lying torn with the sharp bronze,
and my three brothers, whom a single mother bore with me

and who were close to me, all went on one day to destruction.
And yet you would not let me, when swift Achilles had cut down
my husband, and sacked the city of godlike Mynes, you would not
let me sorrow, but said you would make me godlike Achilles'
wedded lawful wife, that you would take me back in the ships
to Phthia, and formalize my marriage among the Myrmidons.
Therefore I weep your death without ceasing. You were kind
  always."

This is the last that will be seen of Briseis, the innocent cause of so
much destruction. The devastation unleashed by her abduction is also
of a pattern, like the plague instigated by the abduction of Chryseis at
the opening of the *Iliad*, and the Trojan War itself, instigated by the
abduction of Helen. In its recitation of the loss of all her protective kin,
Briseis' speech recalls that of Andromache to Hektor. Now the fate of
Briseis, bereft of her champions and among strange men, presages that
of Hektor's wife.

From the moment of his speech of reconciliation, Achilles is intent
only on war and urges immediate action. This prompts a fussy and much-
criticized interlude, introduced by Odysseus, dedicated to the dangers
of fighting on an empty stomach. Later, also at some length, Odysseus
repeats his concern. Possibly there is some inside joke at play, concerning this ever-practical hero's attention to his belly. Achilles' own needs
are met by Athene, who drops "delicate / ambrosia and the nectar" inside
his breast, so that his strength will not fail. These belabored, anxious
explanations about food and, to a lesser extent, earlier concerns about
the state of Patroklos' body, which Thetis has promised to preserve, evoke
a tin-eared copy editor's fretting over all the wrong details: How did the
men keep their strength? Please explain. What about the flies on
Patroklos' body? Various dutiful explanations have been mounted over
centuries to justify this rare stretch where Homer "nods," but it is fair to
say that most readers could do without it: "More than 180 lines have now

passed since luncheon stole the limelight, and nothing has been achieved," as one commentator remarked dryly.[25]

At length, however, the moment for which Achilles has been agitating arrives, and as the newly invigorated Achaeans muster amid the gleam of bronze helmets and shields, Achilles, his heart filled with "sorrow beyond endurance" and "raging at the Trojans," arms for war. This is the last and most magnificent of the *Iliad*'s four, thematically similar but psychologically distinct arming scenes; "Paris arms for shame, Agamemnon for security, Patroclus for loyalty and friendship, but Achilles arms in anger and grief," as one commentator observed:[26]

> "He . . . caught up the great shield, huge and heavy
> next, and from it the light glimmered far, as from the moon.
> And as when from across water a light shines to mariners
> from a blazing fire, when the fire is burning high in the mountains
> in a desolate steading, as the mariners are carried unwilling
> by storm winds over the fish-swarming sea, far away from their
>   loved ones;
> so the light from the fair elaborate shield of Achilles
> shot into the high air. And lifting the helm he set it
> massive upon his head, and the helmet crested with horse-hair
> shone like a star, the golden fringes were shaken about it
> which Hephaistos had driven close along the horn of the helmet.
> And brilliant Achilles tried himself in his armour, to see
> if it fitted close, and how his glorious limbs ran within it,
> and the armour became as wings and upheld the shepherd of the
>   people.
> Next he pulled out from its standing place the spear of his father,
> huge, heavy, thick, which no one else of all the Achaeans
> could handle, but Achilles alone knew how to wield it,
> the Pelian ash spear which Cheiron had brought to his father
> from high on Pelion, to be death for fighters in battle.

* * *

Mounting his chariot, beside his charioteer, Achilles cries out, scolding his immortal horses: "'Take care to bring in another way your charioteer back,'" he says sarcastically, and "'not leave him to lie fallen there, as you did to Patroklos.'" Achilles was not present to witness the impenetrable, silent grief of the horses at the death of Patroklos. As has been seen, Homer eschews the magical and fantastic elements known to other traditions, and never more scrupulously than in his presentation of Achilles. But now there appears one of the most nakedly outlandish events of the epic: Hera puts a voice in Xanthos, so that the horse can speak, and once again the divine gifts of Peleus to his son serve as a haunting reminder of the cost to him of this war:

> Then from beneath the yoke the gleam-footed horse
> answered him,
> Xanthos, and as he spoke bowed his head, so that all the mane
> fell away from the pad and swept the ground by the cross-yoke;
> the goddess of the white arms, Hera, had put a voice in him:
> "We shall still keep you safe for this time, o hard Achilles.
> And yet the day of your death is near, but it is not we
> who are to blame, but a great god and powerful Destiny.
> For it was not because we were slow, because we were careless,
> that the Trojans have taken the armour from the shoulders of
> Patroklos,
> but it was that high god, the child of lovely-haired Leto,
> who killed him among the champions and gave the glory to Hektor.
> But for us, we two could run with the blast of the west wind
> who they say is the lightest of all things; yet still for you
> there is destiny to be killed in force by a god and a mortal."[27]

On Olympos, Zeus summons his own assembly to address the pivotal developments on the Trojan plain, developments that represent the fulfillment of his own plans. "'I think of these men though they are dying,'" he allows to the other immortals. Achilles, if left to his own devices and powers, will make short work of the Trojans; therefore, Zeus announces, he is revoking his command that the gods keep out of the war. "'Go down, wherever you may go among the Achaeans and Trojans / and give help to either side,'" he urges, and then characterizes Achilles' prowess in the most dangerous of all possible terms: "'I fear against destiny he may storm their fortress.'"

Zeus' remarkable pronouncement gives promise of a thrilling turn of events; surely it marks the commencement of the much-anticipated *aristeía* of Achilles, "a man like the murderous war god." Instead Homer nods again, and Zeus' order for the gods to mingle among the armies becomes the pretext for divine buffoonery. Aidoneus, lord of the dead, jumps from his throne and screams aloud in fear that all hell will, literally, break loose. Poseidon and Apollo square off against Athene and the war god Enyalios, as does Hera against Artemis. Less bellicose gods make uncomfortable appearances, such as Leto, the mother of Apollo and Artemis; "generous Hermes," the god of boundaries and messenger of the gods; and crippled Hephaistos.

Nor does the first action of Achilles himself satisfy the dramatic expectations raised by the extended, momentous prelude. To be sure, the son of Peleus approaches like an open-jawed, foaming-mouthed, furious, glaring lion against Aineias, one of Troy's elite heroes. But this first encounter of Achilles' return—his first martial performance in the epic—threatens to be merely a battle of words. Achilles hails his enemy with cheerful, taunting words, at odds with the dark anger and grief he bears: "'Does the desire in your heart drive you to combat / in hope you will be lord of the Trojans, breakers of horses, / and of Priam's honour. And yet even if you were to kill me / Priam would not because of that rest such honour on your hand. / He has sons.'" The two heroes embark upon a kind of slanging match—flyting,[28] playing the dozens— referencing each other's genealogy and ability to use words of insult;

possibly this awkwardly placed encounter makes knowing reference to a tradition dedicated to the exploits of Aineias and his anger with *his* king.[29] At last the two heroes close to exchange actual blows. Cowering under his shield, as the long Pelian ash spear whistles over his head, Aineias is at length rescued, and spirited away to safety, by Poseidon.[30]

Many lines pass, therefore, before Achilles embarks upon the kind of standard slaughter that characterizes the epic way of war. Cutting a swath through the Trojans, he kills a brother of Hektor, Polydoros, and suddenly finds himself in sight of Hektor himself, "'the man who beyond all others has troubled my anger.'" But the ensuing, greatly anticipated encounter between the epic's two contending heroes is also disconcertingly anticlimactic. "'Son of Peleus, never hope by words to frighten me / as if I were a baby,'" Hektor retorts to Achilles' challenge. "'I myself understand well enough / how to speak in vituperation and how to make insults.'" For a bewildering moment, there hovers the possibility of a repeat of the kind of war of words Achilles waged with Aineias. Achilles hurls his spear, however, and a brief exchange follows, and once again the gods intervene to whisk his enemy to safety; on this occasion, it is Apollo who sweeps Hektor away in a thick mist.

The convoluted action transpiring since Thetis' delivery of armor to Achilles has neither furthered the narrative nor heightened dramatic expectations. One can only assume that the broad entertainment afforded by divine foolery and clever references to other epic stories was not felt by ancient audiences to dissipate the dramatic tension—and this consideration is in itself enlightening. Despite the summaries that we possess of the lost epics of the Trojan Cycle, and the many scattered references in later literature, we today know very little about how these other traditions told their stories. But comparison with epics in other times and other cultures suggests they may have looked a lot like the interludes here that accompany Achilles' *aristeía*. Distracting as they are, these "un-Homeric" passages, then, serve modern audiences well—as reminders that the traditional story elements of the *Iliad* did not of themselves guarantee greatness.

The *Iliad* does not regain its high tone and gravitas until the end of Book Twenty, when Achilles' *aristeía* is under way in earnest. There is now nothing amusing about his confrontations with the enemy as he storms across the Trojan plain "as inhuman fire sweeps on in fury," slashing through the Trojan forces, his chariot axle-high in blood and his immortal team of horses trampling underfoot the dead. Achilles' own hands are "spattered with bloody filth" as he drives the terror-stricken Trojans into the river Skamandros (also called Xanthos), leaping in after them so none can escape.

> He, when his hands grew weary with killing,
> chose out and took twelve young men alive from the river
> to be vengeance for the death of Patroklos, the son of Menoitios.
> These, bewildered with fear like fawns, he led out of the water.

These will fulfill his vow to "'behead twelve glorious / children of the Trojans'" before the pyre of Patroklos. And it is here, by the tamarisk-lined river, that Achilles meets a Trojan named Lykaon blundering out of the water.

Lykaon is a son of Priam by a concubine, and as evil fate would have it, this is his second encounter with Achilles, who had captured him in a night raid during some earlier stage of the war. At that time, Achilles had spared his life and sold him in Lemnos, where eventually he was redeemed by a family friend. Now, as Achilles prepares to make his kill, Lykaon runs under the upheld Pelian ash spear. Grasping it with one hand, he clasps Achilles' knees in supplication with the other, begging that his life be spared again for ransom:

> So the glorious son of Priam addressed him, speaking
> in supplication, but heard in turn the voice without pity:

"Poor fool, no longer speak to me of ransom, nor argue it.
In the time before Patroklos came to the day of his destiny
then it was the way of my heart's choice to be sparing
of the Trojans, and many I took alive and disposed of them.
Now there is not one who can escape death, if the gods send
him against my hands in front of Ilion, not one
of all the Trojans and beyond others the children of Priam.
So, friend, you die also."

Buried in the pathos of Lykaon's death is a revelatory fact: in the days before Patroklos' death, it was Achilles' "'heart's choice to be sparing.'" Achilles' actions—and character—in the early days of the war have remained more or less obscure, falling as they do outside the *Iliad*'s chosen time frame. Yet sufficient small hints of the kind of man he was can be gleaned from other incidents in the epic and tend to substantiate his claim that he is now a changed man. The departure of Briseis from his shelter is one such example, who, captive though she was, leaves "all unwilling," and there is the testimony of Andromache, whose father Achilles slew "but did not strip his armour, for his heart respected the dead man." Nor does it appear that bloodlust overwhelmed Achilles in the heat of these early battles. The self-portrait he offers during both his confrontation with Agamemnon in Book One and the Embassy in Book Nine is that of a weary man engaged in the exhausting work of war, which he performs expertly but without much appetite: "'Always the greatest part of the painful fighting is the work of my hands.'" When, therefore, Achilles tells Lykaon that "'it was the way of my heart's choice to be sparing / of the Trojans,'" this is not a rhetorical flourish to make the death of Lykaon more pathetic. Achilles the warrior was once gallant and chivalrous; since the death of Patroklos, he is a different, murderous man.

In his study of combat trauma on American veterans of the Vietnam War, Dr. Jonathan Shay was struck by how vividly and realistically the descriptions of Achilles' actions and state of mind after the death of

Patroklos resembled those of the veterans under his psychiatric care. This was particularly striking of the phenomenon, triggered by some incident—injustice, betrayal, loss of a friend—of the so-called berserk state. As one veteran recalled:

> I just went crazy. I pulled him out into the paddy and carved him up with my knife. When I was done with him, he looked like a rag doll that a dog had been playing with. . . . I lost all my mercy. I felt a drastic change after that. . . . I couldn't do enough damage. . . . For every one that I killed I felt better. Made some of the hurt went [sic] away. EVERY TIME YOU LOST A FRIEND IT SEEMED LIKE A PART OF YOU WAS GONE. Get one of them to compensate what they had done to me. I got very hard, cold, merciless. I lost all my mercy.[31]

Combat trauma undoes character.[32] The cosmic reach of Achilles' furious, raging *aristeía* is evoked by the striking similes clustering around him since his return: fire blazes around his head like the signal flares of a besieged city; his eyes glitter "like sunflare"; his shield glimmers like fire across the water, like moonlight; his helmet shines like a star. These elemental images set up Achilles' elemental battle with one of the few foes capable of threatening him—the river Skamandros, a force of nature. Its eddying waters clogged with the bodies of men Achilles has slaughtered, Skamandros raises his voice in protest and indeed supplication: "'O Achilles, your strength is greater, your acts more violent / than all men's,'" the river implores. "'For the loveliness of my waters is crammed with corpses, I cannot / find a channel to cast my waters into the bright sea / since I am congested with the dead men you kill so brutally. / Let me alone, then; lord of the people, I am confounded.'"

Achilles' slighting response—that he will not leave off killing until Hektor "'has killed me or I have killed him'"—goads Skamandros into hostile action, and, rearing his waters, he comes at Achilles in a dangerous wave. Scrambling out of the river, Achilles makes an undignified dash across the plain, with the river, now surging out of its banks, in fierce pursuit. The lengthy episode is another of the nonheroic interludes that perplexes Achilles' *aristeía*. Its outlandish, fabulous tone, so uncharacteristic of Homer, leads one to suspect an older myth lurking behind the episode, one in which the warrior hero did actual battle against powers of nature and monsters, as in Near Eastern archetypes where a hero battles the Flood.[33]

At length, Hera calls on her lame son for help, and Hephaistos makes a spectacular and unexpected appearance as pure Fire, parching the plain, drying the land, and burning the many corpses:

> Then he turned his flame in its shining
> into the river. The elms burned, the willows and tamarisks,
> the clover burned and the rushes and the galingale, all those
> plants that grew in abundance by the lovely stream of the river.

Blighting the kind of peaceful landscape he so lovingly evoked on Achilles' shield, Hephaistos brings his involvement in Achilles' fate full circle. He cannot keep death from the son of Thetis, but he can fulfill the smith's traditional epic role of protecting young heroes. This swift, startling scene is also the *Iliad*'s only description of the physical damage done to the plain of Troy, and it unnervingly conjures timeless images of the scorched-earth tactics that invading armies inflict upon their enemies' land.

Achilles' savage scamper over the plain drives the Trojans before him, back to Troy. Simultaneously the gods terminate their own battles, and abruptly, with little prelude, return to Olympos. Watching from the battlements of his doomed city, Priam groans aloud and calls for the guards to open the city gates for his routed army. One warrior, Agenor, holds his ground, inspirited by Apollo, the only god who has not left for Olympos, but who stands close by the Trojan, "leaned there on an oak tree with close mist huddled about him." Thus unnaturally emboldened, Agenor calls out to Achilles:

> "You must have hoped within your heart, o shining Achilles,
> on this day to storm the city of the proud Trojans.
> You fool! There is much hard suffering to be done for its winning,
> since there are many of us inside, and men who are fighters,
> who will stand before our beloved parents, our wives and our
>   children,
> to defend Ilion."

But this is not true—the fighters have fled; everyone has fled. Even the gods have fled. Moments later, Agenor has also fled, spirited away by Apollo "in a dense mist," out of the battle and Achilles' range. Apollo himself takes on the likeness of Agenor and in this impersonation goads Achilles into giving chase, leading him away from the walls of Troy and allowing the terrified Trojans to bolt for the city.

Playful on the surface, the interlude of futile chase directly pits Achilles against his own most implacable and malevolent enemy. No god hates him more personally than does Apollo.[34] Dubbed "the most Greek" of the gods, Apollo of later classical times embodied the physical perfection of male youth and the cool rationalism and serene aloofness of the cultivated soul. In the *Iliad*, the traits that will later closely define him are discernible but not necessarily prominent.[35] The god who sends the devastating plague in Book One, Apollo is also the god who can recall it— who can *loigón amúmein*, or "ward off destruction"—a prelude to his later attribute as a healer. He is the "God of Afar," the god of withdrawal, at a distance from man, for whom he manifests disdain. His preferred dwelling is among the Hyperboreans, mysterious dwellers of the Far North, away from the imperfect, impure world of man.[36] To round out his civilized virtues, Apollo is the god of music, associated particularly with the lyre. Reference is made to this skill by Hera, when she reminds Apollo that at the marriage of Achilles' parents, "'you too feasted among them / and held your lyre, o friend of the evil, faithless forever.'"[37]

The traits that define Apollo—bringer and averter of destruction, healing powers, aloofness and withdrawal, youthful beauty, skill in the lyre—have a striking counterpart in the *Iliad:* these are the traits that also define Achilles, the most beautiful hero at Troy, whose wrath has wrought plaguelike destruction, who was taught healing arts by Cheiron, and who is discovered by the Embassy in his tent "delighting his heart in a lyre."[38] That their actions as well as attributes are parallel is made clear in the opening lines of the *Iliad,* which foretell how both god and man direct their divine wrath at the same person, Agamemnon.[39] A tradition survives of an alternative proem for the *Iliad* that made this yet more explicit:

> Sing for me now Muses, who have your homes on Olympos,
> how wrath [*mēnis*] and anger took hold of the son of Peleus,
> and the shining son of Leto; for angered at the king . . .[40]

These striking similarities are of profound, tragic importance. In myth, "the gods often have a mortal double who could almost be mistaken for the god except for the fact that he is subject to death, and indeed is killed by the god himself."[41] That Apollo will be Achilles' slayer, as he was the slayer of Patroklos, has long been known to Achilles. His mother has told him "'that underneath the battlements of the armoured Trojans / I should be destroyed by the flying shafts of Apollo'"; another trait Achilles shares with Apollo, to a limited degree, through his divine mother, is the gift of prophecy.[42]

Now, as Achilles gives chase to Apollo, the plain of Troy belongs to these two, the hero and the dark angel who shadows him so closely.[43] Once the fleeing Trojans are safely battened inside the city walls, Apollo abruptly reveals his disguise in mocking triumph: "'Why, son of Peleus, do you chase me, with those swift feet?'"

"'You have thwarted me,'" Achilles retorts, "'most malevolent of all the gods,'" and as Apollo vanishes to Olympos, Achilles turns back to the walls of Troy. Suddenly the plain has emptied of the clamorous throngs. The Achaeans draw near Troy's battlements, but as a silent and inconsequential presence. The great panorama of battle has telescoped down to a small, hard point, and there are only two persons visible on the plain—indeed, only two in the entire cosmos: Achilles and somewhere, not yet quite in focus, alone and very small, Hektor.

The narrative point of view shifts starkly to Hektor and the inner turmoil of his soul. As Achilles approaches the Skaian Gates, murderous and invincible, it dawns on the Trojan hero, as it has never before, that there is an alternative to standing his ground. His nerve breaks; "trembling took hold of Hektor," and, with the most swift-footed of all heroes in pursuit, he runs.

There can be few passages in all of literature that evoke with such fierce veracity the complexity of a soldier's courage. Like Achilles', Hektor's character has been undone. "I have learned to be valiant," Hektor told Andromache, during their interlude together that now seems a very long time ago. At length, aided, deceitfully, by Athene, Hektor draws once more on this learned, unnatural knowledge and recollects himself.

"Courage is a moral quality," wrote Lord Moran in 1945, in his classic examination of the same, drawing upon his memory of behavior he had witnessed—and medically treated—in the trenches of an earlier war; "it is not a chance gift of nature like an aptitude for games. It is a cold choice between two alternatives."[44] Hektor's choice and its tragic consequences occupy the entirety of Book Twenty-two—all of which follows here. And when at the last he determines to stand firm, the engagement commences between two noble men who both, when the *Iliad* opened, had wanted only to live.

The Death of Hektor

So those who had fled terrorized like fawns into the city
dried off their sweat and drank and slaked their thirst,
slumped on the splendid ramparts. The Achaeans, however,
drew near the walls with shields inclined against their shoulders;
and there ruinous fate bound Hektor to stand firm,
before the Skaian Gates of Ilion.

Now Phoibos Apollo hailed Peleion:
"Why, son of Peleus, do you chase me, with those swift feet,
you a mortal, I an undying god? You must not yet
know that I am divine, you rage after me so strenuously.
Is it of no concern, this business with the Trojans, whom you scattered
    in fear—
who are by now cowering in the city, while you slope off here?
You will never kill me; I am not marked by fate."
Then greatly stirred, swift-footed Achilles answered him:
"You have thwarted me, most malevolent of all the gods, you who
    strike from afar,
turning me here away from the city walls; otherwise many would
have bitten the dirt before they arrived at Ilion.
Saving them, you have robbed me of great glory,
lightly, without fear of retribution;
I would pay you back, if that power were in me."

The translation of this chapter is the author's. Use of Lattimore's translation resumes
on page 192.

So speaking, he made toward the city, intent on great things,
straining like a prizewinning horse who with his chariot
runs effortlessly, stretching over the flat—
so swiftly did Achilles move his feet and knees.
Old Priam first beheld him with his eyes
as, shining like a star, Achilles streaked across the plain,
the star that comes at summer's end, its clear gleaming
in the milky murk of night displayed among the multitude of stars
—the star they give the name Orion's Dog;
most radiant it is, but it makes an evil portent
and brings great feverish heat on pitiful mortal men—
just so did his bronze breastplate shine about Achilles running.
The old man cried out and hammered his head
with his hands; crying mightily, he called,
imploring his beloved son; for he before the gates
continued to stand firm, intent on combat with Achilles.
To him the old man called piteously, reaching out his hands:
"Hektor, for my sake, do not wait for this man
on your own, without allies, lest you push your fate,
broken by Peleion; he is so much stronger
and is pitiless; would that he were as dear to the gods
as he is to me—in short order would the dogs and vultures devour him
prostrated, and bitter pain would leave my heart.
This is the man who has bereaved me of many sons, brave sons,
killing them, or selling them to the outlying islands.
Even now there are two, Lykaon and Polydoros,
whom I cannot see in the city of the cowering Trojans,
sons whom Altes' daughter Laothoë bore me, a queen among women.
If they are alive somewhere among the army, then
I will ransom them for bronze or gold; all this is inside—
old, illustrious Altes endowed his daughter richly.
But if they have already died and are in the house of Hades,

this is grief to my heart, grief to their mother, we who bore them;
but to the rest of the people, it will be grief less lasting
than if you also should die, broken by Achilles.
Come inside the walls, my child, that you may save the
Trojan men and Trojan women; do not make a gift of glory to
the son of Peleus, who will rob you of your very life.
And on me—wretched and still sentient—have pity,
born to ill fate, whom on the threshold of old age father Zeus son of
    Kronos
will blight in unendurable fate, when I have seen
the destruction of my sons, the abduction of my daughters,
my chambers ravaged, and innocent children
hurled to the ground in the terror of battle;
my daughters-in-law abducted by the wicked hands of Achaean men,
and I myself, last of all, at my very gates, my dogs
will rip raw, when some man with sharp bronze
stabbing or casting will strip the spirit from my limbs—
the dogs I raised in my halls and fed at my table as guardians of my
    gates,
these, maddened by the drinking of my blood,
will sprawl in my doorway. All is decorous for the young man
slain in war, torn by sharp bronze,
laid out dead; whatever shows, everything is seemly when he dies.
But when the dogs defile the white head and white beard
and the private parts of a dead old man—
this is most pitiable for wretched mortals."
So the old man spoke, and pulled his white hair with his hands,
tearing it from his head. But he did not persuade the heart of Hektor.
Now in turn his mother wailed, raining tears,
loosening her robe, with a hand she exposed her breast
and raining tears addressed him with winged words:
"Hektor, my child, be moved by this and have pity on me,

if ever I used to give you my breast to soothe you
—remember those times, dear child, defend yourself against this
   deadly man
from inside the walls; don't stand as champion against him,
my stubborn one. If he cuts you down, I will surely never
mourn you on your deathbed, dear budding branch, whom I bore,
nor will your worthy wife. But a long way from us
by the ships of the Achaeans the running dogs will eat you."
Thus both of them weeping addressed their dear son,
repeatedly beseeching. But they did not persuade the heart of Hektor,
but he awaited Achilles, who was looming huge as he drew near.
As a snake by its hole in the mountains waits for a man,
having tasted evil poisons, and an unendurable gall comes upon it,
and it shoots a stinging glance, coiled by its hole,
so Hektor keeping his spirit unquelled did not retreat
and leaned his shining shield against the jutting tower;
agitated, he spoke to his great-hearted spirit:
"O me, if I enter the gates and walls
Poulydamas will be the first to reproach me,
who bade me lead the Trojans to the city,
that baneful night when Achilles the godlike rose,
but I was not persuaded. It would have been far better if I had.
Now since I have destroyed my people by my recklessness,
I dread the Trojan men and the Trojan women with their trailing
   robes,
lest some other man more worthless than me say:
'Hektor, trusting in his strength, destroyed his people'—
thus they will speak. It would be far better, then, for me
to confront Achilles, either to kill him and return home
or to die with honor at his hands, before my city
—but what if I put aside my studded shield
and my strong helmet, leaned my spear against the walls,

and, going out alone, approached noble Achilles
and pledged to him Helen and the possessions with her?
All those things—as much as Alexandros carried away to Troy
in his hollow ships, which was the beginning of our quarrel—
to give to the sons of Atreus to lead away; and in addition
to divide everything else with the Achaeans, whatever this city holds,
and after that to make a formal oath with the Trojan council
not to hide anything, but to divide it all, equally,
whatever wealth this dear city guards within—
but why does my spirit recite these things?
I could set forth to meet him and he not pity me,
nor even respect me, but kill me naked as I was,
as if I were a woman, since I would have put off my armor.
It is not now possible from rock or oak, in the country way,
to chatter to him those things that a young girl and youth
chatter to each other, a girl and youth—
no, it is better to engage with him as quickly as possible;
we shall see to whom the Olympians give glory."
Thus his thoughts churned as he waited, and Achilles drew near
equal to the War God, the helmet-shaking warrior,
brandishing his Pelian ash spear above his right shoulder,
terrifying. The bronze glinted around him like the flare
of blazing fire or of the sun rising.
And as he watched him, trembling took hold of Hektor; and he could
   no longer endure
there to stand his ground but left the gates behind, and, terrified,
   he ran.
The son of Peleus charged for him, trusting in the swiftness of his feet;
as a mountain hawk, lightest of all things on wings,
easily swoops after a terror-stricken dove,
which, away from under, flees, but crying sharply near
he swoops continuously and his spirit drives him to take her,

so Achilles flew straight for him, ravenous, and Hektor fled
under the walls of Troy, working his swift knees.
Past the watch place and the wild fig tree twisted by wind,
always away from the walls, along the wagon path they ran,
and reached the two fair-flowing streams, where the two springs
gush forth from the whirling waters of Skamandros.
One flows with warm water, enveloped with steam smoke
that comes from it as if from a burning fire.
The other even in summer runs as cold as hail,
or snow water, or ice that forms from water.
Near to these there are the broad washing hollows
of fine stone, where their lustrous clothes
the Trojan wives and their beautiful daughters washed
in those days before, in peacetime, before there came the sons of the
    Achaeans.
By this place they ran, one fleeing, the other behind pursuing.
Outstanding was he who fled ahead—but far better he who
    pursued him
swiftly, since it was not for a sacral animal nor for an ox hide
they contended, prizes in the races of men—
but they ran for the life of Hektor breaker of horses.
As when prizewinning horses with their uncloven hooves
tear around the turning post—a great prize awaits,
a tripod, or a woman, in those games held when a man has died—
so three times around the city of Priam they whirled
in the swiftness of their feet, and all the gods looked on.
To them the father of men and gods spoke the first word:
"Alas, it is a dear man whom my eyes see
pursued around the wall; my heart grieves
for Hektor, who has burned many thigh cuts of sacral oxen to me,
both on the summit of Ida of the many glens and at other times
on the heights of his citadel. But now godlike Achilles

pursues him in the swiftness of his feet around the city of Priam.
But come, you gods, consider and take council
whether we shall save him from death or,
noble though he is, at the hands of Peleion Achilles break him."
Then the gray-eyed goddess Athene answered him:
"O father of the bright thunderbolt and black clouds, what have you
    said?
This man who is mortal, consigned long ago to fate—
you want to take him back and free him from the harsh sorrow of
    death?
Do so; but not all the other gods will approve."
In answer, Zeus who gathers the clouds addressed her:
"Take heart, Tritogeneia, dear child. I did not now
speak in earnest; I am willing to be solicitous of you.
Act in whatever way your mind intends, nor hold back any longer."
So speaking, he urged Athene, who had been eager even before;
and she went, slipping down from the peaks of Olympos.

Relentlessly, swift Achilles kept driving Hektor panicked before him,
as when a dog in the mountains pursues a deer's fawn
that he has started from its bed through glens and dells,
and though, cowering in fright, it eludes him beneath a thicket,
the dog runs on, tracking it steadily, until he finds it—
so Hektor could not elude Achilles of the swift feet.
Each time he made to dash toward the Dardanian Gates,
under the well-built tower,
in the hope that men from above might defend him with thrown
    missiles,
each time did Achilles, outstripping him, turn him back
toward the plain and he himself sped ever by the city.
As in a dream a man is not able to pursue one who eludes him,
nor is the other able to escape, nor he to pursue,

so Achilles for all the swiftness of his feet was not able to lay hold of
    him, nor he escape.
How then could Hektor have eluded his fated death
had not Apollo for the last and final time joined closely with him,
to rouse his spirit and make swift his knees?
And shining Achilles was shaking his head at his men,
nor allowed them to let fly their sharp spears at Hektor,
lest whoever was making the throw claim glory, and himself come
    second.
But when for the fourth time they came to the springs,
then Zeus the father leveled his golden scales
and placed in them two portions of death that brings enduring grief,
that of Achilles and that of Hektor breaker of horses;
he lifted them, holding by the middle, and the measured day of Hektor
    sank,
headed to Hades, and Phoibos Apollo abandoned him.

Then the gray-eyed goddess Athene came up to the son of Peleus
and standing near addressed him in winged words:
"Now I hope, illustrious Achilles, beloved of Zeus,
to carry honor for us two back to the Achaean ships,
after breaking Hektor, insatiate though he may be for battle;
he can no longer get clear of us,
not if Apollo the far-shooter should suffer countless trials for his sake,
groveling before Father Zeus of the aegis.
But you now stop and catch your breath, while I
make my way to Hektor and convince him to fight man to man."
Thus spoke Athene, and Achilles obeyed and rejoiced in his heart
and stood leaning on his bronze-flanged ash spear.
She left him and came up to shining Hektor
in the likeness of Deïphobos, in form and steady voice.
Standing close, she spoke winged words:

"My brother, swift Achilles presses you hard,

pursuing you around the city of Priam in the swiftness of his feet.

But come, let us stand firm and defend ourselves, holding fast."

Then great Hektor of the shimmering helm addressed him in turn:

"Deïphobos, even before you were far dearest to me

of my brothers, those sons whom Hekabe and Priam bore.

Now I am minded to honor you even more in my heart—

you who dared for my sake, when you saw me with your eyes,

to quit the walls where the others remain inside."

Then the gray-eyed goddess Athene spoke to him:

"My brother, our father and lady mother implored me greatly,

entreating in turn, and the companions about them,

to remain there—for so great is the dread of all;

yet my inner spirit was harrowed with impotent grief.

But now let us two press straight forward and go to battle,

and let there be no restraint of our spears, so that we shall see if
    Achilles,

killing us both, will bear our bloodied arms

to his hollow ships, or if he will be broken by your spear."

Thus spoke Athene, and with cunning led him on.

But when, as they advanced, they were close to one another,

great Hektor of the shimmering helm spoke first:

"No longer, son of Peleus, shall I flee from you, as before

I fled three times around the great city of Priam nor could then endure

to withstand your charge. But now my spirit stirs me

to hold firm before you. I will take you, or be taken.

But come, let us swear an oath upon our gods, for they

will be the best witnesses and protectors of agreements.

I will not, outrageous though you are, dishonor you if Zeus grants me

to be the survivor and to take of you your life.

But when I have stripped you of your splendid armor, Achilles,

I will give your body back to the Achaeans; and do you the same."

Then, looking at him from beneath his brows, Achilles of the swift feet
    spoke:
"Hektor, you who have done unforgettable deeds—not to me propose
    your agreements.
As there are no pacts of faith between lions and men,
nor do wolves and lambs have spirit in kind,
but they plot evil unremittingly for one another,
so it is not possible that you and I be friends, nor for us two
will there be oaths; before that time one of us falling
will sate with his blood the shield-bearing warrior god.
Recollect your every skill. Now the need is very great
to be a spearman and brave warrior.
There will be no further escape for you, but soon Pallas Athene
will break you by my spear. Now you will pay in one sum
for all the sorrows of my companions, those whom you killed, raging
    with your spear."
He spoke, and, weighing his long-shadowed spear, he let it fly.
But, holding it in his sight as it came at him, shining Hektor avoided it,
for as he watched, he crouched and the bronze spear flew over
and stuck in the earth; but Pallas Athene snatched it up
and gave it back to Achilles, escaping the notice of Hektor, shepherd of
    the people.
And Hektor addressed illustrious Achilles:
"You missed! In no way, then, godlike Achilles,
was it from Zeus you knew my fate—you only thought you did,
and you turn out to be a glib talker, a manipulator of words
—fearing you, you thought I would forget my courage and defenses.
But you will not fix your spear in my back as I flee,
but drive it through my breast as I come at you,
if god grants this to you. Now you in turn dodge my spear,
bronze-pointed; would that you carried the whole of it in your flesh.
Then would this war be lighter to bear for the Trojans,

with you dead. For you are their greatest evil."
He spoke, and weighing his long-shadowing spear, he let it fly
and hurled at the middle of the son of Peleus' shield, nor did he miss;
but the spear glanced off the shield, for a long way. And Hektor was
   angry
that his swift cast flew from his hand in vain,
and he stood dejected, nor did he have any other ash-shafted spear.
Raising his great voice, he called Deïphobos of the pale shield
and asked him for his long spear—but Deïphobos was not near him.
And Hektor understood within his heart and spoke aloud:
"This is it. The gods summon me deathward.
I thought the warrior Deïphobos was by me,
but he is inside the walls, and Athene has tricked me.
Hateful death is very near me; it is no longer far away,
nor is there escape. And for some long time this has been pleasing
to Zeus and to Zeus' son who shoots from afar, who before this
protected me willingly enough. Yet now destiny has caught me.
Then let me not die without a struggle and ingloriously,
but while doing some great thing for even men to come to hear of."
So speaking, he drew his sharp sword
that hung down by his side, huge and strong-made,
and, collecting himself, he swooped like a high-flying eagle,
an eagle that plunges through lowering clouds toward the plain
to snatch a soft lamb or a cowering hare;
so Hektor swooped brandishing his sharp sword.
But Achilles charged, his spirit filled with
savage passion. Before his breast he held his covering shield,
beautiful and intricately wrought, and nodded with his shining
four-horned helmet; splendid horsehair flowed about it,
of gold, which Hephaistos had set thickly around the helmet crest.
As a star moves among other stars in the milky murk of night,

Hesperus the Evening Star, which stands forth as the most beautiful in
    heaven,
so the light shone from the well-pointed spearhead that Achilles
was shaking in his right hand, bent upon evil for Hektor,
surveying his handsome flesh, where it might best give way.
So far the brazen armor protected his flesh,
the beautiful armor that he stripped after slaying the life of
    Patroklos—
but at that point where the collarbone holds the neck from the
    shoulders, there showed
his gullet, where death of the soul comes swiftest;
and at this point shining Achilles drove with his spear as Hektor
    strove against him,
and the spearhead went utterly through the soft neck.
Heavy with bronze as it was, the ash spear did not sever the windpipe,
so that he could speak, making an exchange of words.
He fell in the dust. And shining Achilles vaunted:
"Hektor, you surely thought when you stripped Patroklos
that you were safe, and you thought nothing of me as I was absent—
pitiable fool. For standing by, his far greater avenger,
I remained behind by the hollowed ships—
I who have broken the strength of your knees. You the dogs and birds
will rip apart shamefully; Patroklos the Achaeans will honor with
    funeral rites."
Then with little strength Hektor of the shimmering helm addressed
    him:
"By your soul, by your knees, by your parents,
do not let the dogs devour me by the ships of the Achaeans,
but take the bronze and abundance of gold,
the gifts my father and lady mother will give you;
give my body back to go home, so that

the Trojans and the Trojan wives will give my dead body its portion of
the fire."
Then, looking at him from under his brows, Achilles of the swift feet
answered:
"Do not, you dog, supplicate me by knees or parents.
Would that my passion and spirit would drive me
to devour your hacked-off flesh raw, such things you have done;
so there is no one who can keep the dogs from your head,
not if they haul here and weigh out ten times and twenty times the
ransom and promise more,
not if Dardanian Priam seeks to pay your weight in gold,
not in any way will your lady mother
mourn you laid out upon your bier, the child she bore;
but the dogs and the birds will devour you wholly."
Then, dying, Hektor of the shimmering helm addressed him:
"Knowing you well, I divine my fate; nor will I persuade you.
Surely the soul in your breast is iron.
Yet now take care, lest I become the cause of the god's wrath
against you,
on that day when Paris and Phoibos Apollo
destroy you, great warrior though you are, at the Skaian Gates."
Then the closure of death enveloped him as he was speaking,
and his soul flew from his limbs and started for Hades,
lamenting her fate, abandoning manhood and all its young vigor.
Shining Achilles addressed him, dead though he was:
"Lie dead. I will take death at that time when
Zeus and the other deathless gods wish to accomplish it."
He spoke and pulled his bronze spear from the dead body,
and, laying it aside, he stripped the bloodied armor from Hektor's
shoulders.
But the other sons of the Achaeans ran up around him
and admired Hektor's physique and beauty,

nor was there a man who stood by him without inflicting a wound.
And thus each would speak, looking at his neighbor:
"Well, well; he is softer to handle, to be sure,
this Hektor, than when he torched our ships with blazing fire."
Thus they would speak, and stabbed him as they stood by.
But when shining Achilles of the swift feet had stripped him of arms,
he stood amid the Achaeans and pronounced winged words:
"O friends, leaders, and counselors of the Achaeans;
since the gods gave me this man to break,
who committed evil deeds, more than all the other Trojans together,
come, let us go under arms and scout around the city
so that we may learn the disposition of the Trojans, what they have in
    mind,
whether they will abandon their high city now this man is dead,
or desire to remain, although Hektor is no longer with them
—but why does my spirit recite these things?
There lies by the ships a dead man, unmourned, unburied
—Patroklos. I shall not forget him as long as I am
among the living and my own knees have power in them.
And if men forget the dead in Hades,
I will remember my beloved companion even there.
But come now, Achaean men, singing a victory song,
let us return to our hollowed ship and bring him along.
We have achieved great glory; we have slain shining Hektor,
whom the Trojans worshipped throughout their city as a god."
He spoke, and conceived a shocking deed for shining Hektor:
behind both feet he pierced the tendon
between heel and ankle and fastened there ox-hide straps,
and bound him to his chariot and let the head drag along.
Lifting his glorious armor, Achilles mounted his chariot
and whipped the horses to begin, and they two, not unwilling, took off.
A cloud of dust rose as Hektor was dragged, his blue-black hair

fanning around him, his head lolling wholly in the dust
that before was handsome; so Zeus gave him to his enemies
to be defiled in the land of his own fathers.
His head was wholly befouled by dust; and now his mother
ripped her hair and flung her shining veil
far away, shrieking her grief aloud as she looked on her child.
His beloved father cried out pitiably, and around them the people
were gripped by wailing and crying throughout the city
—it was as if the whole of
lofty Ilion, from its topmost point, were consumed with fire.
With difficulty the people restrained old Priam in his grief
as he strove to go forth from the Dardanian Gates.
Thrashing in the muck, he entreated all,
calling off each man by name:
"Hold off friend, for all your care for me, and let me
leave the city to go to the ships of the Achaeans.
I will entreat this reckless man of violent deeds,
if somehow he may respect my age and pity
my years. Even his father is of such years,
Peleus, who bore him and raised him to be a destruction
to the Trojans; and beyond all men he has inflicted hardship on me.
For so many of my flourishing sons he killed;
I did not mourn as much for all of them, for all my grief,
as for this one, bitter grief for whom will carry me down to the house
    of Hades—
Hektor. Would that he died in my arms.
We would have glutted ourselves with crying and weeping,
his mother, she, ill-fated woman, who bore him, and I."
Thus he spoke lamenting, and thereupon the people mourned.
And Hekabe led the Trojan women in the close-pressed lament:
"My child, I am nothing. Why should I live now, grievously suffering,

when you are dead? You who were night and day my
triumph through the city, a blessing to all,
to the Trojans and the Trojan women throughout the community,
who used to receive you like a god.
For you were to them, indeed, their glory,
while you lived; and now death and fate have overtaken you."
Thus she spoke, crying. But Hektor's wife knew nothing.
For no trusty messenger had come to her
announcing that her husband remained outside the walls,
and she was weaving at her loom in the corner of her high-roofed
    house
a double-folded cloak of crimson and working intricate figures in it.
She called through the house to her attendants with the lovely hair,
to set a great tripod over the fire, so that
there would be a warm bath for Hektor when he returned home from
    battle—
poor wretch, she did not know that far from all baths
gray-eyed Athene broke him at the hands of Achilles.
Then she heard the keening and groaning from the tower,
and her limbs shook, and the shuttle fell to the ground,
and she called back to her maids with the beautiful hair:
"Come, both of you follow me; I will see what trouble has happened.
I hear the voice of Hektor's worthy mother,
the heart in my own breast leaps to my mouth, my limbs beneath me
are rigid; something evil is come near the sons of Priam.
May my word be far from all hearing, but terribly
I fear that shining Achilles has cut my bold Hektor
from the city, on his own, and driving him toward the plain
has stopped him of that fateful ardor
which possessed him, since he never remained in the ranks of men
but rushed far to the front, yielding in his courage to no one."

Thus speaking, she raced through the hall like a madwoman,
her heart shaking, and her two maids ran with her.
But when she reached the tower and the crowd of men,
she stood on the wall, staring around her, and saw him
dragged before the city. Swift horses
dragged him, unconcernedly, to the hollow ships of the Achaeans.
Dark night descended over her eyes,
she fell backward and breathed out her soul;
far from her head she flung her shining headdress,
the diadem and cap, and the braided binding,
and the veil, which golden Aphrodite gave her
on that day when Hektor of the shimmering helm led her
out of the house of Eëtion, when he gave countless gifts for her dowry.
In a throng around her stood her husband's sisters and his brothers'
    wives,
who supported her among themselves, as she was stricken to the point
    of death.
But when then she regained her breath and the strength in her breast
    was collected,
with gulping sobs she spoke with the Trojan women:
"Hektor, I am unlucky. For we were both born to one fate,
you in Troy, in the house of Priam,
and I in Thebes, under forested Plakos,
in the house of Eëtion, who reared me when I was still young,
ill-fated he, I of bitter fate. I wish that he had not begotten me.
Now you go to the house of Hades in the depths of the earth,
leaving me in shuddering grief,
a widow in your house. The child is still only a baby,
whom we bore, you and I, both ill-fated. You will
be, Hektor, no help to him, now you have died, nor he to you.
For even if he escapes this war of the Achaeans that has caused so
    many tears,

there will always be for him pain and care hereafter.
Other men will rob him of his land;
the day of orphaning cuts a child off entirely from his agemates;
he is bent low in all things, his cheeks are tearstained.
In his neediness, the child approaches his father's companions;
he tugs one by the cloak, another by his tunic;
pitying him, one of them offers him a little cup,
and he moistens his lips yet does not moisten his palate.
But a child blessed with both parents will beat him away from the
      feast,
striking him with his hands, reviling him with abuse:
'Get away—your father does not dine with us'—
and, crying, the boy comes up to his widowed mother
—Astyanax, who before on his father's knees
used to eat only marrow and the rich fat of sheep,
then, when sleep took him and he left off his childish play,
he would slumber in a bed in his nurse's embrace,
in his soft bedding, his heart filled with cheery thoughts.
Now he will suffer many things, missing his dear father
—Astyanax—'little lord of the city'—whom the Trojans called by this
      name,
for you alone defended their gates and long walls.
Now beside the curved ships, away from your parents,
the writhing worms devour you when the dogs have had enough
of your naked body; yet there are clothes laid aside in the house,
finely woven, beautiful, fashioned by the hands of women.
Now I will burn them all in a blazing fire,
for they are no use to you, you are not wrapped in them,
—I will burn them to be an honor to you in the sight of the Trojan men
      and Trojan women."
So she spoke, crying, and the women in response mourned.

Everlasting Glory

Achilles has killed Hektor. He has won the climactic battle of this great epic, as he has won his confrontation with Agamemnon. The wrath of Achilles was the dramatic theme of the *Iliad*, and that wrath has now been retired and "unsaid." Surely, by all convention, the *Iliad* will end here, with the triumphant return of its vindicated hero. But the *Iliad* is not a conventional epic, and at the very moment of its hero's greatest military triumph, Homer diverts his focus from Achilles to the epic's two most important casualties. Patroklos and Hektor: it is to the consequences of their deaths, especially to the victor, that all action of the *Iliad* has been inexorably leading.

At the Achaean camp, Achilles has dumped Hektor's corpse "on his face in the dust" by Patroklos' bier. While the other Achaeans returned to their ships, the Myrmidons, under Achilles' direction, have been processing around the body of Patroklos, weeping. Achilles himself orchestrates a stupendous sacrifice, and oxen, sheep, pigs, and bleating goats are slaughtered for the funeral feast and their blood "ran and was caught in cups" as an offering to Patroklos, a gesture possibly calculated to return to him his life and color.[1] Still filthy with blood and grime from battle, Achilles refuses to wash until he has cremated Patroklos, and he gives orders for work teams to set forth "'with the dawn'" to cut timber for the funeral pyre. At last, worn with weariness and grief, he falls asleep by the seashore, with the sound of the waves washing over him:

> and there appeared to him the ghost of unhappy Patroklos
> all in his likeness for stature, and the lovely eyes, and voice,

and wore such clothing as Patroklos had worn on his body.
The ghost came and stood over his head and spoke a word to him:
"You sleep, Achilles; you have forgotten me; but you were not
careless of me when I lived, but only in death. Bury me
as quickly as may be, let me pass through the gates of Hades.
The souls, the images of dead men, hold me at a distance,
and will not let me cross the river and mingle among them,
but I wander as I am by Hades' house of the wide gates.
And I call upon you in sorrow, give me your hand; no longer
shall I come back from death, once you give me my rite of
    burning.
No longer shall you and I, alive, sit apart from our other
beloved companions and make our plans, since the bitter destiny
that was given me when I was born has opened its jaws to take me.
And you, Achilles like the gods, have your own destiny;
to be killed under the wall of the prospering Trojans."

The ghost of Patroklos begs a last request: that his bones and ashes be placed with those of Achilles, when he, too, dies. In his sleep, Achilles responds to Patroklos, imploring him to stay, "'if only for a little'"—but the spirit vanishes, going "underground, like vapour, / with a thin cry." Starting awake, Achilles wonders aloud, "'Even in the house of Hades there is left something, / a soul and an image, but there is no real heart of life in it.'"

In the *Iliad*, the act of dying is described in close detail, as is the treatment of the corpse, the act of mourning, and the state of mind and actions of those left to grieve. The fate of the deceased warrior himself, however, his "essence" as opposed to his corpse, is touched upon directly only here, with the appearance of Patroklos' *psychê* and *eídōlon*—his soul and image.[2] Historically, the Greek practice of cult worship of heroes kept a hero's identity potent after his death, through the worshippers' belief that the dead had power to assist the living; but although hero cults became widespread following the end of Homer's Iron Age, there is no evidence of this practice in the *Iliad*.[3]

More particularly, in the case of its two most important dead heroes, the *Iliad* strenuously eschews any hint that the state of death can in any way be mitigated or that the hero retains any abilities after death. Once the soul, or life force, flees, the inanimate body becomes matter, which, although tenderly handled, washed, anointed, and shrouded, will—barring some rare act of divine intervention—rot and breed flies. The soul departs, going "'down under the gloom and the darkness,'" and although possessions and gifts are cremated along with the corpse, these are only tributes to the dead warrior, not objects he will have any capacity to use in his "journey" to the next existence. In the *Odyssey*, the dreadful impotence and nonbeing of the dead is made explicit; here one learns only that the "'images of dead men'" flutter on the far shore of the unnamed river of the Underworld, presumably the Styx, and that burial or cremation is required to release them wholly.[4] Thus Patroklos does not exist anymore; only his *eídōlon*, or likeness, briefly flickers, caught between memories of Patroklos' life on earth and the urgent need to reach the gray world that now claims him. The simple words of Patroklos' ghostly image ensure that the audience understands, whatever may be said or done afterward in his memory, that death brings the warrior "himself" no reward or glory.

The funeral of Patroklos is performed with barbaric splendor, led by an honor guard of Myrmidons, mounted in full armor behind their chariots, who are followed by "a cloud of foot-soldiers / by thousands." Amid this magnificent procession, the body of Patroklos is borne by the *hetaîroi*—the companions—blanketed with their hair that they have cut as an act of mourning. At the place of the pyre, Achilles cuts his own hair, "which he had grown long to give to the river Spercheios," in Phthia, in fulfillment of a vow Peleus had made to commemorate his son's homecoming; Peleus had lived in expectation of his son's eventual return, it seems, as Thetis had lived in expectation of his imminent death.

Around the pyre, a hundred feet square, are arranged the slaughtered bodies of fat sheep and shambling cattle, in whose blubber the body of Patroklos is wrapped, the better to catch the flames. Four horses and the dogs that had belonged to Patroklos are driven against the pyre and slaughtered, and the whole set fire; now Achilles "also killed twelve noble sons of the great-hearted Trojans / with the stroke of bronze, and evil were the thoughts in his heart against them." When Patroklos' body has been consumed and the fire damped down with wine, his companions gather the bones from the ashes, "weeping, and put them into a golden jar with a double / fold of fat, and laid it away in his shelter, and covered it / with a thin veil; then laid out the tomb and cast down the holding walls / around the funeral pyre, then heaped the loose earth over them / and piled the tomb."[5]

Patroklos' sumptuous funeral accords with heroic burials attested in the literature of different cultures from different ages: Icelandic, Teutonic, Anglo-Saxon, Viking, Vedic, as well as epic Greek—all share a consistent burial pattern. The hero, usually with his armor, is cremated on a pyre;[6] many animals are slaughtered; the funeral ceremonies take place over an extended time of many days; the remains are interred in a tumulus, mound, or barrow. This consistency of detail suggests that the origin of these motifs may have lain not in poetic tradition but in actual burial practice.[7]

The archaeological record supports this view, and broad historical counterparts with Patroklos' funeral can be found in both the Bronze Age Hittite kingdoms and Iron Age Greece—although not in the Greek Bronze Age, where interment in tombs or graves, not cremation, was the burial method of the Mycenaeans. In the recently discovered grave of a Mycenaean military official dating to 1200 B.C.—around the time speculated for the Trojan War—a sword, a spear point, and a knife had been laid beside skeletal remains curled into a fetal position, a poignant reminder that not all burials from the heroic age were heroic.[8]

For many years, it was believed that the closest match to the rites described by Homer were to be found among the Hittites, who cremated their kings on pyres, quenched the embers with wine, and collected the bones, which they then immersed in oil and wrapped in linen.[9] In 1980, however, the spectacular discovery of an Iron Age burial above the town of Lefkandi, on the Greek island of Euboia, revealed that heroic burials had been performed in Greece much nearer to Homer's own time. Under the remains of a monumental building, over 150 feet long by some 45 feet wide and constructed over the charred relics of a great pyre, lay a bronze amphora containing the bones of a thirty- to forty-five-year-old male wrapped in a fine linen robe that, remarkably, had remained intact from the time of interment, just after 1000 B.C. Buried with the "hero" were four horses and a woman richly adorned in gold, who had possibly been sacrificed, along with personal effects that included a sword, a razor, and an iron spearhead[10] (the *heroön* was illegally bulldozed before its thorough excavation by the local landowner, who wanted the site for a vacation home).[11]

When Patroklos' magnificent funeral has been concluded and his bones laid in their urn and his tomb piled over, the Achaeans turn back toward their shelters but are stopped by Achilles. Seating them in assembly, he then directs a stream of treasures to be carried from his ships: tripods, cattle, iron, and women. These will be the prizes awarded in athletic contests held in Patroklos' honor, for chariot racing, footracing, boxing, weight throwing, full-armored close combat, archery, spear throwing. Such games were evoked in the *Iliad* very recently: when Hektor ran from Achilles, it was not for the "prizes in the races of men— / but they ran for the life of Hektor."

Like Patroklos' burial rites, athletic games performed at funerals and religious occasions are attested in the historical record.[12] Boxing and weight lifting were among the contests staged at Hittite religious festivals, for example, although they played only a minor role within the wider pageantry of processions, sacrifice, and ceremonies.[13] On the other hand, athletic games and other competitions were central features of funeral and religious ritual of the Greek Iron Age;[14] this is, after all, the era of the first Olympic Games, whose traditional foundation date is 776 B.C. Just how such contests were seen to honor the dead is not clearly understood, but it appears that they held no deeper ritual significance than the tribute paid by the spectacle and effort of an outstanding performance—an eminently Greek notion. The benefits to the grieving community, on the other hand, are clear. Ritualized, pseudo-military performances of this kind, accompanied by cheers of encouragement and uplifting "award ceremonies" undoubtedly served to reestablish a sense of normalcy and even optimism.[15]

The long set piece, which accounts for most of Book Twenty-three, describing the funeral games held for Patroklos provides us with the only glimpse of the Achaean heroes off duty and "at ease." The individual competitions are humorous, boisterous, and sometimes dangerous, as in the close-combat contest between Diomedes and Aias, which for a chilling moment looks as if it might end in one of their deaths. Pride of place is given to the first and most thrilling competition, the chariot race, for which five heroes stand; as it will turn out, the actions of the spectators are to be as significant as those of the competitors in terms of the light they shed both on Achilles' character and on the anger of heroes.

Of the five contenders, Eumelos, son of Admetos, has the lowest profile, having been mentioned only twice before in the epic, a long while back, in Book Two—once as a leader of an important contingent from Thessaly and once, significantly, as the owner of the "best by far" of mares, "swift-moving like birds, alike in / texture of coat, in age, both backs drawn level like a plumb-line." Shadowy though Eumelos is in the *Iliad*, his family has strong associations with other stories in myth, and he was undoubtedly known to Homer's audience.[16] At any rate, his reintroduction here, thousands of lines after his first fleeting mention, is eloquent evidence of the tight integration of the epic's wide-ranging material.

Diomedes is second to step up, running horses he won in his encounter with Aineias; as often with Diomedes, a whiff of the consummate horse raider accompanies his actions. Menelaos is third, leading "Aithe, Agamemnon's mare, and his own Podargos," a deft summation of his characteristic reliance on his more powerful brother. Fourth is Antilochos, who endures a lengthy stream of advice from his long-winded father, Nestor, which, condensed to its essentials, amounts to "'dear son, drive thoughtfully and be watchful.'" Fifth is Meriones, who despite the fact that he is never fully characterized has a high profile in the epic; with Idomeneus, the lord of Crete, to whom he is henchman, Meriones appears to be an old Minoan relic caught into Mycenaean tradition.[17]

The race begins, and the horses stride away from the ships toward the turning point, a dry stump with two white stones against it, described by Nestor as either "'the grave-mark of someone who died long ago, / or was set as a racing goal by men who lived before our time.'" Is it a grave mark, or is it a goalpost? Given the context—a race by the very grave of Patroklos—the ambiguity is pointed, an ominous reminder that despite what heroes are led to believe, memory of the dead does not always endure.

Soon Eumelos leads—until a broken yoke sends him spinning from his chariot. Entirely heedless of his father's labored advice, Antilochos drives a reckless race, crying out to his horses to overtake Menelaos' mare, "'for fear Aithe who is female / may shower you in mockery.'" His hard-driving tactics frighten careful Menelaos, who loses his nerve and pulls his team aside. "'Damn you,'" cries the fair-haired son of Atreus. "'We Achaeans lied when we said you had good sense.'"

Sitting in the stands, the Achaean assembly strains impatiently to see who is leading as the horses emerge from the dust on the home stretch. A heated argument breaks out between Aias, the son of Oïleus, and Idomeneus:

"Aias, surpassing in abuse, yet stupid, in all else
you are worst of the Argives with that stubborn mind of yours. . . ."
   So he spoke, and swift Aias, son of Oïleus, was rising
up, angry in turn, to trade hard words with him. And now
the quarrel between the two of them would have gone still further,
had not Achilles himself risen up and spoken between them:
"No longer now, Aias and Idomeneus, continue
to exchange this bitter and evil talk. It is not becoming.
If another acted so, you yourselves would be angry.
Rather sit down again among those assembled and watch for
the horses."

Éris—strife—between heroes, it will be recalled, was a favorite theme
of epic. Looked at coldly, stripped of the dignity of their noble epic con-
texts, these quarrels are almost always petty. In the *Cypria*, "Achilles
quarrels with Agamemnon because he received a late invitation" to a
feast; in the *Aethiopis*, "a quarrel arises between Odysseus and Aias over
the armor of Achilles"; the *Odyssey* tells of a quarrel between Achilles
and Odysseus at a festival, not to mention the *Iliad*'s own dramatic action
arising from the "quarrel" between Achilles and Agamemnon.

   Now, at the funeral games, incipient quarrels proliferate. Not only do
Aias and Idomeneus quarrel in the stands, but Menelaos is angry with
Antilochos for his reckless driving, and, in an extended, telling scene,
Achilles momentarily incurs the anger of Antilochos, who finished in
second place, by suggesting that an adjustment of prizes be made to com-
pensate Eumelos for the bad luck of his broken chariot yoke; because of
this accident, "the best man" came in last, as Achilles points out, and he
proposes awarding Eumelos an honorary second prize. At this suggestion, Antilochos stands to argue:

"Achilles, I shall be very angry with you if you accomplish
what you have said. You mean to take my prize away from me. . . ."

But if you are sorry for him and he is dear to your liking,
there is abundant gold in your shelter, and there is bronze there
and animals, and there are handmaidens and single-foot horses."

The proposed redistribution of prizes and Antilochos' indignant response pointedly mirror the themes of the catastrophic quarrel between Achilles and Agamemnon at the beginning of the *Iliad*. As pointed is the contrast between Agamemnon's handling of outspoken challenge to his judgment and authority, and that of Achilles now:

So [Antilochos] spoke, but brilliant swift-footed Achilles, favouring
Antilochos, smiled, since he was his beloved companion,
and answered him and addressed him in winged words:
"Antilochos,
if you would have me bring some other thing out of my dwelling
as a special gift for Eumelos, then for your sake I will do it."[18]

This, the only occasion in the *Iliad* when furious Achilles smiles, serves as a bittersweet reminder of the difference real leadership could have made to the events of the *Iliad*. Agamemnon's panicked prize-grabbing in Book One and even Nestor's rambling "authority" pale beside Achilles' instinctive and absolute command of himself and the dangers of this occasion. As the host of the games in Patroklos' honor, Achilles does not compete, and yet by his graceful assurance he dominates them completely. This is seen most starkly in his handling of Agamemnon himself, who makes a single, brief appearance in the games, as a contender against Meriones in the last of the competitions, for spear throwing. "'Son of Atreus,'" says Achilles, addressing him before the contest is even begun:

" . . . we know how much you surpass all others,
by how much you are greatest for strength among the spear-
   throwers,
therefore take this prize and keep it and go back to your hollow
ships; but let us give the spear to the hero Meriones;
if your own heart would have it this way, for so I invite you."

Coolly forestalling the possibility that the son of Atreus might lose
the competition and instigate yet another face-saving quarrel, Achilles
tactfully intervenes. "He spoke, nor did Agamemnon lord of men disobey
him." A masterpiece of diplomacy, Achilles' short speech reveals the
great leader the Achaeans never had.[19]

The funeral games for Patroklos serve as a kind of epilogue to the
Iliad's Achaean story. The heroes, striving mightily in the peaceable competitions, remain comically true to their heroic, on-the-field-of-battle
characters, and these affectionate and knowing portraits represent the
last time in this epic that most will be seen. With the conclusion of the
games, "the people scattered to go away," and Achilles remains, as it were,
onstage alone.

Weeping again, Achilles recalls Patroklos "and all the actions he had
seen to the end with him, and the hardships / he had suffered; the wars
of men; hard crossing of the big waters." Patroklos' great deeds are never
translated into epic song—*kléa andrōn*—but survive as a close friend's
private reminiscences. After each sleepless night, Achilles arises at dawn
and grimly repeats the one activity he believes will dissipate his grief:
"when he had yoked running horses under the chariot / he would fasten
Hektor behind the chariot, so as to drag him, / and draw him three times
around the tomb of Menoitios' fallen / son."

Patroklos' was not the only unburied corpse. Hektor's mauled body
has lain facedown in the dust since the day he died, and Achilles shows
no sign of relenting on his vow that he will never be given burial. The

plaintive plea of Patroklos' ghost to "'give me my rite of burning,'" without which it cannot pass into the next world, served as an oblique reminder that Achilles' actions maltreat Hektor's *psyché*, as well as his body.

> So Achilles in his standing fury outraged great Hektor.
> The blessed gods as they looked down upon him were filled with
> compassion.

Among the watching gods, a plan to send Hermes to steal the body from Achilles is rejected by the powerful alliance of Hera and Athene, "who kept still / their hatred for sacred Ilion as in the beginning, . . . because of the delusion of Paris / who insulted the goddesses when they came to him in his courtyard / and favoured her who supplied the lust that led to disaster." These few lines are the *Iliad*'s only overt reference to the so-called Judgment of Paris, which anointed Aphrodite as the most beautiful of the goddesses over Hera and Athene; Paris' reward (and bribe) for his judgment was the most beautiful woman in the world, Helen, later of Troy.[20] This judgment, of course, was the cause of the Trojan War. On earth, the wrath of Achilles has ended and new quarrels have been defused, but on Olympos the gods cannot relinquish old grudges. This evocation of the original, now distant but still ongoing divine "quarrel" comes at a critical moment, as attention shifts away from Patroklos' funeral and the Achaeans to the unresolved matter of Hektor's corpse, to Trojan grief, and the fate of Troy.

In a passion, Apollo berates the gods for their disregard of Hektor, who when alive had pleased them with his sacrifices, and even more for their support of "'cursed Achilles,'" who has "'destroyed pity,'" who has no shame, and who "'does dishonour to the dumb earth in his fury.'" Between Apollo's outrage and Hera's cold hatred, Zeus mildly intervenes with a plan; he will summon Thetis, "'so that I can say a close word to her, and see that Achilles / is given gifts by Priam and gives back the body of Hektor." The implementation of the plan summarily outlined by Zeus determines the dramatic action of the remainder of the *Iliad*.

Through Iris the messenger, Zeus' directives are relayed first to Thetis, who, wrapped in a baleful dark cloak, than which "there is no darker garment," obeys his summons. "'You have come to Olympos, divine Thetis, for all your sorrow, / with an unforgotten grief in your heart,'" Zeus greets her, gently. "'I myself know this.'" The gods are angered with Achilles, yet, as Zeus declares to her, "'I still put upon Achilles the honour that he has, guarding / your reverence and your love for me into time afterwards.'" Zeus is ever mindful of his debt to Thetis, yet the moment has arrived at which he must retire his pledge to bring honor to her son. Achilles has had his honor. It is time to move on.

Zeus' directive is quickly telegraphed to all interested parties. Without demur, Thetis flashes from Olympos to join Achilles and declare Zeus' plan. "'So be it,'" Achilles responds abruptly, also without demur. Iris is dispatched to Priam by Zeus, to "'tell him / to ransom his dear son, going down to the ships of the Achaeans / and bringing gifts to Achilles which might soften his anger.'" As Achilles has shown himself to be wholly resistant to appeasement by gifts, Zeus' strategy seems an odd one. It is a strategy, however, tempered by keen knowledge of the hero. As Zeus tells Iris, Achilles "'is no witless man nor unwatchful, nor is he wicked, / but will in all kindness spare one who comes to him as a suppliant.'" Zeus' plan, then, accords with Achilles' essential character, the character he displayed before Patroklos' death. In turn, Priam's first instinctive impulse following the death of his son had been to go to the ships of the Achaeans and there "entreat this reckless man of violent deeds." Zeus' directives, then, do not so much supply the script that Achilles and Priam must enact as provide both stricken men with the means to transcend their grief according to their own almost forgotten natures.

When Iris arrives to deliver Zeus' message to Priam, she finds him sitting in the palace courtyard surrounded by his remaining sons; "and among them the old man / sat veiled, beaten into his mantle. Dung lay thick / on the head and neck of the aged man, for he had been rolling / in it, he had gathered and smeared it on with his hands." Hitherto, Priam has appeared in the epic as an endearing old warrior, affectionately chatting to Helen as they looked out from Troy's battlements over the plain, or riding in, with some pomp, to officiate at the rites attending the duel between Paris and Menelaos. But now, as attention is fully turned, as it has been only once before in the *Iliad,* to Troy, Priam emerges as one of the most compelling and hauntingly memorable of all the epic's many figures.

Like Achilles, Priam is now indifferent to his own fate: "'for myself, before my eyes look / upon this city as it is destroyed and its people are slaughtered, / my wish is to go sooner down to the house of the death god.'" In anger, he lashes out at the Trojans around him, and most of all at his surviving sons, whom an indecent fate has allowed to live, while the best of his sons has died: "'Make haste, wicked children, my disgraces. I wish all of you / had been killed beside the running ships in the place of Hektor.'" Beside him Hekabe, his wife, crazed with grief, cries out against Achilles, "'I wish I could set my teeth / in the middle of his liver and eat it. That would be vengeance / for what he did to my son.'"

Until this point, the epic has been riveted on the spectacle of Achilles' cosmic, unquenchable grief—and, indeed, on the undying divine grief of Thetis—with which, it appeared, there was no equal to be had on earth. But here at Troy, in the courtyard of the doomed city, the grief of ordinary people—the old, beaten king and his aged wife—is a match for the heroic and outsize grief of Achilles. Heroic in his grief, Priam is also heroic in his pathetic mission. Patroklos' body was retrieved from the field by the bitter fighting of the entire Achaean army; Priam will attempt to win the body of his son by abject diplomacy and, save for one companion, the herald Idaios, alone.

Trusting to the word and portent of Zeus, and against the shrill wishes of his wife, Priam sets out in his chariot, ahead of a wagon driven by

Idaios and pulled by mules. In the wagon, carefully chosen from the storeroom, "fragrant / and of cedar" that safeguards his dwindling wealth, is the ransom of "twelve robes surpassingly lovely / and twelve mantles to be worn single, as many blankets, / as many great white cloaks, also the same number of tunics," along with tripods, cauldrons, and talents of gold. Historic Troy VI was a center for textiles, as evidenced by the thousands of spindle whorls discovered on the site by archaeologists, and it is possible that some memory of this fact is reflected in the prominence of clothing and fabrics in the ransom.[21]

It is night when Priam leaves the city, "and all his kinsmen were following / much lamenting, as if he went to his death." Once through the city, on "the flat land," the others turn back and Priam and Idaios set out across the plain.

> And Zeus of the wide brows failed not to notice
> the two as they showed in the plain. He saw the old man and
>   took pity
> upon him, and spoke directly to his beloved son, Hermes:
> "Hermes, for to you beyond all other gods it is dearest
> to be man's companion, and you listen to whom you will, go now
> on your way, and so guide Priam inside the hollow ships
> of the Achaeans, that no man shall see him, none be aware of him,
> of the other Danaans, till he has come to the son of Peleus."

Hermes, son of Zeus and the shy nymph Maia, is a god "resourceful and cunning, a robber, a rustler of cattle, a bringer of dreams, a night watcher, a gate-lurker," as the hymn in his name sings.[22] In the *Iliad*, his most common epithet is *argeiphóntēs*, an obscure term usually translated as "slayer of Argos," the herdsman commissioned to watch over poor Io, one of Zeus' many loves, whom Hera had in fury changed into a cow.[23] Hermes is the god of luck—the Greek word for "windfall" is *hérmaion*—and the god of "jolly and unscrupulous profit," as one scholar puts it;[24]

jolly luck for the thief who escapes detection, bad luck for the man whose house is robbed in the night.

But Hermes' oldest identification is with boundaries. A *hérma* is the heap of stones or cairn that might lie beside a byway, to which passersby add, marking, as it were, their passage. Stone plinths with an upright phallus projecting from the stone, the whole surmounted by the head of the god, were known throughout the classical era simply as *hermes*, potent boundary markers whose symbolism can be traced back to non-human territorial phallic display. "As god of boundaries and of the transgression of boundaries, Hermes is therefore the patron of herdsmen, thieves, graves," and of heralds like Idaios.[25] The most momentous boundary that can be crossed is, of course, the divide between the living and the dead, and it is as a *psychopompós*, "guide of the souls," that Hermes appears memorably in the *Odyssey*, conducting the souls of dead men down to Hades:

> . . . and Hermes
> the kindly healer led them along down moldering pathways.
> They went along, and passed the Ocean stream, and the White
>   Rock,
> and passed the gates of Helios the Sun, and the country
> of dreams, and presently arrived in the meadow of asphodel.
> This is the dwelling place of souls, images of dead men.
> —*Odyssey*, 24.9–14

Strangely, for centuries after this striking appearance in the *Odyssey*, Hermes is only infrequently depicted as a conductor of souls, in art as well as literature. It may be that the role of *psychopompós* was not an "authentic" attribute but was invented by Homer for the *Odyssey*, inspired by the god's well-established roles of night adventurer and messenger. In any case, the outline of the inspiration can be discerned in the *Iliad*, in the mystical, otherworldly journey of old Priam. Much lamented by his kinsmen "as if he went to his death," Priam travels through the night to retrieve the dead body of his son; and it is by the river, just past the "great tomb of Ilos," that Hermes, the guide to Hades, looms out of the darkness.[26]

Both men are terrified, and Idaios urges flight. But Hermes, in "the likeness of a young man, a noble, / with beard new grown, which is the most graceful time of young manhood," takes Priam by the hand and addresses him. Pretending to be one of the Myrmidons and a henchman of Achilles, he reassures Priam on one point—that Hektor's body lies intact and unspoiled.

"'You seem to me like a beloved father,'" says Hermes, and in his respectful, kindly treatment of the frightened old man he appears as the most humane of all the gods in the *Iliad*. Taking the reins, Hermes mounts beside Priam in his chariot, and as the wagon lumbers behind them, he guides the little delegation across the plain to the Achaean fortifications, where, drifting sleep over the sentries as they prepare for dinner, he crosses the defensive ditch, arriving at the "towering / shelter the Myrmidons had built for their king." Constructed of great pine timbers and thatched with meadow grass, the shelter is guarded by a heavy gate; a single bar secures the door to the inner courtyard, "and three Achaeans could ram it home in its socket / and three could pull back and open the huge door-bar; three other / Achaeans, that is, but Achilles all by himself could close it." This Hermes opens for Priam, and when the old man and his wagon are safely inside, he reveals himself as a god, bestows last advice, and vanishes.

The *Iliad*'s great scenes are carefully anticipated and subtly prepared for—but once upon their threshold, there is no dawdling. Suddenly Priam stands before Achilles.

> [Priam] found him
> inside, and his companions were sitting apart, as two only,
> Automedon the hero and Alkimos, scion of Ares,

were busy beside him. He had just now got through with his dinner, with eating and drinking, and the table still stood by.

"'No longer shall you and I, alive, sit apart from our other / beloved companions and make our plans,'" Patroklos' ghost had lamented to Achilles, and the time for sitting apart would surely have been now, with dinner completed, and the other companions busy. Priam has come to Achilles at the most psychologically propitious moment. Silently, he slips to Achilles' knees and takes hold of and kisses his "dangerous and man-slaughtering" hands. As Achilles looks on in wonderment, Priam speaks to him "in the words of a suppliant":

> "Achilles like the gods, remember your father, one who
> is of years like mine, and on the door-sill of sorrowful old age.
> And they who dwell nearby encompass him and afflict him,
> nor is there any to defend him against the wrath, the destruction.
> Yet surely he, when he hears of you and that you are still living,
> is gladdened within his heart and all his days he is hopeful
> that he will see his beloved son come home from the Troad.
> But for me, my destiny was evil. I have had the noblest
> of sons in Troy, but I say not one of them is left to me.
> Fifty were my sons, when the sons of the Achaeans came here.
> Nineteen were born to me from the womb of a single mother,
> and other women bore the rest in my palace; and of these
> violent Ares broke the strength in the knees of most of them,
> but one was left me who guarded my city and people, that one
> you killed a few days since as he fought in defence of his country,
> Hektor; for whose sake I come now to the ships of the Achaeans
> to win him back from you, and I bring you gifts beyond number.
> Honour then the gods, Achilles, and take pity upon me
> remembering your father, yet I am still more pitiful;

I have gone through what no other mortal on earth has gone
   through;
I put my lips to the hands of the man who has killed my children."
   So he spoke, and stirred in the other a passion of grieving
for his own father. He took the old man's hand and pushed him
gently away, and the two remembered, as Priam sat huddled
at the feet of Achilles and wept close for manslaughtering Hektor
and Achilles wept now for his own father, now again
for Patroklos. The sound of their mourning moved in the house.

Before Hermes took his leave of Priam, he had offered last advice: to
entreat Peleion "'in the name of his father, the name of his mother / of
the lovely hair, and his child.'" In the event, Priam evokes only Achilles'
father, and indeed the shadow of Peleus looms large over this final chapter of the *Iliad.* Priam steps into Achilles' shelter like "one who has murdered / a man in his own land, and he comes to the country of others"—
in fact, like Peleus, who according to tradition came to Thessaly and
Phthia as a suppliant exile after killing his half brother. And it is in receiving Priam that Achilles most closely emulates his father; where other
traditions appear to have sung of Peleus' heroic deeds, the *Iliad* knows
him only as the father of Achilles and the recipient of the striking stream
of other suppliant-exiles who wended their way to Phthia—Phoinix,
Patroklos, the obscure Epeigeus.[27]

Achilles is Pēleídēs, Pēleíōn—"son of Peleus"—but also Aiakidēs, "of
the line of Aiakos," Aiakos being Peleus' own father: "Godlike Aiakos,
finest of earth-men. He accomplished what was right for the Gods,"
according to Pindar, for whom Aiakos was also "foremost in hand and
in counsel."[28] It was for his judgment and just counsel that later traditions attest that Aiakos won special status in Hades, and Plato names
him as one of the three judges of the dead.[29] Priam's symbolic journey
to the land of the dead, then, concludes here, in the house of Achilles

Aiakidēs who, like his father's father, has power to pass judgment on the fate of the dead, in this case on the fate of Hektor's body and, by association, Hektor's restless *psyché.*[30]

And it is by speaking of Peleus that Achilles attempts to console Priam. "'Such is the way the gods spun life for unfortunate mortals, / that we live in unhappiness,'" he says, and then embarks upon a paradigm of his own, about the fate of Peleus—Peleus, blessed with shining gifts from the gods themselves, rich, lord of the Myrmidons, and with an immortal wife:

"But even on him the god piled evil also. There was not
any generation of strong sons born to him in his great house
but a single all-untimely child he had, and I give him
no care as he grows old, since far from the land of my fathers
I sit here in Troy, and bring nothing but sorrow to you and your
    children."

The ransom of Hektor is effected without delay, but accompanied by small incidents that reveal the consistency of Achilles' character. When Priam presses the ransom on him with a little too much fervor, Achilles' anger briefly flares: "'I myself am minded / to give Hektor back to you,'" he warns, adding that "'it does not escape me / that some god led you to the running ships of the Achaeans.'" Removing the ransom from the wagon, his companions leave cloaks and a tunic to shroud the corpse, and Achilles ensures that his maids wash Hektor's body out of sight of Priam. His tact is less to spare Priam's sensibilities than a precaution against the eruption of Priam's latent paternal anger at the sight of his son, which, in turn, would surely cause "the deep heart of Achilles [to] be shaken to anger." As in his elegant forestalling of Agamemnon's possible defeat in competition at the funeral games, Achilles demonstrates profound knowledge of the disposition of men's souls, including his own.

When the body of Hektor has been washed, anointed, and decently clad, it is Achilles himself who lifts it and lays it on a litter and with his companions bears it to the wagon. Returning to his shelter, he reports to Priam, "'Your son is given back to you, aged sir, as you asked it.'" Still the deferential host, he urges Priam to join him in a meal, offering an unexpected paradigm from legends of old to illustrate the necessity of eating in the face of grief: even Niobe "'remembered / to eat,'" Achilles says, and recounts at some length the infamous story of the death of Niobe's twelve children at the hands of the children of Leto.[31] A great deal has been written about this incident, which is curious in many regards. In the first instance, the use of anything as conventional as a traditional paradigm, or "old saw," to validate his opinion is highly uncharacteristic of Achilles, who typically speaks his meaning bluntly, stating what he himself knows and he feels: more expected would have been for him to have counseled Priam to eat "as I myself have eaten although worn out with sorrow," or words to this effect. The salient point—that Niobe ate—is not found in any known version of this well-attested myth, and is almost certainly a Homeric adaptation. And if the point—the eating—was not intrinsic, but tacked on—why should Achilles have chosen this particular story?[32]

The essence of Niobe's tragedy, as related by poets from Homer to the lyric poets to the tragedians, is that Niobe, a mortal, compared herself favorably to the goddess Leto, boasting that she had twelve children and Leto only two—Apollo and Artemis. In revenge for this hubris against their mother, the children of Leto slew the children of Niobe, Apollo killing the boys, Artemis the girls. The children did not die gently, but "'nine days long they lay in their blood, nor was there anyone / to bury them, for the son of Kronos made stones out of / the people.'" Niobe herself was turned to stone, and, petrified, she still mourns, in the form of the rock face of Mount Sipylos in Lydia, over which running water courses like tears.[33]

The usual explanation for Achilles' choice of paradigm is that Priam, like Niobe, lost many children, one of whom also lay unburied for many days. Yet the paradigm has meaning for Achilles as well. In both her excessive pride in her offspring and her eternal grieving for their brutal and early deaths, Niobe evokes no one so much as Thetis.[34] The agent of the untimely deaths of both mothers' children is Apollo. One must wonder if lurking behind Apollo's otherwise inexplicable malevolence toward Achilles lies a tradition that Thetis had sung her beloved son's praises somewhat too keenly. The paradigm from Achilles' lips becomes poignant, then, as yet another reminder of his own fast-approaching death.

As he did for the Embassy, so Achilles now prepares dinner for his guest, and he and Priam eat watching each other across the table with mutual wonderment. Priam marvels at the young warrior's "size and beauty, . . . like an outright vision / of gods." Achilles wonders at Priam's brave looks "and listened to him talking." This last is a pregnant, tantalizing line. Of what, one must wonder in turn, could Priam have possibly spoken?

When the meal is completed, Achilles prepares a bed for Priam in the porch of his shelter; this is the second aged visitor to sleep over, the first being Phoinix, following the failed Embassy. It is perhaps mindful of that Embassy that Achilles lets fly a last shot at Agamemnon. " 'Sleep outside, aged sir and good friend,' " he says, "sarcastic," noting that if one of the Achaeans came during the night, " 'he would go straight and tell Agamemnon, shepherd of the people, / and there would be delay in the ransoming of the body.' "

Before the two men turn in, Achilles puts one last question, practical and generous, to Priam: How many days will he need to accomplish Hektor's funeral? Priam's answer as, thinking out loud, he carefully counts on trembling fingers the remaining crushing duties required in the disposal of his son represents a last, masterful touch of characterization of the old king, broken but bound to see this fearful business through. There is wood to be gathered for the pyre, he tells Achilles, adding without irony or anger, "'for you know surely how we are penned in our city'":

> "Nine days we would keep him in our palace and mourn him,
> and bury him on the tenth day, and the people feast by him,
> and on the eleventh day we would make the grave-barrow for him,
> and on the twelfth day fight again; if so we must do."
> Then in turn swift-footed brilliant Achilles answered him:
> "Then all this, aged Priam, shall be done as you ask it.
> I will hold off our attack for as much time as you bid me."
> So he spoke, and took the aged king by the right hand
> at the wrist, so that his heart might have no fear.

Priam and Achilles meet in the very twilight of their lives. Their extinction is certain and there will be no reward for behaving well, and yet, in the face of implacable fate and an indifferent universe, they mutually assert the highest ideals of their humanity. Like all cease-fires, the truce that Achilles pledges for Priam floats the specter of a wistful opportunity.

"Since about tea time yesterday I don't think there's been a shot fired on either side up to now," wrote an anonymous British soldier on Christmas Day 1914, recording the almost surreal suspension of all action early in the Great War that came to be known as the Christmas Truce. Across the trench lines, British and German soldiers spontaneously sang carols, lit candles, and played impromptu soccer games in No-Man's-Land. "We can hardly believe that we've been firing at them for the last week or two—it all seems so strange."[35]

"'I for my part did not come here for the sake of the Trojan / spearmen to fight against them, since to me they have done nothing,'" Achilles declared passionately in the very opening of the *Iliad*. Ten years into the war, the death of Patroklos finally made the stakes of this conflict personal. But by surrendering Hektor, Achilles also surrenders the only shred of real animosity he ever harbored against the enemy. Had Achilles been commander in chief of the Achaean alliance, where, one wonders, would events have gone from here? Perhaps an abrupt recall of troops and the slow exodus back to Greece, and Phthia . . . As it is, the last we see of the *Iliad's* hero is of him sleeping "in the inward corner of the strong-built shelter, / and at his side lay Briseis of the fair colouring." After the extravagance of bloodshed and anguish, matters are more or less back to where they were when the epic quarrel began.

Agamemnon's craven character and the greed that underpins Mycenae's wealth of gold are as well known to the gods as they are to Achilles. Stepping into Priam's dreams, Hermes reappears with a warning, urging the old man to leave the camp before the dawn. As rich as was the ransom Priam paid for Hektor, Hermes says, his remaining sons at Troy " 'would give three times as much ransom / for you, who are alive, were Atreus' son Agamemnon / to recognize you.' "

In short order, Hermes has Priam and Idaios on their way to Troy, taking final leave at the river Xanthos, as "dawn, she of the yellow robe, scattered over all earth." In a brilliant stroke of dramatic pacing, Homer cuts the action suddenly to Troy, where from the height of the citadel Hektor's sister Kassandra sees the small team trudging homeward and cries out to the sleeping city:

"Come, men of Troy and Trojan women; look upon Hektor
if ever before you were joyful when you saw him come back living
from battle."

At the gates of the city, the grieving populace besieges Hektor's bier. One by one, the three women most central to Hektor's life approach to mourn him: Andromache; his mother, Hekabe; and Helen. Calling to the people, King Priam gives orders for the funeral, urging the men not to fear ambush as they range far and wide collecting timber for the pyre, since "'Achilles / promised me, as he sent me on my way from the black ships, / that none should do us injury until the twelfth dawn comes.'" Trusting to Achilles' word—and to his authority to uphold it—the Trojans over the many days undertake the funeral. Again the pyre, the gleaming wine and dampened ashes, again a gathering of bones, wrapped this time in robes of purple and laid in a golden casket; and then the last lines of the *Iliad:*

> They piled up the grave-barrow and went away, and thereafter
> assembled in a fair gathering and held a glorious
> feast within the house of Priam, king under God's hand.
> Such was their burial of Hektor, breaker of horses.

❖

Epic, some may claim, is limited by its genre; nonheroic subjects, such as the lives of women and children, cannot be accommodated within its heroic mandate, and tragedy, for example, picks up where epic must leave off. Yet no subsequent work of literature of any genre has ever made the fate of the entirety of any people more vividly and tragically unambiguous. In the epic's finale, the import of its title becomes clear: the *Iliad* relates the fate of the soon-to-be-extinct city of Ilion. Through the speeches of Andromache and Priam, Homer conjures the individual destructions that will accompany the catastrophic fall of Troy: the Trojan War represents Total War.

The ruins of Troy were still visible in Homer's day, in the mid-eighth century B.C., and perhaps minimally inhabited by local squatters. Around 700 B.C.—conceivably still in Homer's lifetime—Aeolian Greeks migrated over from the nearby island of Lesbos and established a colony amid the ruins. Now settled at Troy, the Greek newcomers possibly supplemented their own traditions of the war with novel local stories.[36] In this regard, a scrap of Luwian, the language of the Trojans, embedded in a thirteenth-century Hittite ritual text is particularly tantalizing:

"ahha-ta-ta alati awienta wilusati
—When they came from steep Wilusa. . . ."[37]

A common Homeric epithet for Ilios—*Wilios*—is *aipeinē, aipús*, "sheer,"
"steep." Was it possible—and why should it not be?—that there was once
a *Trojan* epic about the war?

As ages passed, new generations of colonizers came and went, as well
as squatters and conquerors, leaving levels of habitation on the already
legendary site. A traveler to Troy in the second century B.C. recalled that
"when as a lad he visited the city, . . . he found the settlement so neglected
that the buildings did not so much as have tiled roofs."[38] Still, through
all these ages, the mystique of old Troy—Homer's Troy—persisted, and
according to the third-century-A.D. writer Philostratus, the site was
haunted by the ghosts of its dead heroes.[39]

The fates of these heroes and the *Iliad*'s few heroines were to be the
stuff of later legends. Poets of the epic cycle strode roughshod over the
Iliad's chosen time frame to chronicle remorselessly the full and complete events of the remainder of the war. Arctinus of Miletus, working
around 650 B.C. and according to unsubstantiated legend a pupil of Homer's, is credited with the *Iliad*'s immediate sequel, the *Aethiopis*. An
ancient commentary on the last line of the *Iliad* also records what may
have been the first, lost, transitional lines of the *Aethiopis:*

> So they busied themselves with Hector's funeral. And an Amazon
> came,
> a daughter of Ares the great-hearted, the slayer of men. . . .[40]

In this sequel, Achilles falls in love with the queen of the Amazons,
Penthesilea, a Trojan ally, at the moment that he kills her. He himself
meets his death when an arrow shot by Paris, but apparently guided by
Apollo, strikes him in the ankle. This unlikely mortal wound must surely

reflect the folk tradition that Achilles was invulnerable everywhere except for his foot.[41]

The fall of Troy itself was the subject of two later epics in the Trojan Cycle, the *Little Iliad* and the *Ilias Persis,* or *The Sack of Ilion,* both of which related the stratagem of the Trojan Horse; it is possible that the "horse" reflects a memory from the Bronze Age of Assyrian siege machines, battering rams surmounted by a boxlike casing that protected the men inside as they advanced against a city.[42] This famous decoy was built by one Epeios from wood felled on Mount Ida,[43] and—a pleasing detail recorded by one scholiast—"Arctinus says that it was 100 feet long and 50 feet wide, and that its tail and knees could move."[44] Proclus' summary of the *Sack of Ilion* tells that:

> The Trojans are suspicious in the matter of the horse, and stand round it debating what to do. . . . Some want to push it over a cliff, and some to set fire to it, but others say it is a sacred object to be dedicated to Athena, and in the end their opinion prevails. They turn to festivity and celebrate their deliverance from the war. . . . Sinon holds up his firebrands for the Achaeans, having first entered the city under a pretence. They sail in from Tenedos, and with the men from the wooden horse they fall upon the enemy. . . . They put large numbers to death and seize the city.[45]

The aftermath of the Trojan War, the manner in which the war continued to direct the lives of its survivors, became a powerful theme for later poets and other writers. Through them we learn that Paris was killed by the Greek hero Philoktetes, who had previously been abandoned by his companions on a nearby island; like Paris, Philoktetes was renowned as an archer.[46] Priam was slain in his courtyard by Achilles' son Neoptolemos, whose name means "new war." Priam's daughter Kassandra was raped at Athene's altar by the lesser Lokrian Aias and then taken as booty by Agamemnon to Mycenae, where she met her death at the hands of Agamemnon's wife, Clytemnestra. Another of Priam's daughters, Polyxena, had her throat cut on Achilles' tomb. Priam's wife, Hekabe, was turned into a dog, and her grave became a landmark for sailors, known as Cynossema—"the bitch's tomb." A number of explanations have been offered to make intelligible Hekabe's peculiar, and peculiarly vicious, fate—that she was stoned to death like a dog, that she howled like a dog in grief—but the main point seems to have been to make indelible the depths of abasement to which she had been dragged by loss and enslavement.[47] Andromache, whom the death of Hektor caught while she was at her loom, weaving as her own fate unraveled, was enslaved, too, as she had long feared, handed as a prize to Achilles' son, to whom according to some versions she bore a son; Astyanax, her son by Hektor, was dashed to death from the walls of Troy.[48]

Other epics and later poetry told of the mixed fates of the Achaean veterans. *Nóstoi,* or *Returns,* was the last installment in the Epic Cycle. Homer's *Odyssey,* of course, told of the most famous *nóstos* of all, that of Odysseus, who is portrayed as the ultimate survivor, enduring, resourceful, and "of many wiles." Admirable as the hero of his own epic, elsewhere the resourceful Odysseus is more usually cast as a mendacious, manipulative swindler and, in one tradition, the murderer of Astyanax.[49] Most notorious is the role Odysseus plays in the suicide of Aias, the only Achaean warrior of any standing in the *Iliad* to fight without divine patronage. After Achilles' death, his prized armor was to be awarded to the best of the remaining Achaeans, a competition that came down to two men—Odysseus and Aias. Although widely acknowledged as the best of the Achaeans after Achilles, Aias is defeated by Odysseus, who, with the contrivance of Athena, wins a vote held by the assembled Achaeans.[50] In a fit of divinely induced madness, Aias attempts to kill Odysseus, and when he wakes from his madness, humiliated, he takes his own life, the casualty of yet another epic "quarrel." Odysseus himself, after ten years of wandering, finally made his way home to his island kingdom, Ithaka, where his wife had waited loyally for twenty long years.

Diomedes also endured a delayed homecoming, but to an unfaithful wife. Continuing westward, he eventually settled in Italy.[51] A bloody homecoming awaited Agamemnon at the hands of his wife, Clytemnestra, who murdered him in his bath on the day of his return to Mycenae. The other son of Atreus, Menelaos, and his repentant wife, Helen, live happily ever after, back home in Sparta. The *Odyssey* tells of a visit to them by Odysseus' son, who finds them, middle-aged and domestic, exchanging coy remembrances of momentous events past: "'Sit here now in the palace and take your dinner and listen / to me and be entertained,'" says Helen, and she launches into a reminiscence of Odysseus coming to spy on Troy in disguise. "'Yes, my wife,'" says Menelaos indulgently when she has finished. "'All this that you said is fair and orderly,'" and in turn he recalls how Helen—"'moved by / some divine spirit'"—had almost thwarted the Greek ambush by calling the names of the warriors hidden inside the Trojan Horse, impersonating the voice of each man's wife.[52] For Nestor, too, also returned to the comfort of his palace at Pylos, the Trojan War furnished one more great story of campaigns past, "'in that country'" around the city of Priam, where "'all who were our best were killed in that place.'"[53]

Tellingly, the *Iliad*'s most outstanding Achaean heroes are unambiguously cast as villains in the works of later writers. Agamemnon, Menelaos, and Odysseus make multiple appearances in the plays of Aeschylus, Sophocles, and Euripides as bullying, duplicitous, cold-blooded tyrants; Helen, apart from Euripides' tragicomedy in her name, is usually cursed, especially by other female characters, as an outright whore. Strikingly, the line of Peleus alone generally retains its epic nobility. This is true not only of the reluctant warrior Achilles and Peleus himself but also, unexpectedly, of Achilles' son Neoptolemos, who certainly had blood on his hands. "At Troy he wasn't commonly thought a coward," Andromache, of all people, says heatedly in defense of the young hero in Euripides' tragedy of her name. "He'll do the right thing now—worthy of Peleus / And of Achilles his father."[54] Of Peleus himself, various traditions tell that he was cast out of Phthia by a neighboring king. His fate, then, was that which Priam had evoked in his supplication of Achilles: "And they who dwell nearby encompass him and afflict him, / nor is there any to defend him against the wrath, the destruction."

Writing in the early first century B.C., Strabo summarized the far-reaching consequences of the disastrous war at Troy as it was understood by later history: "For it came about that, on account of the length of the campaign, the Greeks of that time, and the barbarians as well, lost both what they had at home and what they had acquired by the campaign, and so, after the destruction of Troy, not only did the victors turn to piracy because of their poverty, but still more the vanquished who survived the war."[55]

That after the roll of centuries, this same *Iliad*, whose message had been so clearly grasped by ancient poets and historians, came to be perceived as a martial epic glorifying war is one of the great ironies of literary history. Part of this startling transformation can undoubtedly be attributed to the principal venues where the *Iliad* was read—the elite schools whose classically based curriculum was dedicated to inculcating into the nation's future manhood the desirability of "dying well" for king and country. Certain favorite outstanding scenes plucked out of context came to define the entire epic: Hektor's ringing refusal to heed the warning omen, for example—" 'One bird sign is best: to fight in defence of our country' "—or his valiant resolution—" 'not die without a struggle and ingloriously.' " Homer's insistent depiction of the war as a pointless catastrophe that blighted all it touched was thus adroitly circumvented.

The manner in which the Trojan War haunted the memory of the veterans who had survived it is most powerfully evoked by Homer himself. In the *Odyssey*, Odysseus, toward the end of his ten-year voyage home after the fall of Troy, sojourns at the royal court of the Phaiakians.

He has not yet revealed his identity to his hosts when he requests a song from the court bard, Demodokos:

> ". . . sing us
> the wooden horse, which Epeios made with Athene helping,
> the stratagem great Odysseus filled once with men and brought it
> to the upper city, and it was these men who sacked Ilion."
>   —*Odyssey* 8.492–95

The bard complies, singing of how the Greeks broke their ambush and "streamed from the horse and sacked the city." Hearing this story, to the amazement of his Phaiakian hosts, and perhaps also to himself, Odysseus unexpectedly breaks down, overcome by memories:

> As a woman weeps, lying over the body
> of her dear husband, who fell fighting for her city and people
> as he tried to beat off the pitiless day from city and children;
> she sees him dying and gasping for breath, and winding her body
> about him she cries high and shrill, while the men behind her,
> hitting her with their spear butts on the back and the shoulders,
> force her up and lead her away into slavery, to have
> hard work and sorrow, and her cheeks are wracked with pitiful
>   weeping.
> Such were the pitiful tears Odysseus shed from under
> his brows.
>   —*Odyssey* 8.523–32

This, then, is Homer's own last word on the legendary Trojan War.

◈

Amid the deposits found at the heroic burial at Lefkandi was a gold pendant disk that had once adorned the woman buried with the hero.

Elaborately mounted and decorated with granular work, it was found lying on the throat of the female skeleton, with the gold and faience beads that had secured it broken and scattered.[56] When examined, this piece of jewelry was found to predate the burial itself by nearly seven hundred years. An old Babylonian heirloom, it had been handed down for over twenty generations and brought to Greece, somehow, at some time.

This small relic is a concrete reminder of the tenacity with which things of value can be retained, even through turbulent times and migrations. In such a way did the scattered shards of Mycenaean history end up in Homer's *Iliad*: Aias' towering shield, silver-studded swords, the well-built walls of Troy and Mycenae's wealth in gold—these details of times long past were preserved and passed on in faithful stories.

But handed down with the reminiscences of Mycenaean glory were also memories of more recent and more painful times. The *Iliad* speaks casually of suppliant exiles who have fled their homes after murdering men of high estate, the selling of captives into slavery, the looting of cities, threats of usurpation, all of which provide murky glimpses into the period of upheaval in which its tradition was forged.[57] It is to such actual memories that we may owe the *Iliad*'s most haunting images. Priam's predictions that he will live to see '"innocent children / hurled to the ground in the terror of battle'" and that his own body will be ripped raw by his dogs, pitifully revealing his old man's private parts—the shocking specificity of such scenes arise, surely, not from poetic invention but historic memory. The slaughter and enslavement of conquered peoples are commonplaces of war, like broken treaties and inept commanders, but historic counterparts can also be found for the less generic events that most characterize the *Iliad*. Priam's Embassy to Achilles for his son, for example, is echoed in a Hittite text recording the mission of a suppliant parent for her son: "I would certainly have marched against him and destroyed him utterly, but he sent forth his mother to meet me," records Mursili II in a document written in the late fourteenth century B.C. "And since a woman came to meet me and fell at my knees, I gave way to the woman."[58]

"The Greeks at the beginning of their history passed though the very fires of hell," wrote the great scholar Gilbert Murray of the long and difficult period of migration following the fall of the Mycenaean world. "They knew, what Rome as a whole did not know, the inward meaning and the reverse side of glory."[59]

Kléos—glory, fame, renown—stands at the heart of epic. The equation that valorous death wins compensation in glory is very ancient, widely attested in Indo-European and other poetry. The safeguarding and bestowal of such fame is the privilege of poets like Homer—Achilles' glory is everlasting because he is the hero of the *Iliad*.[60] The cultivation of this handy equation would be the work of future ages, as it had been of ancient ages past. One need look no further than the Dardanelles, Homer's "Hellespont," where, facing the very plain of Troy, war cemeteries memorialize the thousands who died in the criminally mismanaged Gallipoli campaign of 1915, with exactly this equation. "Their name liveth for evermore," read the serried headstones of Gallipoli. "Their glory shall not be blotted out."

It was this ancient formula that Homer, through Achilles, confronted head-on. "'I carry two sorts of destiny toward the day of my death,'" Achilles told the Embassy:

> "Either,
> if I stay here and fight beside the city of the Trojans,
> my return home is gone, but my glory shall be everlasting;
> but if I return home to the beloved land of my fathers,
> the excellence of my glory is gone, but there will be a long life
> left for me, and my end in death will not come to me quickly.
> And this would be my counsel to others also, to sail back
> home again."

Life is more precious even than glory. Achilles never wavers in this judgment. It is not, after all, for glory that he sacrifices his life, but for Patroklos.[61] Achilles' judgment is pointedly revisited and pointedly reemphasized in the *Iliad*'s sequel, the *Odyssey*. In an emotional scene at the heart of that epic, Odysseus descends to Hades, where he brushes against the shadowy souls of heroes from the Trojan War. While the *Aethiopis* told how "Thetis snatches her son from the pyre and conveys him to the White Island,"[62] a kind of small paradise for heroes, Homer takes pains to underscore, again, that Achilles cannot escape his wholly mortal fate.

" 'Son of Laertes and seed of Zeus, resourceful Odysseus,' " the ghost of Achilles hails his old companion; " ' . . . how could you / endure to come down here to Hades' place, where the senseless / dead men dwell, mere imitations of perished mortals?' "

" 'Son of Peleus,' " Odysseus answers, with careful reverence, " 'far the greatest of the Achaeans, Achilles' ":

". . . no man before has been more blessed than you, nor ever
will be. Before, when you were alive, we Argives honoured you
as we did the gods, and now in this place you have great authority
over the dead. Do not grieve, even in death, Achilles."
So I spoke, and he in turn said to me in answer:
"O shining Odysseus, never try to console me for dying.
I would rather follow the plow as thrall to another
man, one with no land allotted him and not much to live on,
than be a king over all the perished dead."
—*Odyssey* 11.473ff.[63]

What if Achilles had honored his own first impulse, returned to Phthia, and grown old? Perhaps he would have restlessly paced out his life in the court of his father; perhaps, like disillusioned veterans of later wars, he would have taken to the woods and mountains of his childhood, surrounded by that inscrutable band of brothers, the Myrmidons. As it is, the conclusion of the *Iliad* makes clear that Achilles will die in a war that holds no meaning for him whatsoever.

Thus was the centuries-old martial tradition inherited by Homer ultimately resolved. The stirring, bloody battles, the heroic speeches, and the pride of a warrior's *aristeía*—all have been faithfully retained, along with the dramatic outlines of the ancient story. The *Iliad* never betrays its traditions.

But the *Iliad* also never betrays its subject, which is war. Honoring the nobility of a soldier's sacrifice and courage, Homer nonetheless determinedly concludes his epic with a sequence of funerals, inconsolable lamentation, and shattered lives. War makes stark the tragedy of mortality. A hero will have no recompense for death, although he may win glory.

ACKNOWLEDGMENTS

My first and most obvious debt of gratitude is to the University of Chicago Press for its generous permission to include large segments of Richmond Lattimore's translation of the *Iliad;* it is difficult for me to imagine this book without this text.

A number of individuals have, over the years, provided me with memorable insights or experiences that pertain to this book. Jenny Lawrence sent me on my first journey to Troy for *Natural History* magazine. Similarly, an assignment for *National Geographic* resulted in meetings with many remarkable scholars; I recall in particular an afternoon at Cambridge with the late John Chadwick, a towering figure in the decipherment and study of Linear B; a delightful lunch in Athens with Dr. Spyros Iakovidis, field director of excavations at Mycenae; and an unforgettable day, from before dawn almost to day's end, with the late Manfred Korfmann, director of the new excavations at Troy.

I had the great good fortune to study under the direction of two remarkable Homeric scholars while working toward my doctorate at Columbia University. I am possibly one of a small subset of doctoral candidates who actually enjoyed the writing of their dissertation, thanks in enormous part to the kindness, attention, and insights of my supervisor, Laura Slatkin, who continued to mentor many nonclassical works I undertook long after I left Columbia. The breadth and depth of expertise that Richard Janko brought to any subject was legendary even when I was at Columbia, and I am grateful to him now for the time he took from a demanding schedule generously to read my manuscript. His comments were unfailingly valuable, and my book is the better for them.

A number of public lectures served as test runs for this book, and I am grateful to each venue—and, again, to Jenny Lawrence, whose idea the first lecture series was. I would like to express my gratitude to the New York Society Library, the Century Association, the late Mrs. Astor's Reading Group, and to Jean Strouse, director of the Dorothy and Lewis B. Cullman Center for Scholars and Writers at the New York Public Library, who organized a lecture at the library. Most of these lectures were enhanced by actor Simon Prebble's thrilling readings from the *Iliad*, and I am grateful to him for being so very instrumental in each evening's success.

My particular thanks are due to my editor, Wendy Wolf, for her deft work in navigating me through my own scholarship; it was also she who directly goaded me into undertaking this book, aided and abetted by my agent, Anthony Sheil, and so, at journey's end, I now recognize my debt to them both. Also at Viking, my thanks are due to Bruce Giffords and Carla Bolte for their outstanding work on the challenging demands of editorial production and design, respectively.

Closer to home, I would like to thank Laura Rollison, Joyce Bruce, Gary McCool, and the staff of Lamson Library, Plymouth State University, for their invaluable assistance in obtaining the many far-flung books and articles this work required. I would also like to thank Belinda and John Knight and Linda Baker Folsom for their unfailing support on the home front.

Finally, I thank my sister, Joanna Alexander, and my mother, Elizabeth Kirby, for entertaining my Iliadic thoughts over the years, and my brother-in-law, Ron Haskins, for insights drawn from combat experience; and George Butler for reminding me, repeatedly, that I have profited more than Homer from his story.

NOTES

Preface

1. The most rigorous and detailed attempt to date the *Iliad*, through statistical analysis of the incidence of key linguistic features in the Homeric poems relative to other early poetry, was made by Richard Janko, *Homer, Hesiod and the Hymns* (Cambridge, 1982), and yielded a range of 750–725 B.C. This mid- to late-eighth-century date is widely accepted. For arguments for a later date, around 670–660 B.C., see M. L. West, "The Date of the *Iliad*," *Museum Helveticum* 52 (1995), 203–19.
2. Paraphrased from Trevor Bryce, *Life and Society in the Hittite World* (Oxford, 2004), 98.
3. Appian 3.2.13, quoted from Katherine Callen King, *Achilles: Paradigms of the War Hero from Homer to the Middle Ages* (Berkeley and Los Angeles, 1987), 118.
4. The tracking of the reception of the *Iliad*, and especially of Achilles, to medieval times has borrowed liberally from King, above.
5. George Steiner, "Homer in English translation," in Robert Fowler, ed., *The Cambridge Companion to Homer* (Cambridge, 2007), 365.
6. For the history of the translation of Homer's poems, see Simeon Underwood, *English Translators of Homer: From George Chapman to Christopher Logue* (Plymouth, UK, 1998).
7. Strabo, *Geography* 1.3.2, in Horace Leonard James, trans., *Strabo: Geography*, vol. 1 (Cambridge, MA, 1917), 179.

The Things They Carried

The title of this chapter was inspired by Tim O'Brien's landmark book on Vietnam, *The Things They Carried*.

1. *The Contest of Homer and Hesiod*, in M. L. West, ed. and trans., *Homeric Hymns. Homeric Apocrypha. Lives of Homer* (Cambridge, MA, 2003), 319ff.
2. M. L. West, *Indo-European Poetry and Myth* (Oxford, 2007), 229ff.
3. These characteristics paraphrased from M. L. West, "The Rise of the Greek Epic," *Journal of Hellenic Studies* 108 (1988), 158.
4. Carol G. Thomas and Craig Conant, *The Trojan War* (Westport, CT, 2005), 41.
5. "There is a distinct lack of secondary information available for the Mycenaean army. This is a conspicuous omission in the study of ancient warfare,

given the very militaristic character of Mycenaean culture." Nicolas Grguric, *The Mycenaeans c. 1650–1100 B.C.* (Botley, Oxford, 2005), 6; this slender illustrated "school text" gives probably the most comprehensive account available of the Mycenaean army and warfare.

6. While there are numerous highly specialized studies of specific aspects of the Mycenaean world, the most accessible overview is K. A. and Diana Wardle, *Cities of Legend: The Mycenaean World* (London, 1997). Nic Fields, *Mycenaean Citadels c. 1350–1200 B.C.* (Botley, Oxford, 2004), is a well-illustrated, up-to-date guide to the great Mycenaean sites. The story of the Linear B tablets is excitingly told by John Chadwick, *The Decipherment of Linear B* (Cambridge, 1990). After Michael Ventris cracked the code, he and Chadwick were largely responsible for making the contents of the Linear B tablets accessible to the world; for the documents themselves, see M. Ventris and J. Chadwick, *Documents in Mycenaean Greek,* 2nd ed. (Cambridge, 1973).

7. Chadwick, *The Decipherment of Linear B,* 159ff. The pathos and historical implications of the Trojan entry are discussed in Michael Wood, *In Search of the Trojan War,* rev. ed. (London, 2005), 182f.

8. The different categories of women's work are described in John Chadwick, "The Women of Pylos," in J.-P. Olivier and Th. G. Palaima, eds., *Texts, Tablets and Scribes: Studies in Mycenaean Epigraphy and Economy* (Salamanca, 1988), 43–96.

9. For Mycenaean interference in Anatolia, see Trevor Bryce, *Life and Society in the Hittite World* (Oxford, 2004), 259; the transportation of Anatolian inhabitants is discussed at p. 102.

10. For a summary of evidence of contact between the Mycenaeans and Hittites, see Wolf-Dietrich Niemeier, "Mycenaeans and Hittites in War in Western Asia Minor," in Robert Laffineur, ed., *POLEMOS: Le contexte guerrier en Égée à l'Âge du Bronze* (Liège, 1999), 141–55; and Wood, 182ff.

11. The topography of Troy is described in Manfred Korfmann, "Troy: Topography and Navigation," in Machteld J. Mellink, ed., *Troy and the Trojan War* (Bryn Mawr, PA, 1986), 1–16. For the likelihood of malaria, and Trojan health in general, see J. Lawrence Angel, "The Physical Identity of the Trojans," in Mellink, 63–76, especially 67; figs. 24–26. Skeletal remains for the Trojans of any era are slight—forty-five samples from Troy VI to VIIb, mostly from cremations. An infant:child:adult death ratio is calculated at 6:2:10, "possibly better than in contemporary Greece" (p. 68).

12. After a lapse of nearly two centuries, additional levels were built from around 800 B.C. on into Roman times.

13. For a guide to Troy, see Nic Fields, *Troy c. 1700–1250 B.C.* (Botley, Oxford, 2004). The detailed and excellent field reports from the ongoing excavation at Troy, under the auspices of the University of Tübingen and, until his untimely death in 2005, under the direction of Manfred Korfmann, have been published since 1991 in the periodical *Studia Troica.* Wood, 46ff., gives the best, very readable account of the history of excavation on the site from Heinrich Schliemann onward. H. Craig Melchert, ed., *The Luwians* (Leiden, 2003), contains a collection of essays about Luwian culture and history.

14. The extent and significance of Troy VI became the subject of an unexpectedly heated debate that would have been entertaining had it not been so vituperative. In brief, Frank Kolb, a colleague of Manfred Korfmann's, the director of new excavations at Troy, claimed that Korfmann's reconstructions of the scale and importance of Troy were "fragments of fantasy." The spectacle of the battle of Bronze Age professors drew bemused and bewildered media to a conference convened in Tübingen in 2002; wonderful it is to find passion running so high over a 3,200-plus-year-old archaeological site! The debate led to one happy result, which was a rigorous perusal of all evidence to date pertaining to the archaeology and history of the site by a team of Anatolian specialists. Their assessment, in favor of Korfmann, is a succinct overview of the archaeological record. See D. F. Easton, J. D. Hawkins, A. G. Sherratt, and E. S. Sherratt, "Troy in Recent Perspective," *Anatolian Studies* 52 (2002), 75–109. Kolb's argument is presented in Frank Kolb, "Troy VI: A Trading Center and Commercial City?," *American Journal of Archaeology* 108 (2004), 577–614.

15. Manfred Korfmann, "Troia: A Residential and Trading City at the Dardanelles," in R. Laffineur and W.-D. Niemeier, eds., *POLITEIA: Society and State in the Aegean Bronze Age*, vol. 1 (Liège, 1995), 173–83, and plates XXIII–XXXIII.

16. See Kyriacos Lambrianides and Nigel Spencer, "Unpublished Material from the Deutsches Archäologisches Institut and the British School at Athens and Its Contribution to a Better Understanding of the Early Bronze Age Settlement Pattern on Lesbos," *Annual of the British School at Athens* 92 (1997), 73–107; and Nigel Spencer, "Early Lesbos between East and West: A 'Grey Area' of Aegean Archaeology," *Annual of the British School at Athens* 90 (1995), 269–306, especially 273ff.

17. More specifically, Wilusa was one of four kingdoms in western Anatolia referred to in the archives as "the Arzawa Lands." Trevor Bryce, *The Trojans and Their Neighbours* (Abingdon, Oxon, 2006), 107ff. Bryce and Michael Wood (*In Search of the Trojan War*), 214ff., discuss the nature of Troy's relationship to the Hittite Empire and its status within Anatolia.

18. See Trevor R. Bryce, "Ahhiyawans and Mycenaeans—an Anatolian Viewpoint," *Oxford Journal of Archaeology* 8, no. 3 (1989), 297–310.

19. The early Greek form of *Ilios* would have been *Wilios*, using the roughly *w*-sounding "digamma," a letter that is present in Linear B and still "felt" in the Homeric poems, principally by certain metrical anomalies that are resolved if the lost letter is reinserted; once common to all Greek dialects, it fell out of use in each at different times. Confirmation of the Hittite geographical and political landscape was made only relatively recently with the translation of a key monumental and much-weathered cliff face inscription; see J. D. Hawkins, "Karabel, Tarkondemos and the Land of Mira: New Evidence on the Hittite Empire Period in Western Anatolia," *Würzburger Jahrbücher für die Altertumswissenschaft* 23 (1998), 7–14; and J. D. Hawkins, "Tarkasnawa King of Mira: 'Tarkondemos,' Boğazköy Sealings and Karabel," *Anatolian Studies* 48 (1998), 1–31.

20. For the full, fragmented text of this letter, see John Garstang and O. R. Gurney, *The Geography of the Hittite Empire* (London, 1959), 111–14; the reference to Wilusa is at IV 7–10, p. 113.

21. On the seal, see J. David Hawkins and Donald F. Easton, "A Hieroglyphic Seal from Troia," *Studia Troica* 6 (1996), 111–18.

22. For evidence of Troy's trade, see Bryce, *The Trojans and Their Neighbours*, 122ff.

23. Manfred Korfmann, "Beşik Tepe: New Evidence for the Period of the Trojan Sixth and Seventh Settlements," in Mellink, 17–28 and figs. 14–23.

24. For the sparse evidence of a Mycenaean presence in the Black Sea region and an examination of the several obstacles to Mycenaean penetration, see Marta Guzowska, "The Trojan Connection or Mycenaeans, Penteconters, and the Black Sea," in Karlene Jones-Bley and D. G. Zdanovich, eds., *Complex Societies of Central Eurasia from the 3rd to the 1st Millennium B.C.*, vol. 2 (Washington, D.C., 2002), 504–17. Korfmann points out that as late as 1908, the British Admiralty's *Black Sea Pilot* stated that the stiff, contrary wind coming out of the Dardanelles "lasts sometimes so long that it is not a rare occurrence to see 200 or 300 vessels . . . waiting a favourable and enduring breeze"; Korfmann, "Troy: Topography and Navigation," 7. Benjamin W. Labaree, "How the Greeks Sailed into the Black Sea," *American Journal of Archaeology* 61, no. 1 (1957), 29–33, argues that knowledgeable navigation could have exploited monthly variations in shifting southerly winds in both the Bosporus and Black Sea.

25. This possibility is raised by Richard Janko, "Go away and rule" (a review of Joachim Latacz's *Troy and Homer: Towards a Solution of an Old Mystery*), *Times Literary Supplement*, April 15, 2005, 6–7.

26. The first sack of Troy at the hands of Herakles is referred to at *Iliad* 5.628–51; see P.B.S. Andrews, "The Falls of Troy in Greek Tradition," *Greece & Rome*, 2nd series, vol. 12, no. 1 (April 1965), 28–37; Andrews suggests that a horse raid was the motive for the Trojan War. For the failed expedition to Troy, in which the Greeks mistakenly landed near the wrong city, see the *Cypria*, argument 7; Strabo passes censorious judgment on the escapade: Strabo, *Geography* 1.1.17. The event has an intriguing parallel in Hittite texts: L. A. Gindin and V. L. Tsymbursky, "The Ancient Greek Version of the Historical Event Reflected in a Hittite Text," *Vestnik Drevnej Istorii* 176 (1986), 81–87 (English summary of the Russian on p. 87). Rhys Carpenter has argued that the two Achaean attempts on Troy represent two traditions: "one school (shall we call it the Aeolic?) attaching Troy and its river to Teuthrania at Pergamon above the Kaikos [River], the other (shall we call it the Ionic?) to the Hellespont at Ilios on the Scamander"; Rhys Carpenter, *Folk Tale, Fiction, and Saga in the Homeric Epics* (Berkeley and Los Angeles, 1958), 57ff. The story of the first, botched landing is the subject of a recently discovered fragment of a poem by Archilochus: "Gladly did the sons of the immortals and brothers, whom Agamemnon was leading to holy Ilium to wage war, embark on their swift ships. On that occasion, because they had lost their way, they

arrived at that shore. They set upon the lovely city of Teuthras, and there, snorting fury along with their horses, came in distress of spirit. For they thought they were attacking the high-gated city of Troy, but in fact they had their feet on wheat-bearing Mysia...." (P. Oxy, LXIX 4708, D. Obbink, trans.). The translation as well as images of this exciting new papyrological find can be seen at www.papyrology.ox.ac.uk/POxy/monster/demo/Page1.html.

27. Thucydides 1.11–12, in *History of the Peloponnesian War,* Rex Warner, trans., rev. ed. (New York, 1972), 42.

28. *Iliad* 9.328–29. On the traditions associated with these other raids and their sublimation to the Panhellenic *Iliad,* see Gregory Nagy, *The Best of the Achaeans: Concepts of the Hero in Archaic Greek Poetry* (Baltimore, 1979), 140f. For the numerous associations of Lesbos in particular with the Trojan War tradition, see Emily L. Shields, "Lesbos in the Trojan War," *Classical Journal* 13 (1917–18), 670–81.

29. For the end of the Mycenaean world and the Dark Age that followed, see Carol G. Thomas and Craig Conant, *Citadel to City-State: The Transformation of Greece, 1200–700 B.C.E.* (Bloomington, IN, 1999); and Robin Osborne, *Greece in the Making: 1200–479 B.C.* (London, 1996). A classic study of the archaeological evidence of this period of great transition is V.R.d'A. Desborough, *The Last Mycenaeans and Their Successors: An Archaeological Survey c. 1200–1000 B.C.* (Oxford, 1966). For the Dark Ages, see again V.R.d'A. Desborough, *The Greek Dark Ages* (New York, 1972); and A. M. Snodgrass, *The Dark Age of Greece: An Archaeological Survey of the Eleventh to Eighth Centuries B.C.,* rev. ed. (Edinburgh, 2000). For Mycenaean Boiotia, see John M. Fossey, *Topography and Population of Ancient Boiotia,* vol. 1 (Chicago, 1988), especially 424ff.; for Thessaly, Bryan Feuer, *The Northern Mycenaean Border in Thessaly* (Oxford, 1983). Also Desborough, *The Greek Dark Ages,* 87ff., discusses the Thessalian migration. The evidence for the arrival of the Mycenaeans on Lesbos and their apparent coexistence with the Lesbian population is discussed in Spencer, "Early Lesbos between East and West," 269–306, and especially 275f.

30. For the evolution of the epic and the Aeolic phase, see especially West, "The Rise of the Greek Epic," 151–72; and Paul Wathelet, "Les phases dialectales de l'épopée grecque et l'apport de l'éolien," *Eikasmos* 14 (2003), 9–26. A succinct précis of this complex linguistic history is given with much clarity in Richard Janko, *The "Iliad": A Commentary, Volume IV: Books 13–16* (Cambridge, 1992), 15ff. ("The Aeolic Phase of the Epic Tradition").

31. On the import of Troy's proximity, see, for example, Bryce, *The Trojans and Their Neighbours,* 189.

32. For Anatolian phraseology in the *Iliad,* see, for example, Emile Benveniste, *Indo-European Language and Society,* Elizabeth Palmer, trans. (Coral Gables, FL, 1973), 371ff., on the Aeolo-Phrygian word for "the people" of the king in Homer; and Jaan Puhvel, "An Anatolian Turn of Phrase in the *Iliad,*" *American Journal of Philology* 109 (1988), 591–93. Intriguingly, despite waves of migrations that continued over several generations, the archaeological

record indicates that the Mycenaean newcomers did not displace native Lesbian culture, and one must surmise that the immigrant usurpers were not wholly intolerant of Anatolian ways. The relationship between the native inhabitants of Lesbos and the Aeolian colonizers in the Archaic Age, but with implications for the late Bronze/Dark Ages, is also examined in Nigel Spencer, "Multi-dimensional Group Definition in the Landscape of Rural Greece," in Nigel Spencer, ed., *Time, Tradition and Society in Greek Archaeology: Bridging the "Great Divide"* (London and New York, 1995).

33. Contacts between Lesbos and Ionic Euboia, the long, thin island that parallels mainland Greece, makes the latter a likely site for this transference, a likelihood borne out by certain elements in the *Iliad* itself: West, "The Rise of the Greek Epic," 166f. For compelling evidence of Euboian diffusion of the Homeric epics, see Thomas and Conant, *The Trojan War,* 65ff.

34. Similar transferences across languages of other cultures are described in West, "The Rise of the Greek Epic," 171f.

35. For the Homeric poets: Demodokos, at the court of the Phaecians, is found at *Odyssey* 8.43ff., 8.254ff., and 8.486ff.; Phemios, in Ithaka, at 1.153ff. and 22.330ff.

36. The "Homeric" "Hymn to Delian Apollo" also perpetuates this tradition: "Think of me in future, if ever some long-suffering stranger comes here and asks, 'O Maidens, which is your favorite singer who visits here, and who do you enjoy most?' Then you must all answer with one voice . . . 'It is a blind man, and he lives in rocky Chios: all of his songs remain supreme afterwards.'" (vv. 166ff.); in West, *Homeric Hymns,* 85.

37. But see Andrew Dalby, "The *Iliad,* the *Odyssey,* and Their Audiences," *Classical Quarterly* 45 (1995), 269–79, who argues that the audiences were more humble.

38. On the Book divisions, see Nicholas Richardson, *The "Iliad": A Commentary, Volume VI: Books 21–24* (Cambridge, 1996), 20f.; for the argument that the poet himself made the Book divisions, see Bruce Heiden, "The Placement of 'Book Divisions' in the *Iliad,*" *Journal of Hellenic Studies* 118 (1998), 68–81.

39. Herodotus, *The Histories,* 2.116.

40. The principal source of our knowledge of the lost epics is Proclus' *Chrestomathy,* or "compendium of useful knowledge," reproduced in M. L. West, ed. and trans., *Greek Epic Fragments: From the Seventh to the Fifth Century B.C.* (Cambridge, MA, 2003). It is clear from the distribution of the subjects of these epics that they were carefully composed around the Homeric poems; in other words, these poems deferred to Homer. For a survey of the possible dates and authorship of the Trojan War epics, as well as what can be gleaned of the lost epics themselves, see West, ibid., 12ff. The relationship of the lost epics to the poems of Homer is discussed in Jonathan S. Burgess, *The Tradition of the Trojan War in Homer and the Epic Cycle* (Baltimore, 2001). A succinct overview of the cycle is given in Malcolm Davies, *The Greek Epic Cycle* (London, 2003).

41. The seeds of Homer's tragic vision of the war appear to have been inherent in the wider body of epic tradition. In the lost epic *Cypria,* for example, it is

stated that Zeus' plan was "to relieve the all-nurturing earth of mankind's weight by fanning the great conflict of the Trojan War, to void the burden through death." *Cypria*, fragment 1, in West, *Greek Epic Fragments*, 81f.; see also Hesiod, *Catalogue of Women or EHOIAI*, vv. II.3ff., in Glenn W. Most, ed. and trans., *Hesiod: Volume 2, The Shield. Catalogue of Women. Other Fragments* (Cambridge, MA, 2007), fragment 155 (continued), 233. The *Iliad* itself appears to allude to this tradition; see G. S. Kirk, *The Iliad: A Commentary, Volume I: Books 1–4* (Cambridge, 1985), sub. v. 5, 53, for echoes between the *Cypria* and the *Iliad*'s proem; and R. Scodel, "The Achaean Wall and the Myth of Destruction," *Harvard Studies in Classical Philology* 86 (1982), 33–50; and also J. Marks, "The Junction Between the *Kypria* and the *Iliad*," *Phoenix* 56 (1–2) (2002), 1–24. The Eastern antecedents of "the myth of destruction" are also discussed in M. L. West, *The East Face of Helicon: West Asiatic Elements in Greek Poetry and Myth* (Oxford, 1997), 480ff.; and Walter Burkert, *The Orientalizing Revolution*, Margaret E. Pinder and Walter Burkert, trans. (Cambridge, MA, 1992), 100ff. The application of this myth to the story of the Trojan War "must date from the time when it had become obvious that the Trojan war, though successful, was the beginning of the end for the Mycenaean age": T.B.L. Webster, *From Mycenae to Homer* (New York, 1964), 181. Evidence that the Trojan War was perceived as pointless and destructive by the wider Trojan War Epic Cycle, as well as by the *Iliad*, has recently been examined by Ruth Scodel, "Stupid, Pointless Wars," *Transactions of the American Philological Association* 138 (2008), 219–35.

42. *Iliad* 1.152ff.; 1.277ff; 1.293ff.

Chain of Command

1. G. S. Kirk, *The Iliad: A Commentary, Volume I: Books 1–4* (Cambridge, 1985), sub. vv. 29–31, 56, quotes Aristarchus and is the modern commentator.

2. Ibid., sub. v. 39, 57; Apollonius Sophistes is the scholiast. For Apollo Smintheus, see Simon Pulleyn, *Homer: "Iliad" I* (Oxford, 2000), sub. v. 39, 134ff.

3. On the cycle, see "The Things They Carried," note 41. For the epic theme of *neîkos*, or quarrel, between heroes, see Gregory Nagy, *The Best of the Achaeans: Concepts of the Hero in Archaic Greek Poetry* (Baltimore, 1979), 22ff.

4. Quotes are respectively *Cypria*, argument 9, p. 77; *Aethiopis*, argument 1, p. 111; *Aethiopis*, argument 4, 113; all in M. L. West, ed. and trans., *Greek Epic Fragments: From the Seventh to the Fifth Century B.C.* (Cambridge, MA, 2003).

5. Hesiod, *Catalogue of Women or EHOIAI*, in Glenn W. Most, ed. and trans., *Hesiod: Volume 2, The Shield. Catalogue of Women. Other Fragments* (Cambridge, MA, 2007), fragment 155 (continued), 231f.; the story is also told by Stesichorus, in David A. Campbell, *Greek Lyric III: Stesichorus, Ibycus, Simonides, and Others* (Cambridge, MA, 2001), fragment 190, 91.

6. On the scepter, see Kirk, sub. vv. 234–39, 77f.

7. "Fifty were the fast-running ships wherein Achilles / beloved of Zeus had led his men to Troy, and in each one / were fifty men, his companions in arms, at the rowing benches" (*Iliad* 16.168–70). *Cypria*, argument 12, refers to "Zeus' plan to relieve the Trojans by removing Achilles from the Greek alliance"; West, *Greek Epic Fragments*, 81. This indicates an entirely different dramatic motivation for the absence of Achilles, one in which there is no quarrel, no anger, and no intervention by Thetis.

8. On the best-guess meaning of "hecatomb," see Kirk, sub. v. 65, 60.

9. On Homer's reticence for the outlandish, see Jasper Griffin, "The Epic Cycle and the Uniqueness of Homer," *Journal of Hellenic Studies* 97 (1977), 39–53. Briareus is named, along with two other monstrous brothers, by Hesiod, in his *Theogony* ("The Genealogy of the Gods"), as an essential ally of Zeus in his battle for supremacy with the Titans; see, for example, *Theogony*, 149, in Glenn W. Most, ed. and trans., *Hesiod: Volume 1, Theogony. Works and Days. Testimonia* (Cambridge, MA, 2006), 15. Another tradition, preserved in a fragment of a lost epic entitled *Titanomachy* ("The Battle of the Titans," by Eumelus), states that Aigaion "fought on the side of the Titans" against Zeus, not for him. West, *Greek Epic Fragments*, 225f.

10. In Greek mythology, Zeus' father, Kronos, learning that one of his children was destined to overthrow him, swallowed them all—save Zeus, for whom his wife substituted a stone wrapped in swaddling clothes to deceive him. Later Kronos was induced to vomit back his children, and, led by Zeus, they indeed overpowered him. Kronos in his turn had come to power by overthrowing and castrating his father, Uranus; the entire intricate story is related in Hesiod, *Theogony*, 453ff., in Most, *Hesiod: Theogony*, 39ff. The Hittite Song of Kumarbi relates some of the same themes of the duping and castration of a primordial god; see M. L. West, *The East Face of Helicon: West Asiatic Elements in Greek Poetry and Myth* (Oxford, 1997), 277ff.

11. On the function of stories of the men of old, particularly of a hero's father, in heroic society, see Bruce Karl Braswell, "Mythological Innovation in the *Iliad*," *Classical Quarterly*, n.s., 21, no. 1 (1971), 16–26; and Caroline Alexander, "Appeals to Tradition in the *Iliad*, with Particular Reference to Achilles," dissertation, Columbia University, 1991.

12. *The Odes of Pindar*, C. M. Bowra, trans. (London, 1969), 52f.

13. The implications of this transforming myth were exposed and movingly explored in a landmark work by Laura M. Slatkin, *The Power of Thetis: Allusion and Interpretation in the "Iliad"* (Berkeley and Los Angeles, 1991); for the validity of drawing upon a reference as late as Pindar for evidence of an Iliadic tradition, see her note 26, p. 76f. Thetis' destiny is also an important dramatic element in Aeschylus' *Prometheus Bound*, vv. 907ff.

14. Similar delusional dreams attend many military ventures; compare the report of a U.S. Marine commander from Task Force Tarawa that, on their approach to Nasiriya, in southern Iraq, in March 2003, they had been led to believe that the city's defenders would lay down their weapons and "put flowers in our gun barrels, hold up their babies for us to kiss and give us the keys

to the city." Tim Pritchard, "When Iraq Went Wrong," *New York Times*, December 5, 2006.

15. *Xíphos=qi-si-pe-e* in the Linear B tablets; see Kirk, sub. vv. 2.45, 118.

16. The testing of the army is a motif found in literature and mythology of the ancient Near East, where it functions as a method of weeding out cowards before engaging in battle. See, for example, West, *The East Face of Helicon* 207f.

17. It was Thersites who featured in another epic quarrel with Achilles; the *Aethiopis* states that "Achilles kills Thersites after being abused by him and insulted over his alleged love" of the Amazon queen (*Aethiopis*, argument 1), and the Iliadic passage is undoubtedly an allusion to a well-established epic hatred between the two men. For Thersites as the mirror opposite of Achilles—the worst (*aískhistos*) of the Achaeans as opposed to the best—see Nagy, 259ff.

18. On the origins of Thersites, see P. Chantraine, "À Propos de Thersite," *L'Antiquité Classique* 32 (1963), 18–27.

19. James F. McGlew, "Royal Power and the Achaean Assembly at *Iliad* 2.84–393," *Classical Antiquity*, 8, no. 2 (October 1989), 290.

20. "Agamemnon's leadership is so disastrous, and his blunders often so obvious, that it has seemed unnecessary to inquire any further into Homer's point." Dean C. Hammer, "'Who Shall Readily Obey?': Authority and Politics in the *Iliad*," *Phoenix* 51, no. 1 (1997), 4.

21. On changing leadership patterns in the eighth century B.C., see, for example, Carol G. Thomas and Craig Conant, *Citadel to City-State: The Transformation of Greece, 1200–700 B.C.E.* (Bloomington, IN, 1999), 132ff.

Terms of Engagement

1. "The Asian meadow beside the Kaÿstrian waters" where the wildfowl gather can be identified with the floodplain of the river that still bears this name flowing just outside of Ephesus, on the Aegean coast of Turkey. J. V. Luce, *Celebrating Homer's Landscapes: Troy and Ithaca Revisited* (New Haven, CT, 1998), 15ff.

2. For the various explanations of the aegis and its association with the thunder god, see Richard Janko, *The "Iliad": A Commentary, Volume IV: Books 13–16* (Cambridge, 1992), sub. vv. 308–11, 260f.

3. For the Homeric similes, see William C. Scott, *The Oral Nature of the Homeric Simile* (Leiden, 1974). Less technical and more accessible is G. P. Shipp, *Studies in the Language of Homer*, 2nd ed. (Cambridge, 1972). Also Carroll Moulton, *Similes in the Homeric Poems* (Göttingen, 1977), especially 27ff., on the cascade of images in Book Two.

4. This line, the translation of 2.488, is a substitution for Lattimore's translation, which reads (with preceding verse), "Who then of those were the chief men and the lords of the Danaans? / *I could not tell over the*

multitude of them nor name them." The emendation makes less ambiguous the fact that "the multitude" *(plēthùn)* does *not* refer to "a multitude of leaders" but to "the multitude," the masses—i.e., the troops. For this clarification and its implications, see Bruce Heiden, "Common People and Leaders in *Iliad* Book 2: The Invocation of the Muses and the Catalogue of Ships," *Transactions of the American Philological Association* 138 (2008), 127–54.

5. For the range of scholarly opinion, see A. Giovannini, *Étude historique sur les origines du catalogue des vaisseaux* (Berne, 1969), who believes that the Catalogue dates from around the seventh century B.C.; and R. Hope Simpson and J. F. Lazenby, *The Catalogue of Ships in Homer's "Iliad"* (Oxford, 1970), whose balanced presentation of the archaeological evidence leads them to advocate a Mycenaean origin for the record of place-names, later reworked by the tradition. Similarly, Mark W. Edwards, "The Structure of Homeric Catalogues," *Transactions of the American Philological Association* 110 (1980), 81–105, argues that while a list of place-names is authentically Mycenaean, the descriptive elements attached to them are not. A succinct but detailed survey of the scholarship and Catalogue itself is made by G. S. Kirk, *The "Iliad": A Commentary, Volume I: Books 1–4* (Cambridge, 1985), 168–240.

6. Recently, Linear B tablets found at Thebes confirm the existence of a previously unlocatable site—Elēon—which is named in the Catalogue: "they who held Eleon and Hyle and Peteon" *(Iliad* 2.500). For the names recorded in the Theban tablets and the region they describe, see Louis Godart and Anna Sacconi, "La géographie des états mycéniens," *Comptes rendus de l'Académie des Inscriptions et Belles-Lettres* (1999), 2:527–46; for the individual towns, see E. Visser, *Homers Katalog der Schiffe* (Stuttgart and Leipzig, 1997), 261–66.

7. A list of late forms is given in Shipp, 235ff. On the Catalogue's use of the late Ionian *nées* for "ship"; see Kirk, 171.

8. The possibility of such a muster roll, on the other hand, is hinted at by other Bronze Age documents. Linear B tablet #53 An12 from Pylos gives "a list of the numbers of rowers to be provided by various towns for an expedition to Pleuron": *e-re-ta pe-re-u-ro-na-de i-jo-te* (for the Greek *erétai Pleurōnáde ióntes")—*"rowers to go to Pleuron"; thirty men are listed, a figure suggestive of a ship's complement. See M. Ventris and J. Chadwick, *Documents in Mycenaean Greek,* 2nd ed. (Cambridge, 1973), 183f.; also given in Kirk, 239.

9. The Catalogue is organized into three tours, or circuits: central and southern Greece; Crete, Rhodes, and the Dodecanese Islands; and, with vaguer precision, northern Greece and Thessaly. Lists reminiscent of the Catalogue survive in records and documents from other parts of the Bronze Age world. A poem commemorating the feats of Ramses II in the Battle of Kadesh, fought between Egyptians and Hittites around 1275 B.C., for example, contains a battle list not of ships but of chariots:

Then he caused many chiefs to come,
Each of them with his chariotry,
Equipped with their weapons of warfare:
The chief of Arzawa and he of Masa,
The chief of Irun and he of Luka,
He of Dardany, the chief of Carchemish,
the chief of Karkisha, he of Khaleb,
The brothers of him of Khatti all together,
Their total of a thousand chariots came straight into the fire.

Translation from Miriam Lichtheim, *Ancient Egyptian Literature: A Book of Readings* (Berkeley, 1976), vol. 2: *The New Kingdom*, 66f. The "Dardany" of the list, incidentally, are almost certainly the Dardanians, one of the Homeric names for the Trojans: see Trevor Bryce, *The Trojans and Their Neighbours* (Abingdon, Oxon, 2006), 136.

The Greek historical record has preserved tribute lists and lists of religious festival sites from the classical era and later, suggesting that the Catalogue's original, prosaic function could have been along such census-taking lines. Giovannini, 53ff., discusses these political and religious lists from the fifth century B.C. onward, noting in particular the tours made by envoys to cities whose religious significance afforded them the status of "receivers of sacred envoys." There are, then, a variety of known reasons that a compilation of place-names *could* have been composed in the late Bronze Age. Regarded with sufficient veneration to be safeguarded over the centuries, this Panhellenic overview of Mycenaean political geography would later have been adapted into poetic form, embellished with striking but often safely generic epithets—"strong-founded," "of the great vineyards," "the sacred"—and given a regal, nostalgic place in the developing Panhellenic epic.

10. The weight the Catalogue gives to the various contingents does not accord with their importance in the *Iliad*: The Boiotians, who receive one of the most lavish entries in the Catalogue, are hardly referred to elsewhere in the *Iliad*, for example, while the entries for the Myrmidons and Salamis island-ers, contingents led respectively by the *Iliad*'s all-important heroes Achilles and Aias, receive markedly scant treatment. A Boiotian origin or influence has been speculated on the grounds that "catalogue poetry" was a favorite Boiotian genre. The Boiotian poet Hesiod was celebrated for poetry that is essentially long poetic lists: of the generations of the gods (*Theogony*), myth-ological genealogies (*EHOIAI* or *Catalogue of Women*), movements of the stars (*Astronomia*), farming lore (*Works and Days*).

11. "To an aural audience [the Catalogue] would be the most impressive part, demonstrating the supreme technique of the singer, and giving information of the highest importance": Minna Skafte Jensen, *The Homeric Question and the Oral-Formulaic Theory* (Copenhagen, 1980), 79.

12. See Heiden, 127–54.

13. See, for example, Ruth Finnegan, *Oral Literature in Africa* (Oxford, 1970), 122f.

14. The scholia (Ab) is cited in Kirk's commentary, sub. v. 776, 241f.

15. Strabo, *Geography* 1.1.11, in Horace Leonard Jones, trans., *Strabo: Geography*, vol. 1 (Cambridge, MA, 1917), 179; his misplacing of Troy is at 13.1.34–36.

16. One commentator has suggested that the Hellespont may be "boundless" (*apeírōn*) because its limit was simply not known: Luce, 44. For a survey of the Troad landscape, see Luce, 21ff., and also 236, note 10.

17. Of the Hill of the Thicket, or more prosaically "Bramble Hill" as G. S. Kirk calls it, "the immortal gods have named it the burial mound of the much leaping or bounding Murine." One scholium states that Murine was an Amazon, but this lone attestation is not very convincing. "Bounding," dancing, or leaping, as Kirk speculates, "sounds like some ritual action" (Kirk, sub. vv. 813–14, 247). The *Cypria* is said to have included a catalogue of the Trojans' allies: *Cypria*, argument 12, in M. L. West, ed. and trans., *Greek Epic Fragments: From the Seventh to the Fifth Century B.C.* (Cambridge, MA, 2003), 81. There is no way of knowing how expansive this was, but the *Iliad*'s own scant catalogue follows here. The fact that the majority of leaders have been given Greek names is evidence that this list does not derive from some lost historical document but was created for the epic. The most accessible guide to the Trojan Catalogue, as for the Catalogue of Ships, is Kirk, 248ff. For its possible echo of west Anatolian alliances in the Bronze Age, see Michael Wood, *In Search of the Trojan War*, rev. ed. (London, 2005), 278f.

18. Hektor's name is first mentioned in the *Iliad* at 1.242, significantly in the words of Achilles: "'Then stricken at heart though you be, you will be able / to do nothing, when in their numbers before man-slaughtering Hektor / they drop and die.'"

19. For the Mycenaean origin of Hektor's name, see Paul Wathelet, *Dictionnaire des Troyens de l'Iliade*, vol. 1 (Liège, 1988), 497ff.

20. On the theme of unequal paired brothers, see K. Reinhardt, "The Judgement of Paris," in G. M. Wright and P. V. Jones, trans., *Homer: German Scholarship in Translation* (Oxford, 1997), 184ff. In the *Iliad*, it is striking that Hektor's primary role has been displaced by that of his brother Paris, who should by dramatic, not to mention moral, right be the defender of the city he has placed in jeopardy, as, similarly, Agamemnon displaces his brother Menelaos, who should also by dramatic and moral right be the leader of the army assembled to regain his wife, Helen.

21. A concise overview of arguments for and against the Homeric invention of Hektor is given in Jonathan S. Burgess, *The Tradition of the Trojan War in Homer and the Epic Cycle* (Baltimore, 2001), 64ff. The theory was first presented by John A. Scott, "Paris and Hector in Tradition and in Homer," *Classical Philology* 8, no. 2 (1913), 160–71; and most energetically rebutted by Frederick M. Combellack—apparently still smarting from the effects of an article written thirty years previously—"Homer and Hector," *American Journal of Philology* 65, no. 3 (1944), 209–43.

22. *Aiólos* defined in Richard John Cunliffe, *A Lexicon of the Homeric Dialect* (Norman, OK, 1963), 12.

23. The term is also used once of the war god Ares, at 20.38. See Kirk's discussion of the term (Kirk, sub. v. 816, 250f.).

24. For "Paris/Alexander," see Wathelet, 814ff.; and for "Priam," ibid., 909f. Paris tends to be the preferred name for Trojans, Alexandros for Greeks. Irene J. F. de Jong, "Paris/Alexandros in the *Iliad*," *Mnemosyne* 40 (1987), 124–28, suggests that Homer, "by keeping the 'Trojan' name 'Paris,' may have intended to introduce a 'realistic' element in the representation of the Trojans as speakers of a foreign language." A treaty drawn up around 1300 B.C. between the Hittite king Muwattalli II and Alaksandu of Wilusa binds the latter, and his sons and grandsons after him, to an oath of loyalty, thus establishing Wilusa as a vassal state of the Hittite king. The question arises, then, as to why the ruler of Anatolian Wilusa—*Wilios*—*Ilios*—bore a Greek name? A possible explanation is hinted at in the treaty itself, in which the Hittite king stipulates that on Alaksandu's death the treaty will continue to bind his heir—"In regard to the [son] of yours whom you designate for kingship—[whether he is by] your wife or by your concubine." In other words, the adopted son of a foreign concubine could be the legitimate ruler of Wilusa. For the treaty, see Gary Beckman, *Hittite Diplomatic Texts*, 2nd ed. (Atlanta, 1999), section 5, 88. It has been suggested that the very particular language in this clause has been tailored to a specific circumstance—such as the possibility that Alaksandu was himself the son of a perhaps foreign concubine, or adopted: see Joachim Latacz, *Troy and Homer: Towards a Solution of an Old Mystery* (Oxford, 2004), 117f. Ironically, then, while the epic may have retained the exotic, Asiatic name "Paris" precisely because it suggested a realistic detail, it is the more familiar "Alexandros" that evokes a historic prince of Troy.

25. Text adjusted from Lattimore's "a red folding robe."

26. The verb "to weave" is *huphaínō*. Examples of the "masculine" use are found at *Iliad* 3.212; 6.187; 7.324.

27. The domestic world of the Trojan women is explored by many scholars. See, for example, Maria C. Pantelia, "Spinning and Weaving: Ideas of Domestic Order in Homer," *American Journal of Philology* 114, no. 4 (Winter 1993), 493–501. A discussion of the role of women, as spinners and weavers and other skilled manual laborers, as gleaned from the Linear B documents, is given in Jon-Christian Billigmeier and Judy A. Turner, "The Socio-Economic Roles of Women in Mycenaean Greece: A Brief Survey from the Evidence of the Linear B Tablets," in Helene P. Foley, ed., *Reflections of Women in Antiquity* (New York, 1981), 1–18.

28. For *ainōs*, see Cunliffe, 12; and Kirk, sub. v. 158, 285.

29. "At the same time a good king and a strong spearfighter": This line was a favorite motto of Alexander the Great.

30. It is interesting to consider what Hittite law made of Helen's situation:

(1) If a man seizes a woman in the mountains (and rapes her), the man is guilty and shall die, but if he seizes her in her house, the woman is guilty and shall die. If the woman's husband catches them (in the act) and kills them, he has committed no offense (clause 197).

(2) If he brings them to the palace gate (*i.e. to the royal court*) and says: "My wife shall not die," he can spare his wife's life, but must also spare the lover. Then he may veil her (clause 198).

From Trevor Bryce, *Life and Society in the Hittite World* (Oxford, 2002), 127f.

31. The *eidōlon,* or phantom of Helen, was famously evoked in a lost poem by the sixth-century-B.C. poet Stesichorus, who, it was claimed, had earlier been struck blind for defaming her; for attestations of the lost poem, see David A. Campbell, *Greek Lyric III: Stesichorus, Ibycus, Simonides, and Others* (Cambridge, MA, 2001), fragment 192–93, 93ff. Herodotus claims he was told of Helen's Egyptian sojourn when he was in Egypt (*The Histories,* 2. 116–20). In the *Odyssey,* Helen evidently has a close connection to Egypt, whether or not she had ever visited there (*Odyssey* 4: 219ff.). Otto Skutsch, "Helen, Her Name and Nature," *Journal of Hellenic Studies,* 107 (1987), 188–93, suggests that "two mythological figures are fused in Helen," the fertility goddess and the phenomenon of St. Elmo's fire, destroyer of ships.

32. Later in the *Iliad,* at 11.138ff., reference is made to the fact that the Trojan Antimachos advocated killing Menelaos "'on the spot'" during his Embassy, but he would seem to have been a lone voice in the Trojan assembly.

33. For a discussion of the similarities between Homeric agreements such as is sworn to between Achaeans and Trojans here, and Near Eastern treaty formats, see Peter Karavites, *Promise-Giving and Treaty-Making: Homer and the Near East* (Leiden, 1992); and Jaan Puhvel, *Homer and Hittite* (Innsbruck, 1991), 9ff.

34. The whisking away of a hero by a deity in time of crisis is a traditional theme in many cultures; see, for example, M. L. West, *The East Face of Helicon: West Asiatic Elements in Greek Poetry and Myth* (Oxford, 1997), 99ff. West describes what appears to be a scene of divine rescue depicted on a silver Cyprian bowl dating to about 700 B.C., evidently based upon a Phoenician story. Others have conjectured that the Aphrodite-Paris-Helen nexus reflects the Indo-European archetype of the Dawn Goddess and her mortal lovers; see Ann Suter, "Aphrodite/Paris/Helen: A Vedic Myth in the *Iliad,*" *Transactions of the American Philological Association* 117 (1987), 51–58; and Deborah Dickmann Boedeker, *Aphrodite's Entry into Greek Epic* (Leiden, 1974).

35. *Cypria,* fragment 10, in West, *Greek Epic Fragments,* 89ff. For the many accounts of Helen's parentage and birth, see Timothy Gantz, *Early Greek Myth: A Guide to Literary and Artistic Sources,* vol. 1 (Baltimore, 1993), 318ff.

36. M. L. West, *Indo-European Poetry and Myth* (Oxford, 2007), 229ff.

37. Helen's speculated pre-epic Greek origins are discussed in Linda Lee Clader, *Helen: The Evolution from Divine to Heroic in Greek Epic Tradition* (Leiden, 1976); and Skutsch, 188–93.

38. On Aphrodite, see Walter Burkert, *Greek Religion: Archaic and Classical,* John Raffan, trans. (Cambridge, MA, 1985), 152ff.

39. Compare the depiction of Paris' seduction of Helen, as given by the lyric poet Alcaeus, writing in the early sixth century B.C.:

> [Paris] . . .
> startled the heart of Argive Helen,
> fluttered it in her breast, and mad about
> that host-cheating Trojan guest she took ship
>   and followed him over the sea,
>
> leaving behind her pretty child,
> leaving her husband's sumptuous bed, for
> [Cypris/Aphrodite] had led her astray with lust,
>   the daughter of Leda and Zeus.

From Anne Pippin Burnett, trans., *Three Archaic Poets: Archilochus, Alcaeus, Sappho* (Cambridge, MA, 1983), 186.

40. On the seduction, see M. W. Edwards, *Homer: Poet of the "Iliad"* (Baltimore, 1987), 196f.

41. "Remembered their warcraft" (4.222)—*Mnēsanto dè chármēs; chármēs* is a vexed word, taken by some commentators to refer to the root *char,* or "joy," and thus meaning "joy in battle," "eagerness for the fray," as, for example, Georg Autenrieth, *A Homeric Dictionary,* Robert P. Keep, trans. (Piscataway, NJ, 2002), 328f. However, the notion of battle joy is so alien to the *Iliad* that most translators and scholars refer to "the *primitive* meaning of the root *ghar* (the Greek *char*), and explain it as the 'glow,' 'burning flame' of battle." See Walter Leaf and M. A. Bayfield, *The "Iliad" of Homer,* vol. 1 (London, 1971), sub. v. 222, 346f. Thus "fighting, battle; spirit, stomach, ardour for the fight; the art of war, war, fighting" (Cunliffe, 418).

42. Kirk, sub. vv. 51–53, 336, claims that Argos "was continuously inhabited from the Bronze Age on, and even seems to have escaped major damage at the end of LHIIIB" (circa 1200 B.C.), but this is a misleading quibble. Archaeological evidence shows that diminished populations hung on at a number of formerly important Mycenaean centers, such as Tiryns, Athens, and Argos, but that these, too, faded toward the end of the twelfth and beginning of the eleventh centuries B.C.; see, for example, Carol G. Thomas and Craig Conant, *Citadel to City-State: The Transformation of Greece, 1200–700 B.C.E.* (Bloomington, IN, 1999), 1–31. Given the general collapse of all major centers in the Argolid and elsewhere on the mainland, the existence of a small, tenacious population hanging on in the ruins of a single settlement would in any case have done little to temper the belief of later generations that they had lost their world.

43. The list of epithets is given in Walter Leaf, *The Iliad*, vol. 1 (London, 1900), sub. v. 222, 170.

Enemy Lines

1. See Wolf-Hartmut Friedrich, *Wounding and Death in the "Iliad": Homeric Techniques of Description*, Gabriele Wright and Peter Jones, trans. (London, 2003), especially the appendix by Dr. K. B. Saunders, who is quoted in the text, 161ff.
2. Both the Kazakh *Epic of Manas* and the Kalmyk *Dzhangariada* are quoted in C. M. Bowra, *Heroic Poetry* (London, 1961), 57f., in turn from *Manas: Kirgizkii Epos* (Moscow, 1946), 335, and *Dzhangariada: Geroicheskaya Poema Kalmykov*, S. A. Kozin, ed. (Moscow, 1944), 219.
3. Seth L. Schein, *The Mortal Hero: An Introduction to Homer's "Iliad"* (Berkeley and Los Angeles, 1984), 72ff., gives an eloquent account of the *Iliad*'s insistence on its heroes' mortality. For evidence of war injuries and their treatment in the Bronze Age, see Robert Arnott, "War Wounds and Their Treatment in the Aegean Bronze Age," in Robert Laffineur, ed., *POLEMOS: Le contexte guerrier en Égée à l'Âge du Bronze* (Liège, 1999), 499–507.
4. On Aineias' origins and destiny, see Timothy Gantz, *Early Greek Myth: A Guide to Literary and Artistic Sources*, vol. 2 (Baltimore, 1993), 713ff. Other sources for Aineias' genealogy are the "Homeric Hymn to Aphrodite" vv. 196–98; and Hesiod, *Theogony* 1008–1010. His heroic tradition is revisited in the last chapter of this book, "Everlasting Glory"; see note 48. The recent DNA discoveries are reported in John Hooper, "Etruscan Mystery Solved," *Guardian*, June 18, 2007, 23.
5. The four instances of Aineias' divine rescue are 5.311ff. (by Aphrodite), 5.445ff. (by Apollo), 20.92f. (an account of a past rescue by Zeus), and 20.318ff. (by Poseidon, who justifies his rescue by referring to Aineias' destiny).
6. The implications of these near misses, or places where the *Iliad* threatens to overturn a traditional story element, are examined by James V. Morrison, "Alternatives to the Epic Tradition: Homer's Challenges in the *Iliad*," *Transactions of the American Philological Association* 122 (1992), 61–71.
7. Diomedes' kingship over Argos makes a muddle of heroic geography, as he would appear to be encroaching upon Mycenaean territory under Agamemnon. For the problems raised by the geography of Diomedes' kingdom, see G. S. Kirk, *The "Iliad": A Commentary, Volume I: Books 1–4* (Cambridge, 1985), 180f.
8. Thebaid, argument 9, in M. L. West, ed. and trans., *Greek Epic Fragments: From the Seventh to the Fifth Century B.C.* (Cambridge, MA, 2003), 51ff.
9. For Diomedes' old tribal origins, see Gilbert Murray, *The Rise of the Greek Epic: Being a Course of Lectures Delivered at Harvard University* (Oxford, 1924), 215ff.
10. *Paiëon* occurs only in Book Five of the *Iliad*: Linear B texts from Knossos have a *Pajawone*. See G. S. Kirk, *The "Iliad": A Commentary, Volume II: Books 5–8*

(Cambridge, 1990), sub. vv. 398–402, 102f.; also Walter Burkert, *Greek Religion: Archaic and Classical*, John Raffan, trans. (Cambridge, MA, 1985), 43.

11. The terminology of death is paraphrased from Jasper Griffin, *Homer on Life and Death* (Oxford, 1983), 91, the most eloquent and moving scholarly account of death in both Homeric epics.

12. The phrase *aísima pareipōn*, translated here as "since he urged justice" (*Iliad* 6.62), is more ambiguous in Greek. *Aísima* has various meanings, from "which is just or right" to "that which is decreed by fate." See, for example, Richard John Cunliffe, *A Lexicon of Homeric Dialect* (Norman, OK, 1963), 14.

13. Of the shield, "it is strange that a hero should set out on a three-mile run through country held by the Trojans carrying so great a weight, and that moreover in a position warranted to make it flay his ankles." H. L. Lorimer, *Homer and the Monuments* (London, 1950), 184. Hektor's shield represents the poetic memory of a genuine Mycenaean piece of armor that was, however, never used in the method described.

14. Psalms 103:15f.

15. Ecclesiasticus, or Sirac, 14:18; see M. L. West, *The East Face of Helicon: West Asiatic Elements in Greek Poetry and Myth* (Oxford, 1997), 364ff., for this and other Eastern elements in the Bellerophontes story.

16. For the symbols and Greek Bronze Age knowledge of Hittite scripts, see Trevor R. Bryce, "Anatolian Scribes in Mycenaean Greece," *Historia* 48, no. 3 (1999); 257–64, especially 261f. For the shipwreck and its contents, see George F. Bass, "Oldest Known Shipwreck Reveals Splendors of the Bronze Age," *National Geographic* (December 1987), 693–733. More recently, the tablet and other finds from the shipwreck are beautifully revealed and discussed in Cemal Pulak, "The Uluburun Shipwreck and Late Bronze Age Trade," in Joan Aruz, Kim Benzel, and Jean M. Evans, eds., *Beyond Babylon: Art, Trade, and Diplomacy in the Second Millennium B.C.* (New York and New Haven, CT, 2008), 288–385. For the Bellerophontes story and some of its implications in the epic, see Murray, 175f. For a detailed commentary on the story's many obscure features, see Kirk, *The "Iliad,"* vol. 2, sub. vv. 152–211, 177ff.

17. Ayaan Hirsi Ali, *Infidel* (New York, 2007), 4, 135. Recitation of her grandmother's clan lineage later saved her from assault at knifepoint by establishing that she was a "sister" of her assailant.

18. Some scholars have seen in Paris' characteristic absence from the field of battle the remnant of a tradition of the "wrath of Paris," akin to that of Achilles. See Johannes Th. Kakridis, *Homeric Researches* (Lund, 1949), 43ff.; and Leslie Collins, "The Wrath of Paris: Ethical Vocabulary and Ethical Type in the *Iliad*," *American Journal of Philology* 108 (1987), 220–32.

19. Aristarchus (Arn/A) is quoted by Kirk, *The "Iliad,"* vol. 2, sub. vv. 433–39, 217.

20. S. Farron, "The Character of Hector in the *Iliad*," *Acta classica* 21 (1978), 39–57, gives a brief survey of scholarly attitudes toward Hektor and presents the argument that Homer deliberately underscored Hektor's military weaknesses in order to make him a sympathetic character.

21. *Little Iliad,* West, *Greek Epic Fragments,* fragment 29, 139ff.

22. On Astyanax in early epic and art, see Jonathan S. Burgess, *The Tradition of the Trojan War in Homer and the Epic Cycle* (Baltimore, 2001), 65ff. and appendix C, 186. For the argument that the death of Astyanax may reflect the Near Eastern practice of child sacrifice in time of siege, see Sarah P. Morris, "The Sacrifice of Astyanax: Near Eastern Contributions to the Siege of Troy," in Jane B. Carter and Sarah P. Morris, eds., *The Ages of Homer: A Tribute to Emily Townsend Vermeule* (Austin, TX, 1995), 221–45; the chapter also gives moving examples of Near Eastern poetry mourning the fall of cities.

23. This harsh reality was recognized even by ancient commentators who remarked on the "indecent violence" suffered by captive women. Immanuel Bekker, *Scholia in Homeri Iliadem* (Berlin, 1825), sub. v. 22.62, p. 589.

Land of My Fathers

1. About the value of ten oxen according to scholarly estimate, see W. Ridgeway, *Journal of Hellenic Studies* 8 (1873), 133.

2. On the lyre itself, see Bryan Hainsworth, *The "Iliad": A Commentary, Volume III: Books 9–12* (Cambridge, 1993), sub. vv. 186–87, 87f.

3. For internal evidence that "the Embassy is among the latest of the ideas and episodes built into the *Iliad*," see ibid., sub. v. 609, 289f. On the competitive response of a poet like Homer to his tradition in general, see James V. Morrison, "Alternatives to the Epic Tradition: Homer's Challenges in the *Iliad*," *Transactions of the American Philological Association* 122 (1992), 61–71.

4. For sources pertaining to the life and career of Peleus, see Timothy Gantz, *Early Greek Myth: A Guide to Literary and Artistic Sources,* vol. 1 (Baltimore, 1993), 222ff.; and for his marriage with Thetis, see ibid., 228ff.

5. The slaying by Peleus of Phokos, his half brother, is attested in fragments of the *Alcmeonis,* a lost epic uncertainly dated to the sixth century B.C.: "There godlike Telamon hit him [Phokos] on the head with a wheel-shaped discus, and Peleus quickly raised his arm above his head and struck him in the middle of his back with a bronze axe." *Alcmeonis* 1, in M. L. West, ed. and trans., *Greek Epic Fragments: From the Seventh to the Fifth Centuries B.C.* (Cambridge, MA, 2003), 59. The story is alluded to, obscurely, by Pindar, *Nemean* 5.7ff. in C.M. Bowra, trans., *The Odes of Pindar* (London, 1969). Another tradition related by Apollodorus, *The Library* 3.13.1–3, also has Peleus as the inadvertent killer of his first father-in-law, Eurytion, in the course of the legendary Kalydonian Boar Hunt. In this tale, after Peleus has been received and purified by Eurytion in Phthia for the murder of Phokos, he marries Eurytion's daughter and has a child with her, Polydore. Although the source is late—Apollodorus wrote in the second century B.C.—the *Iliad* also hints at the tradition, citing "the daughter of Peleus, Polydore the lovely" (16.175).

6. On the remarkable number of sons exiled by their fathers who later become

kings in exile, see Margalit Finkelberg, "Royal Succession in Heroic Greece," *Classical Quarterly*, n.s., 41, no. 2 (1991), 303–16.

7. Pindar, *Nemean* 3. 33ff. On the historic as well as mythic implications for Peleus' sack of Iolkos, see M. L. West, "The Rise of the Greek Epic," *Journal of Hellenic Studies*, 108 (1988), 151–72, and especially, 160.

8. Possible implications of Peleus' court of outlaws are discussed in the chapter "Man Down." The approved treatment of fugitive exiles in Bronze and Iron Age Greece can only be surmised. The Bronze Age Anatolian record, on the other hand, is clear: "If some subject of the king of Ugarit, or a citizen of Ugarit, or a servant of a subject of the king of Ugarit departs and enters the territory of the *hapiru* [semi-autonomous bands of freebooters] of My Majesty, I, Great King, will not accept him but will return him to the king of Ugarit." "Edict of Hattusili III of Hatti concerning Fugitives from Ugarit," in Gary Beckman, *Hittite Diplomatic Texts*, 2nd ed. (Atlanta, 1999), no. 33, 178.

9. *The Library*, 3.13.5, in J. G. Frazer, trans., *Apollodorus. The Library*, vol. 2 (Cambridge, MA, 1976), 67. Apollodorus' account, late as it is, is quoted for its vividness. Pottery evidence from Crete gives evidence of Peleus' capture of Thetis as far back as the mid-seventh century B.C.; Gantz, vol. 1, 229. The earliest literary reference is found in Pindar, *Nemean* 3.33–36 and 4.62–65.

10. See, for example, appendix X in Frazer, 383–88.

11. Some accounts attribute Zeus' decision to other causes. The lost epic *Cypria* held that "it was to please Hera that Thetis shied away from the union with Zeus; and he was angry, and swore to make her live with a mortal man." West, *Greek Epic Fragments, Cypria* fragment 2, 83. In the *Iliad*, however, Hera speaks of Thetis as one "'whom I myself / nourished and brought up and gave her as bride to her husband / Peleus, one dear to the hearts of the immortals'" (24.59–61), and her words imply that this was a loving, not a punitive, transaction.

12. That there was a tradition of a happier union is supported by a fragment of Alcaeus, writing in the sixth century B.C.: "and the love of Peleus and the best of Nereus' daughters flourished; and within the year she bore a son, the finest of demigods"; Alcaeus 42, in David A. Campbell, *Greek Lyric I: Sappho. Alcaeus* (Cambridge, MA, 1982), fragment 42, 257ff.

13. So Pindar:

... And forthwith he [Peleus] scorned her embraces—
He was afraid of his Father's anger, the God of Guests.
But cloud-mover Zeus, King of the Immortals,
Marked well and promised from the sky that soon
He should have for wife
A sea-maiden from the golden-spindled Nereids.

From *Nemean* 5.33ff., in Bowra, *The Odes of Pindar* 39f.

14. Pindar refers to Aiakos' righteousness in *Isthmian* 8.25ff. For his role as a judge of the dead, see Plato, *Gorgias*, 524a.

15. Hesiod, *Catalogue of Women*, 58f., in Glenn W. Most, ed. and trans., *Hesiod: Volume 2, The Shield. Catalogue of Women. Other Fragments* (Cambridge, MA, 2007), fragment 152, 217ff.

16. See, for example, T.B.L. Webster, *From Mycenae to Homer* (New York, 1964), 186, who posits that "it is still possible to see behind Diomede's account of Lycurgus, Glaukos' account of Bellerophon, and Achilles' account of Peleus a shorter poem in which the three heroes were listed probably with others as instances of prosperity which turned to adversity."

    Notable parallels between Thetis and Eos, the goddess of the dawn, offer additional insight into the *Iliad*'s depiction of Peleus as a man defined by sorrowful old age. Linguistic and thematic studies have shown that both goddesses (along with Aphrodite) exhibit attributes of the Indo-European Dawn Goddess prototype. To reduce this comparison to its simplest elements, both Thetis and Eos are associated with the sea, both have unions with mortal men, and both bear mortal children who fight at Troy (for parallels between Thetis and Eos, see Laura M. Slatkin, *The Power of Thetis: Allusion and Interpretation in the "Iliad"* [Berkeley and Los Angeles, 1991], 21ff. and 40–41); the Indo-European origin and traits of the Dawn Goddess are explored in Deborah Dickmann Boedeker, *Aphrodite's Entry into Greek Epic* (Leiden, 1974). According to the Greek tradition, Eos, falling in love with the mortal Tithonos, implored Zeus to grant her lover immortality, which he did; the goddess neglected, however, to ask also for eternal youth on his behalf—in the *Iliad*, Tithonos is mentioned as the brother of Priam and Laomedon of Troy; *Iliad* 20.237. (See Gantz, vol. 1, 36f., for the list of ancient sources of this legend.) The earliest citation, "The Hymn to Aphrodite," dating from the seventh century B.C., relates that while Tithonos was young, "he took his delight in Dawn of the golden throne, the early-born, and dwelt by the waters of Ocean at the ends of the earth; but when the first scattering of grey hairs came forth from his handsome head and his noble chin, the lady Dawn stayed away from his bed." "Hymn to Aphrodite" 5.225ff., in M. L. West, ed. and trans., *Homeric Hymns. Homeric Apocrypha. Lives of Homer* (Cambridge, MA, 2003), 177. The Eos paradigm that Thetis shares may explain the striking absence in the *Iliad* of Thetis from the bed and home of Peleus, as well as the *Iliad*'s portrait of this formerly robust hero as being perpetually "on the door-sill of sorrowful old age": Peleus' youth has passed, and his eternally youthful wife has left him to his aging mortality.

17. Gantz, vol. 1, 229f., for both literary and artistic attestations.

18. *Cypria*, respectively, fragment 4, 85; and argument 1, 69, in West, *Greek Epic Fragments*. Hera's words appear at *Iliad* 24.61–62.

19. Most, *Hesiod: The Shield*, fragment 237, 309. The burning by fire is described, obscurely, in Lykophron, *Alexandra*, 177–79.

20. The tradition of Achilles' being dipped into the Styx by his heel is directly attested only in the works of the first-century-A.D. Roman writer Statius;

Statius, *Achilleid* 1.133–34, 1.268–70, and 1.480–81, but see chapter "Everlasting Glory," note 41.

21. For the story of Demeter, see "Hymn to Demeter," vv. 231ff., in West, *Homeric Hymns. Homeric Apocrypha. Lives of Homer,* 51f. For the story of Meleager, see Bacchylides 5.136ff., in David A. Campbell, *Greek Lyric IV: Bacchylides, Corinna, and Others* (Cambridge, MA, 2006), 149. In an examination of Hittite rites of divine appeasement, Calvin Watkins demonstrates that fire and firebrands are associated with divine anger and that these ritual elements can be discerned behind the story of Meleager. If this is true, it also has bearing on the attempts to appease the anger of Achilles: Calvin Watkins, "L'Anatolie et la Grèce: Résonances culturelles, linguistiques et poétiques," Académie des Inscriptions et Belles-Lettres, *Comptes rendus des séances* 3 (2000), 1143–58; see especially 1146ff.

22. Of Peleus per se, the *Iliad* knows of two offspring: his son, Achilles, and a daughter, Polydore: "One battalion was led by Menesthios of the shining / corselet, son of Spercheios, the river swelled from the bright sky, / born of the daughter of Peleus, Polydore the lovely, / to unremitting Spercheios, when a woman lay with an immortal; / but born in name to Perieres' son, Boros, who married / Polydore formally (16.173–78). The elaborate explanation of the family circumstances—i.e., divine union and human marriage for the sake of appearances—also suggests other now lost traditions about her. One ancient commentator identifies Polydore as the daughter of another Peleus, not the son of Aiakos, although the reference to Spercheios, the landmark river of Peleus' kingdom, belies this. Later writers held her to be the daughter of Peleus' union not with Thetis but with an earlier wife: Polydore "is surely a child of Peleus' first marriage, which Homer suppresses in favor of his union with Thetis; [Achilles] must remain, for him, an isolated figure." Richard Janko, *The "Iliad": A Commentary, Volume IV: Books 13–16* (Cambridge, 1992), sub. vv. 173–78, 341.

23. M. Ventris and J. Chadwick, *Documents in Mycenaean Greek,* 2nd ed. (Cambridge, 1973), 101 and 103f.

24. Both interpretations are advanced in, respectively, L. R. Palmer, *The Interpretation of Mycenaean Texts* (Oxford, 1963), 79; and expanded by Gregory Nagy, "The Name of Achilles: Etymology and Epic," in *Studies in Greek, Italic, and Indo-European Linguistics,* Anna Morpurgo Davies and Wolfgang Meid, eds. (Innsbruck, 1976), 209–37; and Gary B. Holland, "The Name of Achilles: A Revised Etymology," *Glotta* 71 (1993), 17–27.

25. Richard John Cunliffe, *A Lexicon of the Homeric Dialect* (Norman, OK, 1963), 271.

26. Others have regarded Peleus' shadowy presence, evoked only as a reminder of the day Achaeans mustered for the war, as evidence that "Peleus emerges as a kind of communal conscience, who spurs the Achaeans to live up to their warrior ideals": Kevin Crotty, *The Poetics of Supplication: Homer's "Iliad" and "Odyssey"* (Ithaca, NY, 1994), 28.

27. Later in the *Iliad,* an extended description is given of Achilles' great spear hewn from an ash tree grown on the Pelion Mountains, "the Pelian ash spear

which Cheiron had brought to his father / from high on Pelion to be death for fighters" (16.143–44). According to the *Cypria,* Cheiron gave this spear to Peleus as a wedding gift: *Cypria,* fragment 4, in West, *Greek Epic Fragments,* 85.

28. "The Precepts of Chiron," fragment 218, Glenn W. Most, ed. and trans., *Hesiod: The Shield. Catalogue of Women. Other Fragments* (Cambridge, MA, 2007), 297.

29. Comparisons have long been drawn between the approximately 1700 B.C. Akkadian epic of Gilgamesh and the *Iliad,* which share certain broad themes, a pair of heroic friends, and an evocation of the hero's tragic and futile strategies to thwart mortality. In such comparisons, it is usually supposed that Achilles, the hero of the *Iliad,* is the counterpart of Gilgamesh, the hero of the Akkadian epic. In fact, Achilles' wild and strangely innocent upbringing in the mountains is more suggestive of Enkidu, Gilgamesh's comrade.

30. For the suitors' wooing of Helen and oath to her father, see Hesiod, *Catalogue of Women or EHOIAI,* in Most, fragment 155 (continued), 231ff.; and Stesichorus, fragment 190, in David A. Campbell, *Greek Lyric III: Stesichorus, Ibycus, Simonides, and Others* (Cambridge, MA, 2001), fragment 190, 91. The *Cypria* relates how Thetis arranged a rendezvous between Achilles and Helen at an early stage of the war; *Cypria,* argument 11, in West, *Greek Epic Fragments,* 79.

31. Emily Vermeule, *Aspects of Death in Early Greek Art and Poetry* (Berkeley, 1979), 190f. Thetis' father, Nereus, is famously prophetic.

32. Reference is made to Achilles' son at *Iliad* 19.326–27.

33. *Cypria,* fragment 19, in West, *Greek Epic Fragments,* 97ff.

34. Achilles "vixdum exuta pueritia"—"pueritia," or "boyhood," usually ending at age seventeen. J. van Leeuwen, *Commentationes Homericae* (Leiden, 1911), 112.

35. Rhys Carpenter, *Folk Tale, Fiction, Saga in the Homeric Epics* (Berkeley and Los Angeles, 1958), 72 and, for Peleus in general, 71ff.

36. Interestingly, in the *Aethiopis,* Achilles is absent from the war not on account of a quarrel with Agamemnon but because he killed Thersites in anger and had to leave Troy to be purified in Lesbos; *Aethiopis,* fragment 1, in West, *Greek Epic Fragments,* 111. For one reason or another, Achilles in epic, then, is characteristically absent. The story with Thersites also recalls Peleus' striking association with murder and purification.

37. For a summation of distinctive late features in Achilles' characterization, see also M. L. West, "Greek Poetry 2000–700 B.C.," *Classical Quarterly,* n.s. 23 (1973), no. 2, 179–92.

38. M. L. West, *Indo-European Poetry and Myth* (Oxford, 2007), 402ff.

39. Homer "confronted traditional epic with his own new work—the realization of a fundamentally and completely different conception of epic poetry": Alfred Heubeck, "Homeric Studies Today," in Bernard C. Fenik, ed., *Homer: Tradition and Invention* (Leiden, 1978), 13.

40. Paraphrased from Dale S. Sinos, *Achilles, Patroklos and the Meaning of "Philos"* (Innsbruck, 1980), 19f.

41. For the childhood deeds of Herakles, see, for example, Pindar, *Nemean* 1.35f.; and Gantz, vol. 1, 377ff. The deeds of young Achilles are described by Pindar, *Nemean* 3.45ff.

42. For the widely held view that Phoinix was a Homeric invention, see, for example, Frederick E. Brenk, S.J., "Dear Child: The Speech of Phoinix and the Tragedy of Achilleus in the Ninth Book of the *Iliad*," *Eranos* 84 (1986), 77–86, and especially 82; Bruce Karl Braswell, "Mythological Innovation in the *Iliad*," *Classical Quarterly*, n.s., 21, no. 1 (1971), 16–26, especially 22f. On Phoinix's reshaping of the Meleager story, see Lowell Edmunds, "Myth in Homer," in Ian Morris and Barry Powell, eds., *A New Companion to Homer* (Leiden, 1997), 425ff.

43. Phoinix's parable is also wildly tactless. We have met Meleager in passing once before; he is the hero of legend who, as Homer's audience would undoubtedly have known, shared certain fateful circumstances with Achilles. In the well-known story Phoinix does not tell, Meleager's mother had custody of a firebrand, or log, to which her son's life was magically attached; angered with her son, the mother threw the brand on the fire, and Meleager died (see note 21 of this chapter). Meleager's story is a variation on the same theme that has Achilles' mother attempting to render the children of Peleus immortal by laying them in the fire—a deed that in fact killed them. In short, Phoinix's story serves to underscore the thought now uppermost in Achilles' mind—his mortality. The parallels between the story of Achilles' anger and the earlier story of the anger of Meleager are explored in a classic work by Johannes Th. Kakridis, *Homeric Researches* (Lund, 1949), 18ff.

44. See Jasper Griffin, "Homeric Words and Speakers," *Journal of Hellenic Studies* 106 (1986), 36–57; the quote appears on p. 53.

45. On *phthíō*, see Gregory Nagy, *The Best of the Achaeans: Concepts of the Hero in Archaic Greek Poetry* (Baltimore, 1979), 185ff.

46. For the geographical kingdom of Peleus and Achilles, see R. Hope Simpson and J. F. Lazenby, "The Kingdom of Peleus and Achilles," *Antiquity* 33 (1959), 102–5.

In God We Trust

1. Following the Embassy of Book Nine is Book Ten, by convention called "the Doloneia," which was widely held even in antiquity to represent a very skillful non-Iliadic (but possibly Homeric) addition to the *Iliad*. Its subject is a nocturnal, covert mission by Odysseus and Diomedes to the Trojan camp to gain information on the disposition of the enemy, who intercept a Trojan spy, Dolon, on his way to spy out the Greek camp. The night ambush; the "weapons of fear" carried by the two Greeks; the cold-blooded murder of Dolon, whom they had tricked into believing he could save his life by cooperating with them; and the subsequent slaughter of newly arrived Trojan allies under King Rhesos, whose fabulous horses Diomedes drives back to the Achaean camp, conjure a decidedly nonheroic sequence of events, more characteristic of the *Odyssey* than the *Iliad*. Much has been written about

this episode; see, for example, Georg Danek, *Studien zur Dolonie* (Vienna, 1988); and Bernard Fenik, *"Iliad X" and the "Rhesus": The Myth* (Brussels, 1964). For the escapade's resemblance to certain warrior and initiation rites, see Olga Merck Davidson, "Dolon and Rhesus in the *Iliad*," *Quaderni urbinati di cultura classica* 30 (1979), 61–66; and for the episode as an echo of Odysseus' role in the sack of Troy, see Adele J. Haft, "'The City-Sacker Odysseus' in *Iliad* 2 and 10," *Transactions of the American Philological Association* 120 (1990), 37–56.

2. For the identification of the tribes, see Richard Janko, *The "Iliad": A Commentary, Volume IV: Books 13–16* (Cambridge, 1992), sub. vv. 4–7, 42f.

3. As was done by Mary Lefkowitz, *Greek Gods, Human Lives* (New Haven, CT, 2003), 53ff.

4. *Histories*, 2. 53, Aubrey de Sélincourt, trans., *Herodotus: The Histories* (London, 2003), 117.

5. For the evidence of the Linear B tablets, see Walter Burkert, *Greek Religion: Archaic and Classical,* John Raffan, trans. (Cambridge, MA, 1985), 43ff. On the offerings to Poseidon, see John Chadwick, *The Mycenaean World* (Cambridge, 1976), 96ff.

6. On Hera and her association with cows, by way of Zeus, see M. L. West, *Indo-European Poetry and Myth* (Oxford, 2007), 184f.; also Simon Pulleyn, *Homer: "Iliad" I* (Oxford, 2000), sub. v. 551, 260.

7. West, *Indo-European Poetry and Myth*, 136.

8. Burkert, 140; for parallels with the Ugaritic/West Semitic war goddess Anat, see Bruce Louden, *The "Iliad": Structure, Myth, and Meaning* (Baltimore, 2006), 245–85.

9. Athene's skinning of a man named Pallas, in some traditions her father, and wearing of his skin is rare evidence of her darker nature: Burkert, 140, and note 21 on p. 404, for citation of (obscure) sources.

10. For the birth of Athene, see Hesiod, *Theogony*, 886ff., in Glenn W. Most, ed. and trans., *Hesiod: Theogony. Works and Days. Testimonia* (Cambridge, MA, 2006), 75ff.; "Homeric Hymn to Athena" (28 in West), 4f.; and Pindar, *Olympian* 7.35ff., in C. M. Bowra, trans., *The Odes of Pindar* (London, 1969), 165.

11. Athene's other common epithet, *Tritogéneia*, remains obscure. See G. S. Kirk, *The "Iliad": A Commentary, Volume I: Books 1–4* (Cambridge, 1985), sub. vv. 513–16, 394, for a review of attempted explanations.

12. Burkert, *Greek Religion*, 17.

13. West, *Indo-European Poetry and Myth*, 166ff.

14. For the tension between Zeus' original character and the assumed functions of a storm god, see M. L. West, *The East Face of Helicon: West Asiatic Elements in Greek Poetry and Myth* (Oxford, 1997), 114ff.

15. For Ugaritic origin, see Janko, sub. vv. 292–93, 198; and M. L. West, "The Rise of the Greek Epic," *Journal of Hellenic Studies* 108 (1988), 170.

16. Plato, *The Republic*, 378b7ff.; C.D.C. Reeve, trans. (Indianapolis, 2004), 58f.

17. "Longinus," *On the Sublime*, 9.7, in Stephen Halliwell, ed. and trans., *Aristotle "Poetics"*; W. H. Fyfe, trans., rev. by Donald Russell, *Longinus "On the*

Sublime"; Doreen C. Innes, ed. and trans., based on W. Rhys Roberts, *Demetrius "On Style"* (Cambridge, MA, 1999), 189.

18. *Diòs* is the genitive, or possessive, form of the noun "Zeus"—i.e., "of Zeus."

19. Hera's adornment, like the armor of the Homeric heroes, is inspired by styles of different epochs. Her dress would seem to be the *peplos,* a kind of draped and folded length of fabric held by pins, of post-Mycenaean date. Similarly, her mulberry-cluster earrings have a counterpart in finds from an early Dark Age tomb; there is no evidence that the Bronze Age Mycenaeans wore earrings. On the other hand, her zone, or elaborate belt, resembles the gold-edged girdle hung with thirty-five golden pendants discovered in the tomb of a Mycenaean princess. The details of Hera's finery are examined by Janko, sub. vv. 180–85, 176ff.

20. Hera's evocation of Okeanos and Tethus/Tethys is a reference to a theogony in which "Okeanos and Tethus are the primeval parents, not merely the parents of all waters," a theogony whose origin can be traced to Babylonian creation epic; Janko, sub. vv. 200–207, 180ff.

21. Other examples of divine deceptions are found, for example, in Hesiod, *Theogony,* 535ff., relating Prometheus' trick on Zeus; and the "Hymn to Hermes," which relates the many crafty exploits of the newborn god. For Demodokos' song, see *Odyssey* 8.266ff. Aphrodite's determined seduction of the mortal Anchises, related in the "Hymn to Aphrodite," has many undoubtedly conscious resemblances to Hera's seduction of Zeus.

22. Raffaele Pettazzoni, *The All-Knowing God: Researches into Early Religion and Culture,* H. J. Rose, trans. (London, 1956), 145–52; and Jasper Griffin, "The Divine Audience and the Religion of the *Iliad,*" *Classical Quarterly,* n.s. 28 no. 1 (1978), 1–22.

23. See, for example, Odysseus Tsagarakis, *Nature and Background of Major Concepts of Divine Power in Homer* (Amsterdam, 1977), 19ff.

24. My account is taken from David Clarke, *The Angel of Mons: Phantom Soldiers and Ghostly Guardians* (Chichester, 2005); the quotation appears on p. 52 and is based on the account of Private John Ewings, Second Battalion of the Royal Inniskilling Fusiliers, then a thirty-five-year-old private from County Tyrone, who recalled the events at the age of 101, in an interview for the BBC in 1980 (cited in Clarke's book as an interview by Helen Madden, BBC Northern Ireland, May 22, 1980).

25. The poem was in turn rebutted by Hugh MacDiarmid, in "Another Epitaph on an Army of Mercenaries":

It is a God-damned lie to say that these
Saved, or knew, anything worth any man's pride.
They were professional murderers and they took
Their blood money and impious risks and died.
In spite of all their kind some elements of worth
With difficulty persist here and there on earth.

Man Down

1. The list of duties, as well as characterization, of the *therápōn* follows that of P.A.L. Greenhalgh, "The Homeric Therapon and Opaon and Their Historical Implications," *Bulletin of the Institute of Classical Studies of the University of London* 29 (1982), 81–90. The list appears on p. 82.

2. Georg Autenrieth, *A Homeric Dictionary*, Robert P. Keep, trans. (Piscataway, NJ, 2002), 150.

3. The term *hetaîros*, "companion" or "comrade-in-arms," can refer to "a close comradeship between or among equals or a relationship resembling that of knight and squire to mere common participation in warfare": Richard John Cunliffe, *A Lexicon of the Homeric Dialect* (Norman, OK, 1963), 164; see also P. Chantraine, *Dictionnaire étymologique de la langue grecque*, vol. 1 (Paris, 1968), 380f. It can also, apparently, refer to more formal, institutionalized relationships, as is hinted at in a scene in Book Twenty-two, when Andromache imagines Astyanax, orphaned "among his father's *hetaîroi* . . . but one whose parents are living beats him out of the banquet / hitting him with his fists and in words also abuses him: / 'Get out, you! Your father is not dining with us'" (22.492ff.). Collectively, Achilles' Myrmidon *hetaîroi* form a loyal "band" bound to their king, of which Patroklos as an individual *hetaîros* is also a friend and companion; see George John Stagakis, "*Therapontes* and *Hetairoi*, in the *Iliad*, as Symbols of the Political Structure of the Homeric State," *Historia* 15 (1966), 408–19.

4. Hesiod, *Catalogue of Women or EHOIAI*, fragment 147, in Glenn W. Most, ed. and trans., *Hesiod: The Shield. Catalogue of Women. Other Fragments* (Cambridge, MA, 2007), 213ff. The *Cypria* makes mention of Patroklos in regard to his capture of a Trojan named Lykaon (West, *Cypria* fragment 11, 79); this same Lykaon appears toward the end of the *Iliad* in a famously pathetic scene with Achilles. These two references, then—both enlargements of Iliadic characters and incidents—are all that can be gleaned from the surviving epic tradition about Patroklos. On the other hand, he is casually introduced in the *Iliad*, in Book One, not by his name, Patroklos, but simply as "the son of Menoitios," and this has been taken as evidence that his character was already familiar to epic audiences. If so, was he familiar because he had a place in the broader epic tradition or because Homer's version of the Trojan War had already made the son of Menoitios famous? For the view that his character was not merely developed but created by Homer, see, for example, Hartmut Erbse, "Ilias und 'Patroklie,'" *Hermes* 111 (1983), 1–15. Janko, on the other hand, points out that Patroklos carries some "old epithets"—i.e., *hippeús*, "fighting from a chariot," and *hippokéleuthos*, "horse-driving"; Richard Janko, *The "Iliad": A Commentary, Volume IV: Books 13–16* (Cambridge, 1992), sub. v. 20, 317f.; likewise, on the antiquity of the phrase "strength of so-and-so," which extends to Patroklos, see G. S. Kirk, *The "Iliad": A Commentary, Volume I: Books 1–4* (Cambridge, 1985), sub. vv. 658–60, 226.

5. The details of Patroklos' background are gleaned from 18.325–26 and 23.85–87.

6. For the inspiration for Patroklos' name, see Hartmut Erbse, "Achilleus, Patroklos und Meleagros," in Jens Holzhausen, ed., *ψυχή—Seele—Anima: Festschrift für Karin Alt Zum 7 Mai 1998* (Stuttgart, 1998), 1–6.

7. Heroic companionship is discussed in C. M. Bowra, *Heroic Poetry* (London, 1961), 65ff. For Peirithoös and Theseus, see Timothy Gantz, *Early Greek Myth: A Guide to Literary and Artistic Sources*, vol. 1 (Baltimore, 1993), 277ff.

8. A concise overview of the complicated history and different versions of the epic is given in the introduction to Stephen Mitchell's translation, *Gilgamesh* (New York, 2004).

9. On the tradition and pattern of such scenes, see Bernard Fenik, *Typical Battle Scenes in the "Iliad"* (Wiesbaden, 1968), 191; an overview of the compositional function of type scenes is given in Matthew Clark, "Formulas, Metre and Type-Scenes," in Robert Fowler, ed., *The Cambridge Companion to Homer* (Cambridge, 2004), 117–38, especially 134ff.

10. *Cypria*, fragment 4, in M. L. West, ed. and trans., *Greek Epic Fragments: From the Seventh to the Fifth Century B.C.* (Cambridge, MA, 2003), 85.

11. M. L. West, *Indo-European Poetry and Myth* (Oxford, 2007), 157, note 126; *Iliad* quotes are at 16. 866f. and 18. 84f. For the gifts to Peleus, see W. R. Paton, "The Armour of Achilles," *Classical Review* 26 (1912), 1–4; and Janko, 310ff.

12. For such examples from "shamanistic" heroic saga, see Bowra, 6ff.

13. "In the *Iliad* an unkillable warrior would be an absurdity; every man must face death, and no magical armour can be allowed to exempt him from that terrible prospect." Jasper Griffin, *Homer on Life and Death* (Oxford, 1983), 167.

14. Hesiod, *Catalogue of Women*, fragment 145, in Most, 213. The testimony citing Hesiod's account does not give the name of the island, but it can reasonably be supplied as Aigina; see, for example, Gantz, vol. 1, 220. Elsewhere in the Hesiodic corpus, a snippet of a fragment cites a "Myrmidon" as the father of Aktor, who in the *Iliad* is in turn the father of Menoitios, Patroklos' father (fragment 10 [continued]), 61. See also Apollodoros, *The Library* 1.7.3; and Gantz, vol. 1, 168, 222.

15. Theagenes, fragment 17, in Felix Jacoby, *Die Fragmente der Griechischen Historiker* (Leiden, 1998), 4:511.

16. The associations are discussed in Jeffrey S. Carnes, "The Aiginetan Genesis of the Myrmidons: A Note on *Nemean* 3.13–16," *Classical World* 84 (1990–91), 41–44.

17. See Dennis R. MacDonald, "Andrew and the Ant People," *The Second Century* 8 (1991), 43–49; it is also possible that the name of Achilles' famously savage men inspired the name of the cannibal city.

18. For Myrmidons as distinct from Phthians, see Janko, sub. vv. 685–88, 133.

19. Quoted from West, *Indo-European Poetry and Myth*, 448 and 450, respectively. Warrior societies associated with wolves and wolfish acts are well attested in ancient Greece, especially in Arcadia. Typically, initiates into such secret societies must undergo ordeals involving the commission of taboo acts, such

as cannibalism; a notorious example is the "leopard men" of Africa, who dressed in leopard skins to kill and eat people. See, for example, Walter Burkert, *Homo Necans*, Peter Bing, trans. (Berkeley and Los Angeles, 1983), 83ff. For the wolf both as a model of the outlaw on the fringe of society and as exemplifying the warrior ideal, see Mary R. Gerstein, "Germanic *Warg*: The Outlaw as Werwolf," in Gerald James Larson, C. Scott Littleton, and Jaan Puhvel, eds., *Myth in Indo-European Antiquity* (Berkeley, 1974), 131–56. In Homeric epic, a hero is occasionally overcome with "wolfish rage"; see Bruce Lincoln, *Death, War, and Sacrifice: Studies in Ideology and Practice* (Chicago, 1991), 131–37.

20. The numbers are given in C. B. Armstrong, "The Casualty Lists in the Trojan War," *Greece and Rome*, series 2, 16 (1969), 30–31; Patroklos' tally includes twenty-seven named victims and an anonymous cluster of nine men killed in each of three assaults.

21. The extraordinary transport of Sarpedon in death and in particular Hera's earlier statement that a "tomb and gravestone" are "the privilege of those who have perished" have suggested to some scholars that reference is made here to Sarpedon's status as a cult hero; see Gregory Nagy, "On the Death of Sarpedon," in Carl A. Rubino and Cynthia W. Shelmerdine, eds., *Approaches to Homer* (Austin, TX, 1983), 189–217.

22. "The pair of warriors shares some of the starkest, philosophical moments of reflection in the poem"; Carroll Moulton, "The Speech of Glaukos in *Iliad* 17," *Hermes* 109 (1981), 1–8.

23. For the argument that Glaukos and Sarpedon also mirror aspects of Achilles and foreshadow his return, see ibid.

24. Jasper Griffin, "The Epic Cycle and the Uniqueness of Homer," *Journal of Hellenic Studies* 97 (1977), 39–53, especially 40; see also Janko, sub. vv. 777–867, 408f., on the stripping of armor as a folklore motif.

25. Walter Burkert, *Structure and History in Greek Mythology and Ritual* (Berkeley and Los Angeles, 1982), 60; see also Trevor Bryce, *Life and Society in the Hittite World* (Oxford, 2004), 203ff.

26. We have seen that the meaning of *therápōn*, the Greek word describing Patroklos' relationship to Achilles, is "comrade-in-arms," "henchman," or "retainer"; some scholars, however, argue that the word is not Greek in origin, but a Bronze Age adaptation of a Hittite term, *tarpan-*, meaning "ritual substitute." The seminal study of the Hittite word is by Nadia Van Brock, "Substitution rituelle," *Revue Hittite et Asianique* 65 (1959), 117–46, especially 125f.; for possible implications of the Greek borrowing in the wider epic context, see Gregory Nagy, *The Best of the Achaeans: Concepts of the Hero in Archaic Greek Poetry* (Baltimore, 1979), 292f.; also Dale S. Sinos, *Achilles, Patroklos and the Meaning of "Philos"* (Innsbruck, 1980), 29ff.

27. The intensification of threats of mutilation after death that follows the death of Patroklos in Book Twenty, is examined by Charles Segal, *The Theme of the Mutilation of the Corpse in the "Iliad"* (Leiden, 1971), 18ff.

28. This striking image of the horses stilled by grief calls to mind familiar but anachronistic images of the quiet stillness of grave stelae of the classical era; counterparts exist on Iron Age pottery used as grave markers and even on shaft-grave stelae at Mycenae that depict a weathered horse and chariot; Mark W. Edwards, *The "Iliad": A Commentary, Volume V: Books 17–20* (Cambridge, 1991), sub. vv. 434–36, 106.

29. *Aethiopis,* in West, *Greek Epic Fragments,* argument 3–4, 113. The many parallels between Achilles and Memnon and their mothers, Thetis and Eos, are discussed by Laura M. Slatkin, "The Wrath of Thetis," *Transactions of the American Philological Association* 116 (1986), 1–24.

30. For the ways in which the death of Patroklos corresponds to the death of Achilles, see Jonathan S. Burgess, *The Tradition of the Trojan War in Homer and the Epic Cycle* (Baltimore, 2001), 74ff.; and for a comprehensive bibliography of this question, see his note 98, p. 219.

31. In later eras, the extravagance of Achilles' grief invited speculation that he and Patroklos had been lovers. This belief was apparently central to a lost trilogy by Aeschylus (the *Myrmidons, Nereids, Phrygians*) and represented a trend in the fifth century B.C. and later to cast old, established myths in a homosexual light that reflected current social mores. Thus Herakles was made the lover of his companion-in-arms; King Minos became the lover of Theseus; a nephew of Daedalus became the lover of Rhadamanthys, one of the judges of the dead; and so forth. The classic work on the subject is K. J. Dover, *Greek Homosexuality,* rev. ed. (Cambridge, MA, 1989). A late-fourth-century-B.C. tradition devised a passion on Achilles' part for Troilos, one of Priam's sons, who according to authors as early as Ibycus was renowned for his "loveliness of form"; Ibycus, fragment 282.41–46, in David A. Campbell, *Greek Lyric III: Stesichorus, Ibycus, Simonides, and Others* (Cambridge, MA, 2001), 224f. The cyclic tradition, significantly, says nothing about this passion, the *Cypria* noting only that Achilles ambushes Troilos at the shrine of Apollo and slays him; West, *Greek Epic Fragments,* argument 11, 79. For the evolution of the story of Achilles and Troilos, see Gantz, vol. 2, 597ff.

    In the modern era, teachers and scholarship have traditionally laid strenuous emphasis on the fact that Briseis, the woman taken from Achilles in Book One, was his *géras,* his war prize, the implication being that her loss for Achilles meant only loss of honor, an emphasis that may be a legacy of the homoerotic culture in which the classics and the *Iliad* were so strenuously taught—namely, the British public-school system: handsome and glamorous Achilles didn't *really* like women, he was only upset because he'd lost his prize! Homer's Achilles, however, above all else, is spectacularly adept at articulating his own feelings, and in the Embassy he says, " 'Are the sons of Atreus alone among mortal men the ones / who love their wives? Since any who is a good man, and careful, / loves her who is his own and cares for her, even as I now / loved this one from my heart, though it was my spear that won her' " (9.340ff.).

    The *Iliad*'s depiction of both Achilles and Patroklos is nonchalantly heterosexual. At the conclusion of the Embassy, when Agamemnon's ambassadors have departed, "Achilles slept in the inward corner of the strong-built shelter, / and a woman lay beside him, one he had taken from Lesbos, / Phorbas' daughter, Diomede of the fair colouring. / In the other corner Patroklos went to bed; with him also / was a girl, Iphis the fair-girdled, whom brilliant Achilles / gave him, when he took sheer Skyros" (9.663ff.).

The nature of the relationship between Achilles and Patroklos played an unlikely role in a lawsuit of the mid-fourth century B.C., brought by the orator Aeschines against one Timarchus, a prominent politician in Athens who had charged him with treason. Hoping to discredit Timarchus prior to the treason trial, Aeschines attacked Timarchus' morality, charging him with pederasty. Since the same charge could have been brought against Aeschines, the orator takes pains to differentiate between his impulses and those of the plaintiff: "The distinction which I draw is this—to be in love with those who are beautiful and chaste is the experience of a kind-hearted and generous soul"; Aeschines, *Contra Timarchus* 137, in C. D. Adams, trans., *The Speeches of Aeschines* (Cambridge, MA, 1958), 111. For proof of such love, Aeschines cited the relationship between Achilles and Patroklos; his citation is of great interest for representing the longest extant quotation of Homer by an ancient author.

32. The argument that Achilles' unexpected compromise of the loan of his armor "is the linchpin holding the poem's two halves together" is made by Janko, 310; see also Erbse, "Ilias und 'Patroklie,'" 1–15.

33. Jonathan Shay, *Achilles in Vietnam: Combat Trauma and the Undoing of Character* (New York, 1995), 40.

34. The incident at Walter Reed is described by Esther Schrader, "These Unseen Wounds Cut Deep," *Los Angeles Times*, November 14, 2004.

35. John Keegan, *The First World War* (New York, 2000), 426f.

No Hostages

1. A knotty question of concern to more literal-minded scholars is why if Patroklos could wear the armor of Achilles, could Achilles not now wear the armor of Patroklos? Perhaps Patroklos had no armor and was not after all a "companion-in-arms," but a "retainer"? See John Scott, "Achilles and the Armour of Patroklos," *Classical Journal* 13 (1917–18), 682–86. For the view of a mid-twentieth-century man-at-arms, that the preoccupation with stripping fallen warriors of their armor reflects the modern tactic of "recovery battles" to obtain valuable weaponry, see General Sir John Hackett, "Reflections upon Epic Warfare," *Proceedings of the Classical Association* 68 (1971), 13–37.

2. The flame around Achilles' head and his murderous cry have counterparts in other Indo-European myths. See Julian Baldick, *Homer and the Indo-Europeans: Comparing Mythologies* (London, 1994), 84f.

3. The poignancy of this bathing scene is enhanced by its play upon standard epic scenes of hospitality and feasting: "Then when the maids had bathed

them and anointed them with oil, / and put cloaks of thick fleece and tunics on them . . ." (*Odyssey* 4.49f.). On such bathing, see Alfred Heubeck, Stephanie West, and J. B. Hainsworth, *A Commentary on Homer's "Odyssey,"* vol. 1 (Oxford, 1990), sub. vv. 3.464ff, 189.

4. H. L. Lorimer, *Homer and the Monuments* (London, 1950), 73.

5. Readers will be entertained to learn that the modern medical opinion is that Hephaistos' condition is due to "bilateral club foot," a "congenital anomaly"; Christos S. Bartsocas, "Hephaestus and Clubfoot," *Journal of the History of Medicine and Allied Sciences* 27 (1972), 450–51.

6. This is Hephaistos' second catastrophic plunge to earth recalled in the *Iliad*, the first being that described in Book One, when the smith reminds Hera of how Zeus flung him from Olympos when he tried to rescue her from Zeus' punishment (1.586ff.). Possibly, these two falls are "doublets" of each other, one being an early "genuine" tradition and the other a late innovation inspired by the first. Of the two, the second seems most likely to be genuine, in great part because of the very ancient mythic pairing of fire and nurturing water, and because Hera's disgust at her son's lameness is related elsewhere: "My son has turned out a weakling among the gods, Hephaestus of the withered legs, whom I myself bore. I picked him up and threw him in the broad sea." "Hymn to Apollo," vv. 316ff., in M. L. West, ed. and trans., *Homeric Hymns. Homeric Apocrypha. Lives of Homer* (Cambridge, MA, 2003), 95.

7. Other Indo-European examples of the pairing of fire and water are given by M. L. West, *Indo-European Poetry and Myth* (Oxford, 2007), 270ff.

8. See, for example, Walter Burkert, *Greek Religion: Archaic and Classical,* John Raffan, trans. (Cambridge, MA, 1985), 167.

9. The role of the smith as guardian is discussed by Dean A. Miller, *The Epic Hero* (Baltimore, 2000), 260ff., and especially 266f. Hephaistos, by most accounts, has no children of his own; see Timothy Gantz, *Early Greek Myth: A Guide to Literary and Artistic Sources,* vol. 1 (Baltimore, 1993), 77f. The smith of epic and legend is typically childless (Miller, 268), a fact that may have to do with the sacred, taboo nature of his art, which may have isolated him from marriage. In 1984, the author witnessed a traditional, highly ritualized iron smelting in Malawi, in Central East Africa, where the smelting site and all immediately surrounding area was strictly taboo to women; the author was excepted as a *mazungu,* or genderless "white person."

10. Of the many news stories reporting families' purchase of body armor for their sons and husbands in Iraq, see, for example, Associated Press, "Soldiers in Iraq Still Buying Their Own Body Armor," *USA Today,* March 26, 2004.

11. *Aethiopis,* argument 2, in M. L. West, ed. and trans., *Greek Epic Fragments: From the Seventh to the Fifth Century B.C.* (Cambridge, MA, 2003), 111. Evidence from vase paintings from as early as the mid-sixth century B.C. and later poetry indicate that in some traditions the arms Achilles carried with him from Phthia to Troy were not gifts from his father but were another set of armor made by Hephaistos and given to him by Thetis. See, for example, Euripides, *Iphigenia in Aulis,* 1070ff. The different traditions are discussed

in K. Friis Johansen, *The "Iliad" in Early Greek Art* (Copenhagen, 1967), 107ff.

12. Modern attempts to reconstruct the shield of Achilles have foundered on practical details. The usual heroic shield was made of layers, or folds, of tough ox hide stretched over a frame. The "five folds composing the shield" of Achilles, however, were made of five layers of metal: "the god of the dragging feet had made five folds on it, / two of bronze on the outside and on the inside two of tin / and between them the single gold" (20.270ff.). Since in reality only bronze is capable of withstanding the shock of a bronze-headed spear, which would tear through soft tin and gold, the shield's construction appears to owe more to poetry than to fact. On the other hand, the detail and assurance with which the shield's decorative scenes are described suggest that Homer had actual, as opposed to mythic, examples of metal craftmanship in mind. Both "ages of Homer"—the Mycenaean Bronze Age and the eighth century B.C. Age of Iron—provide examples of the decorative metalwork suggestive of the shield. Graves of Mycenae have yielded spectacular metal relics of the late Bronze Age, including diadems, breastplates, and ornamental boxes of beaten gold; bronze daggers with inlay of hunting scenes wrought in silver and gold set in blue-black niello; and intricate cloisonné. Photographs of these famous objects can be found in many books on Greek art; see, for example, Sp. Marinatos and M. Hirmer, *Crete and Mycenae* (New York, 1961), plates xxxv–xxxviii, 95–98. Bronze, however, is worked cold, not on a hot forge with hammer and tongs, and in this essential respect Hephaistos most resembles the ironworker. For possible Iron Age models, see note 17 below. Possibly relics—and memories of relics—of the Mycenaean Bronze Age inform Homer's description of Hephaistos' art, while the Bronze Age techniques that produced such art were unknown: D.H.F. Gray, "Metalworking in Homer," *Journal of Hellenic Studies* 74 (1954), 1–15. For an overview of the techniques reflected in the description of the crafting of the shield, see Mark W. Edwards, *The "Iliad": A Commentary, Volume V: Books 17–20* (Cambridge, 1991), 201ff.

13. Certain features, such as the assembly in the marketplace and agricultural development, are particularly suggestive of the pre-*polis* communities of the eighth century B.C. See, for example, Dean C. Hammer, "'Who Shall Readily Obey?': Authority and Politics in the *Iliad*," *Phoenix* 51, no. 1 (1997), 1–24, and especially 15; and Gregory Nagy, "The Shield of Achilles," in Susan Langdon, ed., *New Light on a Dark Age: Exploring the Culture of Geometric Greece* (Columbia, MO, 1997), 194–208.

14. For the dating of the *Aspis*, see Richard Janko, "The Shield of Heracles and the Legend of Cycnus," *Classical Quarterly* 36, no. 1 (1986), 38–59.

15. Hesiod, *The Shield*, 144ff., in Glenn W. Most, ed. and trans., *Hesiod: The Shield. Catalogue of Women. Other Fragments* (Cambridge, MA, 2007), 13ff.

16. Hugh G. Evelyn-White, *Hesiod, the Homeric Hymns and Homerica* (Cambridge, MA, 1982), xxiv.

17. Significantly, Agamemnon's corselet, with its cobalt serpents and other images of terror, had been given to him as a "guest present" from the king of Kypros (Cyprus) (11.33ff.), and shields and large circular bowls decorated with engravings and hammered relief have been found dating from the eighth and seventh centuries B.C., from Cyprus and Crete. Arranged in circular bands, the scenes of hunting, lion attacks on bulls, pastoral life, and even the siege of a city suggest a pictorial narrative as on Achilles' shield. See Glenn Markoe, *Phoenician Bronze and Silver Bowls from Cyprus and the Mediterranean* (Berkeley and Los Angeles, 1984), 51ff.; and Jan Paul Crielaard, "Homer, History and Archaeology: Some Remarks on the Date of the Homeric World," in Jan Paul Crielaard, ed., *Homeric Questions: Essays in Philology, Ancient History and Archaeology, Including the Papers of a Conference Organized by the Netherlands Institute at Athens (15 May 1993)* (Amsterdam, 1995), 201–88, and especially 218ff.

18. While the elements that constitute the archetypal heroic journey from withdrawal to return—a journey to a mysterious place, tests or trials that must be overcome, a symbolic death, and heroic return—are widely held to be manifest in the "journey" of Achilles, from withdrawal and isolation to reintegration with his community, it should be noted that imaginative rearrangement and special pleading are required to make Achilles fit the archetype—that Patroklos is the companion of his lonely journey, that his trial or test (doing battle with the river Skamandros) follows rather than precedes his return, and so forth. But see William R. Nethercut, "The Epic Journey of Achilles," *Ramus* 5 (1976), 1–17.

19. "To Demeter," in West, *Homeric Hymns*, vv. 302ff., 57ff. For an examination of this pattern, see Mary Louise Lord, "Withdrawal and Return: An Epic Story Pattern in the Homeric Hymn to Demeter and in the Homeric Poems," *Classical Journal* 62 (1967), 241–48. Hittite texts preserve mythic stories of a "vanishing deity" that tell of the departure of a god—often on account of anger—and the disastrous consequences to mankind of his absence; Harry A. Hoffner Jr. and Gary M. Beckman, eds., *Hittite Myths*, 2nd ed. (Atlanta, 1998), 14ff.

20. P. Chantraine, *Dictionnaire etymologique de la langue grecque*, vol. 3 (Paris, 1974), 696f.

21. P. Considine, "Some Homeric Terms for Anger," *Acta Classica* 9 (1966), 15–25, argues that *mēnis* "is a solemn *epic* term for any wrath, divine or human," 21, a weaker reading than Watkins, below.

22. Calvert Watkins, "On μῆνις," *Indo-European Studies* 3 (1977), 686–722; the quote is from 694f.

23. This digressive story tells how Hera tricked Zeus into swearing that a son "'born of the blood of your generation'" that day would be "'lord over all those dwelling about him'" (19.105ff). Hera then induced premature labor in one woman and stayed the birth of Herakles; thus the tyrannical and unworthy Eurystheus came to be lord over the hero Herakles. This digressive story enforces "the theme of a superior hero in the service of an inferior

king," so central to the *Iliad*. See Olga Merck Davidson, "Indo-European Dimensions of Herakles in *Iliad* 19.95–133," *Arethusa* 13 (1980), 197–202, especially 200.

24. Denys Page rightly sees that "the parable of Meleager loses all its colour and significance if it is addressed *to a man to whom it does not apply*—a man who is going to get the full compensation after all." Denys L. Page, *History and the Homeric "Iliad"* (Berkeley and Los Angeles, 1959), 312f.; to Page, the disjunction between Phoinix's paradigm and Achilles' actual circumstances is, bizarrely, evidence of multiple authors at work in the *Iliad,* rather than an ironic highlighting of how little stories of men of old apply to godlike Achilles—and to his revelation at the time of the Embassy that life is more precious than all prizes.

25. Ibid., 314.

26. James I. Armstrong, "The Arming Motif in the *Iliad*," *American Journal of Philology* 79, no. 4 (1958), 337–54; the quote appears on p. 350.

27. Xanthos' voice is stopped by the Erinyes, "the Furies," and this otherwise obscure detail suggests the conflation of different traditions pertaining to Hera and horses, and a prophetic son of Erinys; see Sarah Iles Johnston, "Xanthus, Hera and the Erinyes (*Iliad* 19.400–418)," *Transactions of the American Philological Association* 122 (1992), 85–98.

28. Flyting or "fliting," according to the *Oxford English Dictionary,* is "poetical invective; originally a kind of contest practiced by the Scottish poets of the 16th c., in which two persons assailed each other alternately with tirades of abusive verse"; a good epic example is found in *Beowulf* (499–606).

29. On the meeting of the two traditions, see Gregory Nagy, *The Best of the Achaeans: Concepts of the Hero in Archaic Greek Poetry* (Baltimore, 1979), 265ff.

30. A popular theory holds that the prominence given to Aineias at this key moment in the epic (as also in the "Hymn to Aphrodite") is evidence that Book Twenty and the "Hymn" "were composed for a court of barbarian princes in the Troad who believed themselves descended from Aineias"; Peter M. Smith, "Aineiadai as Patrons of *Iliad* XX and the Homeric 'Hymn to Aphrodite,'" *Harvard Studies in Classical Philology* 85 (1981), 17–58. Smith counters this theory with a close review of the ancient sources relating the story of Aineias after the fall of Troy. This review, however, does not explain Poseidon's statement in the *Iliad* that "'it is destined that he [Aineias] shall be the survivor'" (*Iliad* 20.302).

31. Jonathan Shay, *Achilles in Vietnam: Combat Trauma and the Undoing of Character* (New York, 1995), 78f. In more recent conflicts, the rampage by U.S. Marines in the town of Haditha, on the Euphrates River, in which twenty-four Iraqi civilians were killed, was triggered by the death of a lance corporal in the unit; see, for example, Ellen Knickmeyer, "In Haditha, Memories of a Massacre," *Washington Post,* May 27, 2006.

32. That everything, including Achilles, has changed since Patroklos' death is underscored by a simple refrain that runs through Achilles' speeches from the time of his knowledge of Patroklos' death until the funeral: *nún dé*—"but

now"—i.e., in contrast to all previous time; Samuel Eliot Basset, "Achilles' Treatment of Hektor's Body," *Transactions of the American Philological Association* 64 (1933), 41–65, especially 58f.

33. "When human foes are lacking, heroic man fights against powers of nature or monsters"; C. M. Bowra, *Heroic Poetry* (London, 1961), 49, cites examples of such battles, from Gilgamesh to Beowulf. For Near Eastern archetypes, see Trevor Bryce, *Life and Society in the Hittite World* (Oxford, 2004), 216f.

34. All evidence indicates that Apollo's origins lie in the Near East and that he was a late arrival among the Greek Olympians; his name (like Aphrodite's) does not appear in the Linear B tablets. The suggestive name *-appaliuna* (the text is broken), which some scholars read as a reference to Apollo, appears at the end of a long list of divine witnesses invoked to solemnize a late-fourteenth-century-B.C. treaty between the Hittite king and Alaksandu of Wilusa; see "Treaty 13, Between Muwattalli II of Hatti and Alaksandu of Wilusa," in Gary Beckman, *Hittite Diplomatic Texts*, 2nd ed. (Atlanta, 1999), 92. The treaty's possible reference to "Apollo" is discussed in Trevor Bryce, *The Trojans and Their Neighbours* (Abingdon, Oxon, 2006), 119. Manfred Hutter, "Aspects of Luwian Religion," in H. Craig Melchert, ed., *The Luwians* (Leiden, 2003), 267, is more cautious: "Whether the fragmentary name of the god]appaliunas is identical with Apollo known from Greek sources remains to be seen. It is possible, but there is presently neither a real argument to prove this point nor to make this god a Luwian one." If the association between the names is sound, however, it would be evidence that an Anatolian Apollo was among the guardians of historical Troy, and could account in some part for his malice toward Achilles in the *Iliad*.

35. General discussions of Apollo's origins and character are found in Burkert, *Greek Religion*, 51f. and 143ff.

36. The earliest reference to the Hyperboreans is in a prose outline of a lost poem by Alcaeus (c. 600) by the fourth-century-A.D. rhetorician Himerius, which describes Apollo's journey to the north in a chariot pulled by swans; Himerius, *Orations* 48.10–11, in David A. Campbell, *Greek Lyric I: Sappho. Alcaeus* (Cambridge, MA, 1982), Alcaeus 307(c), 355. For Apollo's withdrawn nature, see Walter F. Otto, *The Homeric Gods*, Moses Hadas, trans. (Boston, 1954), 62ff.

37. Apollo's association with the lyre is given poetic explanation in the Homeric Hymn "To (Delian) Apollo," vv. 130ff., and "Hymn to Hermes," vv. 499ff. Hera's words, however, appear to refer to a tradition touched upon in a surviving fragment of a lost tragedy by Aeschylus, in which a heartbroken Thetis recalls how Apollo knew of Achilles' tragically destined short life but, dissembling at her wedding, "sang that I would be blest with a son / who would live a long life, unacquainted with suffering," as Thetis cries out, in this fragment:

"And, saying all this, he sang a paian in praise of my great good fortune cheering my heart.

And I thought the mouth of Apollo could not lie,
rich as it is with prophetic skill.
But he who sang of this, he who was there at the feast,
he who said these things, he it was who killed
my son."

Translation from Jennifer R. March, "Peleus and Achilles in the *Catalogue of Women*," *Proceedings of the XVIII International Congress of Papyrology, Athens 25–31 May 1986* (Athens, 1988), 345–52. The fragment is in Stephan Radt, ed., *Tragicorum Graecorum Fragmenta, vol 3. Aeschylus* (Göttingen, 1985), fragment 350, 416ff.; the verses are also quoted by Plato in the *Republic* (2.383b). For the argument that the Aeschylean fragment is incompatible with the *Iliad*'s depiction of Thetis as a mother possessed of unwavering foreknowledge of her son's early death, see Jonathan S. Burgess, "Untrustworthy Apollo and the Destiny of Achilles: *Iliad* 24.55–63," *Harvard Studies in Classical Philology* 102 (2004), 21–40; this argument, however, does not take into account the keen sense of betrayal that Thetis bears throughout the epic, nor the fact that although she might indeed have known of her son's early death all the days of his actual life, Apollo's prophecy was sung before his conception.

38. Both also share a shadowy and mostly unexamined relationship with wolves. For Apollo's numerous associations with wolves, see Daniel E. Gershenson, *Apollo the Wolf-god* (McLean, VA, 1991). Achilles' association comes through his grandfather Aiakos; for the sources to this obscure tradition, see Gantz, vol. 1, 227.

39. Robert J. Rabel, "Apollo as a Model for Achilles in the *Iliad*," *American Journal of Philology* 111, no. 4, 429–40. The use of the same diction to describe the ability of Apollo and Achilles (and Zeus and Thetis) to dispatch or ward off destruction is examined by Laura M. Slatkin, "The Wrath of Thetis," *Transactions of the American Philological Association* 116 (1986), 1–24, especially 15f.

40. The proem is discussed in G. S. Kirk, *The "Iliad": A Commentary, Volume I: Books 1–4* (Cambridge, 1985), 52f.

41. Burkert, *Greek Religion*, 202. A number of explanations for the hostility between the two have been offered; the ritual antagonism is examined by Nagy, *The Best of the Achaeans*, 61ff. and 289ff. The possibility of Achilles' anger having been caused by his murder of Trojan Troilos in a sanctuary of Apollo is raised by Malcolm Davies, "The Judgement of Paris and *Iliad* Book XXIV," *Journal of Hellenic Studies* 101 (1981), 56–62, especially 60.

42. Other predictions of his death specifically at the hands of Apollo are given at 19.416f. by Xanthos (who refers to the agents as "'a god and a mortal'"), and at 22.359f. by Hektor. In one tradition, Apollo is also the slayer of Meleager, hero of Phoinix's endlessly tactless paradigm; see Hesiod, *Catalogue of Women or EHOIAI*, in Most, fragment 22.10ff., 75.

43. Achilles' chase under the walls of Troy closely parallels the circumstances

of his own death: "Achilles puts the Trojans to flight and chases them into the city, but is killed by Paris and Apollo," records the blunt summary of the lost *Aethiopis;* West, *Greek Epic Fragments,* argument 3, 113.

44. Lord Moran, *The Anatomy of Courage* (London, 2007), 67.

Everlasting Glory

1. Walter Burkert, *Greek Religion: Archaic and Classical,* John Raffan, trans. (Cambridge, MA, 1985), 60.

2. Indirectly, it has been evoked in the pathetically beautiful words that describe the moment death descends upon both Patroklos and Hektor, when the "soul flew from his limbs and started for Hades, / lamenting her fate, abandoning manhood and all its young vigor" (16.855ff. and 22.362). These verses are also noteworthy for containing a notable archaism: the phrase *lipous' androtēta kaì hēbēn*—"leaving manhood and its young vigor"—does not scan, or fit the hexameter meter, as it stands but was shaped for the Mycenaean or possibly even earlier form **anṛtāta,* suggesting that poets were singing of dying warriors from very ancient times. See Richard Janko, *The "Iliad": A Commentary, Volume IV: Books 13–16* (Cambridge, 1992), sub. vv. 855–58, 420f.

3. Archaeology shows that at the end of the Dark Ages, hero-cult worship spread throughout Greece, into the emerging city-states. The many later descriptions given in surviving literature show that worship at these hero cults was essentially chthonic, or relating to the Underworld—rites that involved the sacrifice of black animals and libations of blood, enacted at dusk around a low hearth. Sometimes the heroes worshipped by the cults were the inventions of a later age, pragmatically calculated to suit a particular location or need, or revered historical personages awarded this ultimate honor; but the most common cults were those for heroes named in epic. For the appearance of hero cult at the end of the Iron Age, see Peter G. Calligas, "Hero-cult in Early Iron Age Greece," in Robin Hägg, Nanno Marinatos, and Gullög C. Nordquist, eds., *Early Greek Cult Practice* (Stockholm, 1988), 229–34; Calligas believes that the contemporary emergence of both hero cult and epic may represent parallel developments rather than be causal. The complexities of different types of cults are reviewed through the archaeological record by A. Mazarakis Ainian, "Reflections on Hero Cults in Early Iron Age Greece," in Robin Hägg, ed., *Ancient Greek Hero Cult* (Stockholm, 1999), 9–36, who argues for epic as the shaping force. For the argument that hero cults arose under the influence of epic but were also related to local burial practices, see J. N. Coldstream, "Hero-Cults in the Age of Homer," *Journal of Hellenic Studies* 96 (1976), 8–17. For discussion of different types of such cults, see Lewis Richard Farnell, *Greek Hero Cults and Ideas of Immortality* (Oxford, 1921); a list of cults named in ancient sources is at 403ff. An examination of the evidence for blood offerings at hero cults suggests that the offering was made as an extension and modification of the common *thysia,* or sacrifice of a burnt offering; "In those cases, the blood may have

functioned as a reference both to the battlefield *sphagia* [sacrificial slaughter] and to the fact that the hero had died, and thus acquired his heroic status, as a consequence of war"; G. Ekroth, "Offerings of Blood in Greek Hero-cults," in V. Pirenne-Delforge and E. Suárez de la Torre, eds., *Héros et héroïnes dans les myths et les cultes grecs: actes du Colloque organisé à l'Université de Valladolid du 26 au 29 mai 1999* (Liège, 2000), (*Kernos*; supplement 10), 263–80; quoted passage is on p. 279. As discussed, some scholars have seen evidence of cult ritual in the description of the death of Sarpedon and the transference of his body to his homeland (16.456f.); see chapter "Man Down," note 22.

4. The Styx is the only river of Hades named in the *Iliad* (2.755, 8.369, 14.271, and 15.37). The *Odyssey*, however, gives a clearer picture of Underworld geography:

"There Pyriphlegethon and Kokytos, which is an off-break
from the water of the Styx, flow into Acheron. There is
a rock there, and the junction of two thunderous rivers."
　　　　　　　　—Odyssey 10.513–15

5. The interment of Patroklos' bones is closely parsed, with a speculative sketch of how the tomb was placed over the pyre, by Angeliki Petropoulou, "The Interment of Patroklos (*Iliad* 23.252–57)," *American Journal of Philology* 109 (1988), 482–95.

6. No armor, however, is cremated with Patroklos; see chapter "No Hostages," note 1.

7. M. L. West, *Indo-European Poetry and Myth* (Oxford, 2007), 496f.; West points out that in all probability the Indo-Europeans "did not practice cremation, which first appears among the Hittites and spreads into Greece and northern Europe from the thirteenth century B.C.E." Quote is on p. 498.

8. "Rare Mycenaean Grave Unearthed," *Friends of Troy Newsletter*, December 2007, p. 2.

9. Trevor Bryce, *The Trojans and Their Neighbours* (Abingdon, Oxon, 2006), 22f.; and Trevor Bryce, *Life and Society in the Hittite World* (Oxford, 2002), 176ff.

10. For the heroic burial of Lefkandi, see Mervyn Popham, E. Touloupa, and L. H. Sackett, "The Hero of Lefkandi," *Antiquity* 56 (1982), 169–74 and plates xxii–xxv. The burials and grave goods are described in more detail by M. R. Popham, P. G. Calligas, and L. H. Sackett, eds., *Lefkandi II: The Protogeometric Building at Toumba, Part 2: The Excavation, Architecture and Finds* (Oxford, 1993), especially 19ff., and plates 15–22. Evidence of the sacrifice of domestic animals, perhaps on their master's pyre, predates Homer; see, for example, the remarkable late Middle Helladic horse burial described by Evangelia Protonotariou-Deilaki, "The Tumuli of Mycenae and Dendra," in Robin Hägg and Gullög C. Nordquist, eds., *Celebrations of Death and*

Divinity in the Bronze Age Argolid (Stockholm, 1990), 85–102. Examples of Iron Age tumuli built over pyres are given in Nicholas Richardson, *The "Iliad": A Commentary, Volume VI: Books 21–24* (Cambridge, 1996), sub. vv. 245–48, 198f.; and cremations, sub. v. 254, 199f. That despite archaeological matches with individual elements of Patroklos' funeral, "no one burial containing all of the elements or on anywhere near the scale" has yet been discovered is emphasized by Dennis D. Hughes, *Human Sacrifice in Ancient Greece* (London, 1991), 66.

11. This outrage was widely covered; see, for example, "Greek Antiquities: Victims of Demand for Housing," *New York Times*, October 2, 1980, p. A12.

12. Again, Mycenaean practices are the least certain: sixteenth-century-B.C. grave stelae, or markers, found at Mycenae depicting a warrior mounted behind a chariot pulled by a straining horse may possibly commemorate athletic contests for the deceased; they may also, however, represent hunting or military scenes; Emily Vermeule, *Greece in the Bronze Age* (Chicago, 1964), 90ff. Other possible evidence of Bronze Age competitions in footracing, boxing, and charioteering is described in Eva Rystead, "Mycenaean Runners—including APOBATAI," in E. B. French and K. A. Wardle, eds., *Problems in Greek Prehistory* (Bristol, 1988), 437–42.

13. Charles Carter, "Athletic Contests in Hittite Religious Festivals," *Journal of Near Eastern Studies* 47, no. 3 (July 1988), 185–87.

14. Many of these festal contests were choral or poetic. In his *Works and Days*, a dour farmer's almanac in verse, Hesiod records how he had sailed across the sea "for the games of valorous Amphidamas—that great-hearted man's sons had announced and established many prizes—and there, I declare, I gained victory with a hymn, and carried off a tripod with handles." Hesiod, *Works and Days*, 654f., in Glenn W. Most, ed. and trans., *Hesiod: Volume 1, Theogony. Works and Days. Testimonia* (Cambridge, MA, 2006), 141.

15. On the social function of the games, see, for example, James M. Redfield, *Nature and Culture in the "Iliad": The Tragedy of Hector* (Chicago, 1975), 210.

16. When Apollo's son Asklepios was killed by a thunderbolt, Apollo revenged himself by killing the Cyclops, a son of Zeus, who had made the bolt. As punishment for this crime, Apollo was sentenced to serve a year as a laborer to a mortal, and it was Eumelos' father, Admetos, who became his—respectful and kind—employer. The horses Eumelos drives were a gift from Apollo to his father; *Iliad* 2.763ff., and see Timothy Gantz, *Early Greek Myth: A Guide to Literary and Artistic Sources*, vol. 1 (Baltimore, 1993), 92.

17. For Meriones' Minoan associations, see T.B.L. Webster, *From Mycenae to Homer* (New York, 1964), 104f., 117f.

18. In the *Iliad*'s immediate sequel, the *Aethiopis*, Antilochos fulfills the role of Patroklos in the *Iliad*, being Achilles' closest companion, whose death Achilles avenges. Some scholars believe that Achilles' smile for Antilochos here is a nod toward this future role; see M. M. Wilcock, "The Funeral Games of

Patroclus," *Bulletin of the Institute of Classical Studies of the University of London* 20 (1973), 1–11.

19. The political implications of the games are well discussed in Dean C. Hammer, "'Who Shall Readily Obey?' Authority and Politics in the *Iliad*," *Phoenix* 51, no. 2 (1997), 1–24, especially 13ff.

20. The authenticity of lines 23 to 30, which include this passage, has been hotly contested since antiquity on account of both linguistic features and sense (i.e., would the gods countenance the stealing of a body? Athene and Hera should not engage in a beauty contest with Aphrodite, and so forth). For a summation of the arguments for and against their inclusion, see Richardson, sub. vv. 23–30, 276ff., whose conclusion is that "it is probably fair to say that the passage as a whole should be regarded as part of the original poem."

21. Bryce, *The Trojans and Their Neighbours*, 124.

22. "To Hermes," in M. L. West, ed. and trans., *Homeric Hymns. Homeric Apocrypha. Lives of Homer* (Cambridge, MA, 2003), vv. 13–15, 115.

23. The term "is usually rendered as 'slayer of Argos,' although this would constitute an unusual linguistic formation (*argei-* instead of *argo-*), and we must allow for the possibility that the myth was generated by the (no longer understood) epithet." Gantz, vol. 1, 109. Several alternative readings are offered: for "dog slayer," watchdogs being the enemy of the night thief, see M. L. West, *Hesiod: Works and Days* (Oxford, 1980), 368f.; and for "dragon" or "serpent slayer," see S. Davis, "Argeiphontes in Homer—The Dragon-Slayer," *Greece & Rome* 22, no. 64 (February 1953), 33–38.

24. Walter F. Otto, *The Homeric Gods: The Spiritual Significance of the Greek Religion* (Boston, 1964), 109.

25. Burkert, *Greek Religion*, 158. On Hermes as the god of boundaries, and breaker of boundaries, see ibid., 156ff.; on herms and their "animal ritual" origins, see Walter Burkert, *Structure and History in Greek Mythology and Ritual* (Berkeley and Los Angeles, 1982), 39ff.

26. For Priam's journey to Hades, see, for example, Cedric H. Whitman, *Homer and the Heroic Tradition* (New York, 1965), 217f. The "Odyssean" overtone of Book Twenty-four is discussed in Richardson, 21ff.

27. The passage is discussed by Bruce Heiden, "The Simile of the Fugitive Homicide, *Iliad* 24.480–84: Analogy, Foiling, and Allusion," *American Journal of Philology* 119 (1998), 1–10.

28. Pindar, *Isthmian* 8.21–24 and *Nemean* 8.7–8, respectively, in C. M. Bowra, trans., *The Odes of Pindar* (London, 1969), 52, 215.

29. Plato, *Gorgias* 524a, where Aiakos is the judge of the dead of Europe, as the others are of the Asian dead; also Gantz, vol. 1, 220f., for other sources.

30. A linguistic anomaly underscores Achilles' relationship with his distinguished grandfather. Priam is instructed to come "to the son of Peleus," a phrase in the Greek rendered by the single word *Pēleïōnáde.*" The use of *-de* to indicate the direction of something is employed by Homer with no other personal name—but is paralleled by the common phrase *Aïdósde*—"to the house of Hades"; see Richardson, sub. v. 338, 308. Achilles' association with

Phthia—"the Waste Land"—his Underworld appearance in the *Odyssey*, and the notable chthonic elements of his role in this last book of the *Iliad* have led some scholars to conjecture that he was once a god of the dead; see Hildebrecht Hommel, *Der Gott Achilleus* (Heidelberg, 1980), especially 25ff.

31. The number of Niobe's children varies; different ancient citations report variously that Hesiod sang of "ten sons and ten daughters" and "nine and ten"; Hesiod, *Catalogue of Women or EHOIAI*, in Glenn W. Most, *Hesiod: Volume 2, The Shield. Catalogue of Women. Other Fragments* (Cambridge, MA, 2007), fragments 126 and 127, respectively, 195. For the possibility that the inconsistency between Homer and Hesiod points to two traditions, see Edm. Liénard, "Les Niobides," *Latomus* 2 (1938), 20–29. The numerous sources for this story are given in Gantz, vol. 2, 536ff.

32. Bruce Karl Braswell, "Mythological Innovation in the *Iliad*," *Classical Quarterly*, n.s. 21, no. 1 (1971), 16–26.

33. For a close examination of the paradigm, see Richardson, sub. vv. 596–632, 339ff.

34. That "the people" were turned to stone is a detail undoubtedly inspired by the petrification of Niobe herself, yet it is interesting that there was a tradition that Thetis caused a wolf to be turned to stone for devouring cattle of Peleus; in another version, the lithification was caused by the wife of Aiakos, Psamathe, who was, like Thetis, a daughter of Nereus; see Gantz, vol. 1, 227.

35. The excerpt from this letter is quoted from Lawrence Van Gelder, "Singer Buys Rare World War I Letter," *New York Times* (November 9, 2006), reporting on the purchase of the anonymous letter by the Irish singer Chris de Burgh. See also Malcolm Brown and Shirley Seaton, *Christmas Truce: The Western Front, December 1914* (London, 2001).

36. The possibility of a continuous habitation of Troy from its fall until Homer's age, and the "narrative" implications, is raised by Michael Wood, *In Search of the Trojan War*, rev. ed. (London, 2005), 298f.

37. Calvert Watkins, "The Language of the Trojans," in Machteld J. Mellink, ed., *Troy and the Trojan War* (Bryn Mawr, PA, 1986), 45–62 (for quotation see 58f.).

38. Strabo, *Geography* 13.1.27, in Horace Leonard Jones, trans., *Strabo: Geography*, vol. 6 (Cambridge, MA, 1929), 53. The traveler was Demetrius of Scepsis, whose lost work on some sixty lines of the Trojan Catalogue was said to have filled sixty books.

39. Philostratus, *Life of Apollonius*, 4.11–13.

40. *Aethiopis*, fragment 1, in M. L. West, ed. and trans., *Greek Epic Fragments: From the Seventh to the Fifth Century B.C.* (Cambridge, MA, 2003), 115.

41. But what part of his foot? Achilles' ankle is most commonly mentioned, although later writers refer to the sole of his foot. The latter accords with Paris' wounding of Diomedes in the flat of his foot in Book Eleven (11.369ff.), which is often taken to be a doublet of his later striking of Achilles; see Bryan Hainsworth, *The "Iliad": A Commentary, Volume III: Books 9–12* (Cambridge,

1993), sub. vv. 369–83, 267. On the exact place and cause of Achilles' death, see Gantz, vol. 2, 625ff. Achilles' heel is referred to only in the work of the first-century-A.D. poet Statius; *Achilleid* 1.133–34, 1.268–70, and 1.480–81.

42. For Near Eastern siege machinery, see Sarah P. Morris, "The Sacrifice of Astyanax: Near Eastern Contributions to the Siege of Troy," in Jane B. Carter and Sarah P. Morris, eds., *The Ages of Homer: A Tribute to Emily Townsend Vermeule* (Austin, TX, 1995), 227ff.

43. *Little Iliad,* argument 4, in West, *Greek Epic Fragments,* 123.

44. *Sack of Ilion,* fragment 1, ibid., 147.

45. Ibid., arguments 1 and 2, 145.

46. The return of Philoktetes was a favorite subject of tragedy; only Sophocles' play of his name has survived. Other traditions have a former wife of Paris play a role in his death; see Gantz, vol. 2, 635ff.

47. On Hekabe's fate, see H. J. Rose, *A Handbook of Greek Mythology* (London, 2000), 235ff. The debasement of Hekabe is the subject of Euripides' fearful tragedy, *Hecuba,* in which her designated master is Odysseus.

48. "A scattering of Classical and later writers recorded their own or others' belief that he [Astyanax] survived Troy's fall and, often in company with Aineias' son Askanios, founded one or more cities in the Troad": Peter M. Smith, "Aineiadai as Patrons of *Iliad* XX," *Harvard Studies in Classical Philology* 85 (1981), 17–58, especially 53ff.

49. "Odysseus kills Astyanax, Neoptolemus receives Andromache as his prize, and they divide up the rest of the booty.... Then they set fire to the city, and slaughter Polyxena at Achilles' tomb"; *Sack of Ilion,* argument 4, in West, *Greek Epic Fragments,* 147. In the *Little Iliad* it is Neoptolemus who kills Astyanax. See page 81 of this work.

50. Both Pindar, *Nemean* 8.23ff., and Sophocles' *Ajax* treat Aias' humiliating loss and death. The *Iliad* declares that Aias was "far the best ... while Achilles stayed angry" (2.278f.); yet when, in Book Three, Helen identifies key Achaean figures to Priam, her offhand dismissal of Aias—"That one is gigantic Aias, wall of the Achaeans, / and beyond him there is Idomeneus (3.229f.)— seems pointedly slighting.

51. The details of Diomedes' journey westward are obscure and confused, as is the tradition that in Italy his men were transformed into birds. See Gantz, vol. 2, 699f., for the various versions and sources; and Irad Malkin, *The Returns of Odysseus: Colonization and Ethnicity* (Berkeley and Los Angeles, 1998), 234ff.

52. *Odyssey* 4.238ff.

53. *Odyssey* 3.103ff.

54. Euripides, *Andromache,* 341ff., in David Grene and Richmond Lattimore, eds. and trans., *Euripides III* (Chicago, 1958), 87.

55. Strabo, *Geography* 1.3.2.

56. For the date of the pendant see Irene S. Lemos, *The Protogeometric Aegean: The Archaelogy of the Late Eleventh and Tenth Centuries B.C.,* (Oxford, 2002), 131f. The significance of the exotic quality and antiquity of the Lefkandi burial goods is discussed in Jan Paul Crielaard, "*Basileis* at Sea: Elites

and External Contacts in the Euboean Gulf Region from the End of the Bronze Age to the Beginning of the Iron Age," in Sigrid Deger-Jalkotzy and Irene S. Lemos, eds., *Ancient Greece: From the Mycenaean Palaces to the Age of Homer* (Edinburgh, 2006), 271–97, especially 286f.

57. See Ione Mylonas Shear, *Kingship in the Mycenaean World and Its Reflection in the Oral Tradition* (Philadelphia, 2004), 82.

58. Quoted from Bryce, *Life and Society in the Hittite World,* 99; and also p. 31 on the quality of royal mercy.

59. Gilbert Murray, *The Rise of the Greek Epic: Being a Course of Lectures Delivered at Harvard University* (Oxford, 1924), 92.

60. The transcendence of death through poetic renown is a complex and vast subject. A landmark work on Greek epic's role in immortalizing dead heroes is Gregory Nagy, *The Best of the Achaeans: Concepts of the Hero in Archaic Greek Poetry* (Baltimore, 1979), especially 174ff. A succinct overview of the Indo-European evidence, and a less formulaic approach, is given by West, *Indo-European Poetry and Myth,* 396ff. and 403ff. Challenging the premise that *kléos áphthiton* is in fact a formulaic survival from Indo-European heroic poetry is Margalit Finkelberg, "Is ΚΛΕΟΣ ΑΦΘΙΤΟΝ a Homeric Formula?," *Classical Quarterly* 36, no. 1 (1986), 1–5. While Anthony T. Edwards, "ΚΛΕΟΣ ΑΦΘΙΤΟΝ and Oral Theory," *Classical Quarterly* 38, no. 1 (1988), 25–30, concurs that this key phrase does not represent a Homeric formula, as the term is usually understood, he also suggests that oral theory of poetics, as is it increasingly refined, indicates that formulaic status neither proves nor disproves the antiquity of a phrase.

61. A decision in favor of glory has wrongly been ascribed to Achilles since ancient times; see Bruno Snell, *Scenes from Greek Drama* (Berkeley and Los Angeles, 1964), 1–22.

62. *Aethiopis,* argument 4, in West, *Greek Epic Fragments,* 113. The tradition that a pleasant fate awaits chosen heroes after death is also found in the *Odyssey,* where Menelaos is told that:

"... it is not the gods' will
that you shall die and go to your end in horse-pasturing Argos,
but the immortals will convoy you to the Elysian
Field, and the limits of the earth, where fair-haired Rhadamanthys
is, and where there is made the easiest life for mortals,
for there is no snow, nor much winter there, nor is there ever
rain, but always the stream of the Ocean sends up breezes
of the West Wind blowing briskly for the refreshment of mortals.
This, because Helen is yours and you are son-in-law therefore
to Zeus."
—*Odyssey* 4.561ff.

That the Homeric epic knowingly, as it were, withheld this happier end from Achilles is significant and consistent.

63. This small scene is also dense with allusions to Achilles' remarkable ances-

try. Odysseus' reference to Achilles' exceptional authority in the Underworld evokes the exceptional authority awarded his forebear, Aiakos, for example (see note 30). Also striking is the exchange between Achilles and Odysseus concerning Peleus, who still lives: to Achilles' moving request that Odysseus "tell me anything you have heard about stately Peleus, / whether he still keeps his position among the Myrmidon / hordes, or whether in Hellas and Phthia they have diminished / his state," Odysseus replies simply, "I have no report to give you of stately Peleus." The *Iliad*'s striking silence about Peleus' deeds, then, is also carried into the *Odyssey*. The tradition that brought Achilles, so to speak, to Troy, was that of the Thessalian refugees. Does the often-expressed concern for affairs back in Phthia, and for the fate of its old rulers, together with Achilles' wistful yearning to return home, reflect the nostalgia of these immigrant exiles for the land they would never see again? "The men of the Migrations had left their fathers' graves behind them. The ghosts whom they ought to have fed and cared for were waiting in the old lands helpless." Murray, *The Rise of the Greek Epic*, 71.

SELECTED FURTHER READING

While a detailed bibliography can be gleaned from the chapter notes, the following is intended as a guide to works on major themes that are readily obtainable and mostly accessible to the general reader.

TEXTS

T. W. Allen and D. B. Monro, eds., *Homeri Opera*, 2 vols. (Oxford, 1920), reprinted 1976.
M. L. West, ed., *Homeri Ilias* (Stuttgart and Leipzig, 1998–2000).

COMMENTARIES

The most comprehensive, thorough, and handy commentary is the six-volume series published by Cambridge University Press, of which the late G. S. Kirk was general editor. While the line-by-line commentary can be technical, the series' many essays on general themes ("The Gods in Homer," "Typical Motifs and Themes") are clear and readable. The different volumes are:

G. S. Kirk, *The "Iliad": A Commentary, Volume I: Books 1–4* (Cambridge, 1985).
———, *The "Iliad": A Commentary, Volume II: Books 5–8* (Cambridge, 1990).
Bryan Hainsworth, *The "Iliad": A Commentary, Volume III: Books 9–12* (Cambridge, 1993).
Richard Janko, *The "Iliad": A Commentary, Volume IV: Books 13–16* (Cambridge, 1992).
Mark W. Edwards, *The "Iliad": A Commentary, Volume V: Books 17–20* (Cambridge, 1991).
Nicholas Richardson, *The "Iliad": A Commentary, Volume VI: Books 21–24* (Cambridge, 1993).

Valuable single-book commentaries are:

Jasper Griffin, *Homer: "Iliad" IX* (Oxford, 1995).
Simon Pulleyn, *Homer: "Iliad" I* (Oxford, 2000).

TRANSLATIONS

Richmond Lattimore, *The "Iliad" of Homer* (Chicago, 1961): the most faithful to Homer's Greek of all translations available in English, both in literal word sense and in epic gravitas. All translations in this book (with the exception of "The Death of Hektor," which is by the author) are from Lattimore's landmark translation.

Robert Fagles, *The "Iliad"* (New York, 1990): colloquial and modern, a translation that many readers have found to be the most accessible.

Simeon Underwood, *English Translators of Homer: From George Chapman to Christopher Logue* (Plymouth, UK, 1998), gives a succinct (seventy-nine-page) discussion of the most important translations and changing sensibilities.

OTHER EARLY GREEK POETRY CITED IN THIS WORK

Epic Cycle: M. L. West, ed. and trans., *Greek Epic Fragments: From the Seventh to the Fifth Century B.C.*, Loeb Classical Library 497 (Cambridge, MA, 2003); see also Malcolm Davies, *The Greek Epic Cycle*, 2nd ed. (London, 2003), a short (ninety-one-page) overview of the many issues associated with these lost poems.

Hesiod: Glenn W. Most, ed. and trans., *Hesiod: Volume 1, Theogony. Works and Days. Testimonia*, Loeb Classical Library 57 (Cambridge, MA, 2006); and *Hesiod: Volume 2, The Shield. Catalogue of Women. Other Fragments*, Loeb Classical Library 503 (Cambridge, MA, 2007).

Homer, *The Odyssey:* translations by Richmond Lattimore (New York, 1967), used in this work, and Robert Fagles (New York, 1996) are to be recommended.

Homeric Hymns: M. L. West, ed. and trans., *Homeric Hymns. Homeric Apocrypha. Lives of Homer*, Loeb Classical Library 496 (Cambridge, MA, 2003).

Pindar: C. M. Bowra, trans., *The Odes of Pindar* (London, 1969).

THE BRONZE AGE AND THE TROJAN WAR

Greece and Mycenae

John Chadwick, *The Mycenaean World* (Cambridge, 1976).
———, *The Decipherment of Linear B* (Cambridge, 1990).
Nic Fields, *Mycenaean Citadels c. 1350–1200 B.C.* (Botley, Oxford, 2004).
K. A. and Diana Wardle, *Cities of Legend: The Mycenaean World* (London, 1997).

Anatolia and Troy

Trevor Bryce, *Life and Society in the Hittite World* (Oxford, 2002).
———, *The Trojans and Their Neighbours* (Abingdon, Oxon, 2006).
Nic Fields, *Troy c. 1700–1250 B.C.* (Botley, Oxford, 2004).
H. Craig Melchert, ed., *The Luwians* (Leiden, 2003).
Studia Troica: interdisciplinary periodical dedicated to Troy and the Troad through

all their many historical phases; includes the annual report of excavations at Troy. Copies can be ordered through the Project Troia Web site: www .unituebingen.de/troia/eng/sttroica.html.

Trojan War

G. S. Kirk, "History and Fiction in the *Iliad*," in *The "Iliad": A Commentary, Volume II: Books 5–8* (Cambridge, 1990), 36–50.

Joachim Latacz, *Troy and Homer: Towards a Solution of an Old Mystery*, translated from the German by Kevin Windle and Rosh Ireland (Oxford, 2004).

Carol G. Thomas and Craig Conant, *The Trojan War* (Westport, CT, 2005).

Michael Wood, *In Search of the Trojan War*, rev. ed. (London, 2005): an excellent, exciting, and well-written overview that navigates the Mycenaean and Hittite sources, modern archaeological findings, and the history of the discovery of the primary sites.

DARK AGE

M. I. Finley, *The World of Odysseus*, rev. ed. (New York, 1982).

Ian Morris, ed., *The Dark Ages of Greece* (Edinburgh, 2009).

Robin Osborne, "Homer's Society," in Robert Fowler, ed., *The Cambridge Companion to Homer* (Cambridge, 2007), 206–19.

A. M. Snodgrass, *The Dark Age of Greece: An Archaeological Survey of the Eleventh to the Eighth Centuries B.C.*, rev. ed. (Edinburgh, 2000): a detailed and necessarily technical overview of the archaeological evidence.

Carol G. Thomas and Craig Conant, *Citadel to City-State: The Transformation of Greece, 1200–700 B.C.E.* (Bloomington, IN, 1999).

ORAL POETRY AND TRANSMISSION OF THE HOMERIC POEMS

No aspect of Homeric scholarship is more vexed or contentious than the so-called Homeric question, which in fact encompasses several central questions regarding authorship and compositional technique of the *Iliad* and the *Odyssey*: Was "Homer" an individual poet, or is the name a misleading term for the long poetic tradition that passed through many anonymous hands? How faithfully, or innovatively, was this tradition passed on? How and when was it finally recorded? In other words, did Homer write? Did he dictate to a scribe? Was the text of the *Iliad* finally fixed, by writing, centuries after "Homer"? Did the same poet compose the *Iliad* and the *Odyssey*?

While many of these questions were raised even in ancient times, modern scholarship is securely dated to the work of Milman Parry, whose methodical analysis of the function and economy of the formulaic language of Homeric poetry securely established the epics' debt to traditional oral-compositional technique. Parry's later work with *guslars*, or professional poets, of Serbo-Croatian heroic poetry, in what was then Yugoslavia, in partnership with his colleague Albert B. Lord, appeared to substantiate his earlier linguistic work. Parry's legacy is most accessible in a single-volume collection of his papers, *The Making of Homeric Verse: The Collected Papers of Milman Parry*, Adam Parry, ed. (Oxford, 1997); due to the necessarily technical nature of his work, nonspecialist readers may find these landmark papers more complex and obscure than rewarding. More suitable for the general reader is Lord's summation, below.

Once taken as conclusive evidence of the strict orality of the Homeric poems *themselves* (as opposed to their undisputed but still-enigmatic debt to traditional oral poetry), Parry's thesis has come to receive more critical scrutiny; in particular, the expertise of nonclassicists with wide experience in living oral traditions has weighed in on the central arguments. Among the questions raised are the extent to which conclusions about Homeric diction are relevant to oral poetic traditions of our own era, the suitability of semiliterate *guslars* performing in urban cafés as a model for a Dark Age poet such as Homer, and the vast and conspicuous gulf between Serbo-Croatian narratives and the monumental epic poems of Homer. Also of greater interest today is the significance of the *Iliad* as an end-of-tradition composition. Such questions are fruitfully addressed, in particular, in the essays of the collection edited by Stoltz and Shannon, below.

The following list of works, many contradicting one another, will stimulate further thought, rather than provide definitive answers to the important, if irresolvable, "Homeric question":

Robert Fowler, "The Homeric Question," in Robert Fowler, ed., *The Cambridge Companion to Homer* (Cambridge, 2004), 220–32.
Richard Janko, "The Origins and Evolution of the Epic Diction" and "The Text and Transmission of the *Iliad*," in *The "Iliad": A Commentary, Volume IV: Books 13–16* (Cambridge, 1992), 8–19 and 20–38, respectively.
Minna Skafte Jensen, *The Homeric Question and the Oral-Formulaic Theory* (Copenhagen, 1980).
G. S. Kirk, *The Songs of Homer* (Cambridge, 1962).
Albert B. Lord, *The Singer of Tales* (Cambridge, MA, 1981).
Gregory Nagy, *Homeric Questions* (Austin, TX, 1996).
Barry B. Powell, "Homer and Writing," in Ian Morris and Barry Powell, eds., *A New Companion to Homer* (Leiden, 1997), 3–32.
———, *Homer and the Origin of the Greek Alphabet* (Cambridge, 1994).
Benjamin A. Stoltz and Richard S. Shannon, eds., *Oral Literature and the Formula* (Ann Arbor, 1976); see especially Ruth Finnegan, "What Is Oral Literature Anyway? Comments in the Light of Some African and Other Comparative Material," 127ff.

CRITICAL STUDIES

As indicated by the chapter Notes, there are many prisms through which to view the *Iliad*. The six-volume Cambridge Commentary, as noted above, has valuable essays on specific themes central to Homeric studies. The works cited below represent particularly insightful, and often moving, treatments of what could be called the epic's defining issues:

Jasper Griffin, *Homer on Life and Death* (Oxford, 1983).

Katherine Callen King, *Achilles: Paradigms of the War Hero from Homer to the Middle Ages* (Berkeley and Los Angeles, 1987).

Gregory Nagy, *The Best of the Achaeans: Concepts of the Hero in Archaic Greek Poetry* (Baltimore, 1979).

James M. Redfield, *Nature and Culture in the "Iliad": The Tragedy of Hector* (Chicago, 1975).

Seth L. Schein, *The Mortal Hero: An Introduction to Homer's "Iliad"* (Berkeley and Los Angeles, 1984).

Jonathan Shay, *Achilles in Vietnam: Combat Trauma and the Undoing of Character* (New York, 1995).

Laura M. Slatkin, *The Power of Thetis: Allusion and Interpretation in the "Iliad"* (Berkeley and Los Angeles, 1991).

Simone Weil, "The *Iliad*, or the Poem of Force," translated by Mary McCarthy, in Christopher Benfey, ed., *War and the "Iliad"* (New York, 2005), 1–37.

INDEX

Hera, 26, 30–31, 110, 205, 261*n.23*
  Achaean cities sacrificed by, 61, 62
  Aphrodite mocked by, 70
  cows associated with, 110, 252*n.6*
  in Deception of Zeus, 113–16, 126,
    154
  Hephaistos thrown from Olympos by,
    152, 259*n.6*
  horses and, 164, 262*n.27*
  intervention in war by, 112–16, 130, 150,
    165, 170, 202
  Judgment of Paris and, 91, 202
  Sarpedon's death and, 120, 136, 138,
    256*n.22*
  Thetis' marriage and, 90, 91, 172,
    247*n.11*, 263*n.37*
  Zeus' pact with, 60–61, 62
Herakles, 99, 232*n.27*, 251*n.41*, 257*n.32*,
  261*n.23*
Hermes, 165, 202, 205–7, 253*n.21*
  with Priam, 205, 206–7, 209, 214
Herodotus, 13, 110, 242*n.31*
heroes:
  Achilles' distinctiveness from tradition
    of, 95–100, 102
  angry, withdrawal of, 87
  cult worship of, 193–94, 265–66*n.3*
  Peleus as outside tradition of, 95
  quarrels between, *see* quarrels between
    heroes
  smith as nurturer and guardian of, 153,
    170, 259*n.9*
  superiority of fathers and, 27
  whisking away of, 57, 242*n.34*
  withdrawal-to-return theme of, 159,
    261*n.18*
  see also specific heroes
Hesiod, 22, 90, 91, 94, 236*n.9*
  Athene's birth in, 111
  on athletic games, 267*n.14*
  catalogue poetry of, 239*n.10*
  divine deception in, 116, 253*n.21*
  on Heracles' shield, 156
  on Menoitios, 127
  on Niobe, 269*n.31*
  on origins of Myrmidons, 133–34,
    255*n.14*
  Theogony of, 110, 253*n.21*
hetaîros, 127, 194, 254*n.3*
Hill of the Thicket, 45, 46, 240*n.17*
Himerius, 263*n.36*
Hippolochos, 107
Hippomolgoi, 109

Hittites, 3–8, 10, 256*n.27*, 263*n.34*
  Ahhiyawa and, 7
  Alaksandu of Wilusa in texts of, 48
  in Battle of Kadesh, 238–39*n.9*
  cremation and, 195, 196, 266*n.7*
  cuneiform of, 74
  divine appeasement and, 249*n.21*
  law of, Helen's situation and,
    241–42*n.30*
  Luwian in ritual text of, 215–16
  mission of suppliant parent and,
    222–23
  Mycenaean contact with, 230*n.11*
  religious festivals of, 196
  Song of Kumarbi of, 236*n.10*
  Trojans related to, 3, 7, 231*n.18*
  "vanishing deity" stories of, 261*n.19*
  Weather God of, 111
  Wilusa as vassal state of, 241*n.24*
Homer, 103, 147
  as blind bard, 12, 234*n.37*
  Embassy's innovative elements and, 87,
    246*n.3*
  as "first geographer," 44
  Hektor as alleged invention of, 46,
    240*n.21*
  Hesiod's borrowing from, 156
  new direction for epic of, 96, 102, 104,
    250*n.39*
  origins of, 2–3, 11
  outlandishness eschewed by, 26, 132,
    164, 236*n.9*
  Patroklos developed by, 127, 254*n.4*
  Phoinix as invention of, 100, 251*n.43*
  Plato's banning of works of, 113
  theogony of, 110
Homeric Hymns, 116, 159, 253*n.21*,
  261*n.19*, 262*n.29*
homosexuality, 257–58*n.32*
honor, 35, 80, 98, 165
  of Achilles, *see* Achilles, honor of
  of Agamemnon, 37, 85
Horace, xii
horses, 7, 43–44, 85, 127, 232*n.27*
  burial of, 196, 266*n.10*
  Diomedes cults and, 69
  divine, 70, 108, 132–33, 137, 143, 147,
    164, 167
  in funeral games, 198, 267*n.12*
  grief of, 143, 147, 164, 257*n.29*
  Hera and, 164, 262*n.27*
  of King Rhesos, 251*n.1*
  Pedasos, 133, 137